GERRY HASSAN is a writer, commentator and Research Fellow at the University of the West of Scotland.

He has written, edited and published numerous books on Scottish and British politics, ideas, policy, social change and futures thinking, leading the Demos *Scotland 2020* and *Glasgow 2020* projects. His books include *After Independence*, *The Strange Death of Labour Scotland*, *Radical Scotland: Arguments for Self-Determination*, *The SNP: From Protest to Power* and *After Blair: Politics after the New Labour Decade*. He regularly writes and appears in Scottish, UK and international media, and his writing can be found at www.gerryhassan.com

Advance Praise For *Caledonian Dreaming*:

*An intelligent, brave and much needed contribution to the debate around the referendum in Scotland. This, along with other great contributions, like Lesley Riddoch's* Blossom, *are hugely important to the general discourse and much needed research into the country we have been, the country we now are and the country we could become.*
ELAINE C. SMITH, actress and campaigner

*This is a remarkable book – balanced and brave, insightful and incisive, intelligently blending the personal and the political. Whatever the referendum result, if Scotland really wants to be 'the best place in the world to grow up', Gerry Hassan's suggestions for 'a new democracy' would be an excellent starting point.*
SUE PALMER, author, *Toxic Childhood*

*Gerry Hassan sets out to challenge the lazy presumptions that are around about Scotland and its future. He invites the reader to think and think again.*
STUART COSGROVE, broadcaster

*Understanding that the old stories we tell ourselves influence the new stories we go on to write, Gerry Hassan has crafted a brilliant book unpacking the political narratives that have shaped modern Scotland in order to create a space to imagine anew. A book about Scotland important to anyone, anywhere, dreaming a new world.*
STEPHEN DUNCOMBE, author, *Dream: Re-imagining Progressive Politics in an Age of Fantasy*

D1392512

*The independence referendum changes what is possible regardless of its outcome. It forces people in Scotland to confront far more directly the nature of their country rather than continue to accept the myths that build up when there is no option to go it alone. In* Caledonia Dreaming *Gerry Hassan skillfully traverses these key myths to show that, if Scotland were to gain independence, it would have to confront internal realities that were hidden when Westminster could be blamed for so much. If the Scots prove the bookies wrong, if events over the summer of 2014 turn so that independence is achieved, then this book demonstrates that the new Scotland will be further from many possible idealised European utopias than many nationalists had ever imagined. It is a key contribution to the debate no matter where you stand.*
DANNY DORLING, author, *Injustice: Why Social Justice Persists,* Professor of Human Geography, Oxford University

*With one bound Scotland could be free! How tempting that looks to the progressive-minded on both sides of the border. If only it were that easy. Gerry Hassan drills down to deeper reasons why the many dysfunctions of British democracy could dog an independent Scotland too. With a non-partisan but beady eye on society both sides of the border, in this clever book here are tougher questions to consider than a mere Yes/No.*
POLLY TOYNBEE, writer and journalist, *The Guardian*

Open Scotland is a series which aims to open up debate about the future of Scotland and do this by challenging the closed nature of many conversations, assumptions and parts of society. It is based on the belief that the closed Scotland has to be understood, and that this is a pre-requisite for the kind of debate and change society needs to have to challenge the status quo. It does this in a non-partisan, pluralist and open-minded manner, which contributes to making the idea of self-government into a genuine discussion about the prospects and possibilities of social change.

Luath Press is an independently owned and managed book publishing company based in Scotland, and is not aligned to any political party or grouping. *Viewpoints* is an occasional series exploring issues of current and future relevance.

# Caledonian Dreaming

## The Quest for a Different Scotland

GERRY HASSAN

with a Foreword by FINTAN O'TOOLE

**Luath** Press Limited

EDINBURGH

www.luath.co.uk

First published 2014
Reprinted 2014

ISBN: 978-1-910021-32-3

The paper used in this book is recyclable. It is made from
low chlorine pulps produced in a low energy, low emissions manner
from renewable forests.

Printed and bound by
Martins the Printers, Berwick-upon-Tweed

Typeset in 11 point Sabon
by 3btype.com

# Contents

Gie aa, and aa comes back
  wi mair nor aa.
Hain ocht, and ye'll hae nocht,
  aa flees awa.

LUVE

**DOUGLAS YOUNG**

# Acknowledgements

Any book like this is assisted and encouraged by a range of people who aid its slow process coming from a set of ideas to its final form. First and foremost, I would like to show my gratitude and pleasure at working with the fantastic team at Luath Press – Gavin MacDougall, Lydia Nowak, Laura Nicol and Tom Bee.

Second, in terms of illustrations I would like to thank Tara Beall, Gerry McCartney, Greg Moodie, Ross Sinclair and Oxfam Scotland for giving permission for work to be used. Third, in electoral facts and figures, Sarah Mackie of the Electoral Commission Scotland was an embodiment of professionalism and support. Fourth, I would like to give my thanks for their encouragement and contribution to this project: Anthony Barnett, Simon Barrow, Eleanor Bell, Paddy Bort, Ross Colquhoun, Phil Denning, Roanne Dods, David Donnison, Stephen Duncombe, Ian Fraser, Michael Gardiner, Doug Gay, Joe Lafferty, Marc Lambert, Steve Lambert, Gayle MacPherson, Doreen MacWhannell, Robin McAlpine, Allan McConnell, James McCormick, Ailsa McKay, Susan McPhee, James Mitchell, Ken Neil, Alison Park, Karine Polwart, David Purdy, Eileen Reid, Eddie Rice, Philip Schlesinger, Martin Sime, Nigel Smith, Francis Stuart, Willie Sullivan, David Torrance, Michael Torrance, Katherine Trebeck, Jean Urquhart, Andy Wightman and Eleanor Yule. Fifth, many thanks to Clara Young for permission to use Douglas Young's poem.

A special thanks and acknowledgement goes to Rosie Ilett who read and proofed the entire text at a near-final stage, and who was a source of inspiration and ideas throughout the course of this project.

Finally, a word on the style of this book. It has been written not as a specialist or academic book for those in the know but for the general informed reader. Therefore, despite what some readers might think, I have deliberately gone out of my way to avoid using obscure phrases or too much jargon. I have also kept references to other works and publications to a minimum. References are only used when absolutely necessary, and the range included indicate the main immediate sources for this book for further reading.

This book has been a pleasure to write and research, coming as it does at an august time, and also as the first in a series of books in the 'Open Scotland' series published by Luath. Many thanks for their commitment and professionalism in bringing this book and the series into being. I hope people find it as enjoyable and stimulating as I have writing it and immersing myself in the reading, ideas and thoughts at this exciting period in our country.

*Gerry Hassan*
gerry.hassan@virgin.net
Glasgow/Drummore
March 2014

# The Art of Growing Up: A Foreword

FINTAN O'TOOLE

IN 1926, THE NEW and fragile Irish state, barely recovering from a civil war, marked the tenth anniversary of the event that led to its foundation: the Easter Rising in Dublin in 1916. The Abbey, now the State's national theatre, staged a new drama by its star playwright, Sean O'Casey, *The Plough and the Stars*. Most people wanted, even needed, an acknowledgment of the nobility of those who had given their lives for an Irish independence that had now been at least partially achieved.

What they got instead was a searing critique of the Rising, which O'Casey dramatised as a product of male vanity and the marginalising of the poor. The insult was deeply intimate: those who led the riotous protests against O'Casey included mothers, widows and sisters of men who had died for Irish independence. As one of them, Hannah Sheehy-Skeffington, asked, how could:

> ... a State-subsidised theatre presume on popular patience to the extent of making a mockery... of a revolutionary movement on which the present structure claims to stand?

The Abbey's co-founder, W.B. Yeats, chose this moment to say something important: this is what independence looks like. Answering a question from the audience at a poetry reading, he suggested a vital distinction between national vanity and national pride:

> The moment a nation reached intellectual maturity, it became exceedingly proud and ceased to be vain and when it became exceedingly proud it did not disguise its faults... but when it was immature it was exceedingly vain, and did not believe in itself, and so long as it did not believe in itself, it wanted other people to think well of it, in order that it might get a little reflected confidence. With success came pride, and with pride came indifference as to whether people were shown in a good light or a bad light on the stage.

*Caledonian Dreaming* is a shock to Scottish vanity and a beacon of Scottish pride. It doesn't argue for independence, it embodies it. Gerry Hassan shows what intellectual maturity looks like: the clarity of vision and the honesty of purpose to live without the comfort of self-aggrandising myths. It strips away the protective clothing that all national movements love to wear and presents a Scotland denuded of some of its most cherished illusions. But just as bravely, it is not ashamed of that nakedness. Hassan's vision is as hopeful as it is unflinching, as full of possibilities as it is empty of fantasy.

The great trap of nationalism is the tendency to define 'us as 'not them'. Nationalist movements need to imagine their country as both distinctive and unified. These are tricky tasks and the easiest way to get around them is to caricature one's own country as the opposite of a caricature of the oppressor. Irish nationalism did this only too well: Britain was Protestant, monarchical, English-speaking industrial and urban, so Ireland had to be Catholic, republican, Gaelic-speaking, agricultural and rural. Scotland, in the 21st century, has a more sophisticated version of this reversal: England is all those things summed up in Thatcherism so Scotland embodies all the virtues of anti-Thatcherism: tolerant, social democratic, egalitarian, civic, open.

The problem with this Scottish version of the 'not them' double caricature is that it is so damned attractive. The Irish nationalist brand was largely reactionary and backward-looking. The Scottish version appeals to values that any progressive person would like to see embodied in a future state. There's a warmth and decency to Scotland's 'not them' that is lacking in so many other historic and contemporary nationalisms – and which make it all the more insidious. It is a sugar-coated hallucinogen.

Even a nice version of 'not them' traps a country in the immaturity of national vanity. A mature sense of national pride, on the other hand, demands a much more exacting examination of 'us'. How well do the self-regarding myths map on to the lived reality? In what sense do 'we' form a single entity? Who gets to be 'us' and who is consigned to being another, internal, 'them'? Can all oppression and injustice be blamed on 'them' or do they not perhaps have roots in our own hierarchies and habits? *Caledonian Dreaming* is wide awake to these questions.

At the heart of Hassan's argument is a brilliant teasing-out of a relatively simple truth: national independence is not an event but a process. And a process with no simple beginning and no possible end. In this sense, he sees independence as being already well under way in a gradual maturing of self-government. And he also sees it as a struggle that will have to continue even if there is a great moment of 'liberation' in 2014. It is the struggle for truly meaningful democracy, which is to say a democracy in which every citizen shares the right to a dignified private and public existence and every citizen takes on the endless responsibility of renewing and deepening the collective processes that make this possible.

This is a great challenge but Scotland also has a great opportunity. Very few countries ever get the chance to become independent without inheriting the corrosive, distorting, disabling effects of violence. That this is taken for granted in Scotland doesn't mean that it is not an extraordinary blessing.

Scotland also has the opportunity to become more mature and take responsibility without the baggage of national vanity and the heady rush of illusions that quickly become the toxic sludge of post-independence disillusionment. This is the art of growing up: far more important than any formal constitutional standing. There could be no better harbinger of these possibilities than this bracing, searching, discomfiting and ultimately exhilarating book.

CHAPTER ONE

# Scotland is Changing: A Nation in Transition

> Empathy is what keeps us together. It's all really about people getting on with other people. And if you bring a kid up in a war zone, you're going to get a warrior.
>
> KARYN MCCLUSKEY, Head of Scottish Violence Reduction Unit,
> *The Guardian*, 19 December 2011

THESE ARE UNPRECEDENTED times to live in: of immense and complex change and uncertainty, and a set of crises and challenges in how institutions, politics and the mainstream media try to understand and explain these.

It is not an accident then that in the UK and most of the West, there is a widespread suspicion of traditional power and elites: whether bankers, politicians or many professional groups.

This is an age of flux and movement – of the emergence of new radical voices and forces, of the rise of populist and xenophobic parties across Europe, and the inability of conventional politics and the orthodoxies and dogmas which have dominated recent decades, to offer any plausible answer to the times we live in (Coggan, 2013; Mair, 2013).

These are also dramatic times for Scotland – witness the independence debate, the historic referendum in September 2014, and the possible end of the United Kingdom as we have come to know it – an eventuality which would carry with it consequences far beyond the shores of Scotland and the UK.

There is a short-term political account of how all this happened, focused on the SNP unexpectedly winning an overall majority in the Scottish Parliament 2011 elections, but much deeper and historic forces are at work. These include the long-term evolution of autonomy and distinctiveness in Scottish society, and what I call 'voice' both within the UK and Scotland. Another factor has been the nature of the UK, the values and priorities it has chosen to embrace, and the vision of society it has increasingly chosen to champion.

This makes where the Scotland of 2014 finds itself and where it might go the product of a host of factors which have potent roots and which are not going to go away or be resolved whatever the result of the referendum vote. This is one crucial point both Scottish and UK audiences need to reflect on, that the dynamics which have brought this debate to where it is will not disappear post-referendum. There is no tidy or final conclusion to this, whatever Scotland's formal constitutional status.

Despite this, much of the tone, particularly that of certain politicians and parts of the mainstream media, deliberately poses the debate in an alienating and apocryphal black and white style – in terms of continuity and stability versus uncertainty and rupture.

This is inaccurate in at least two ways. First, the independence debate despite the Yes/No vote is not some modern equivalent of a Victorian duel of two sparing gentlemen or Cold War Mutual Assured Destruction (MAD). Instead, there is an element of ambiguity and continuity between the two offers. Second, and more importantly, the future cannot be future proofed. Indeed, we are continually told by 'official' voices that we cannot count on the social provisions experienced by previous generations in the future, and while that can be contested, the future is going to involve upheaval and uncertainty whatever Scotland 'decides' in 2014.

There is a bigger story to this. Look at the Scotland of recent years. It hasn't exactly been a society of peace and calm. Some of the central pillars of public life have crashed and burned.

There was the Royal Bank of Scotland (RBS), once the fifth biggest bank in the world, which had to be nationalised to save it, but which has hardly cleaned up its ethical behaviour since. Then Glasgow Rangers FC, previously Scotland's most successful football club, went into liquidation, and are currently working their way through Scotland's lower leagues. Most recently, the Catholic Church has been tainted by a series of sexual scandals which have involved some of its most senior and high-profile figures.

These were all on their own tumultuous events, yet taken together they describe a society in flux, dramatic change and that old certainties no longer hold. They also point to the systemic abuse of power, dysfunctional leadership and wider issues in culture whether in business, football or churches.

Despite all of this, the Scotland presented to us in our mainstream politics, media and public life is one divorced from these dramatic changes. It is one of continuity, of dismissing each of the above as one-offs and the product of individual factors and inexcusable behaviour – of Fred Goodwin, David Murray and Keith O'Brien and the like. This is a culture of restoration of authority and of Scotland pre-crash, and wishing to continue collusion with powers, its uses and abuses, despite all that has happened.

Strangely, the way the independence debate is often portrayed is as one divorced from these changes – as if it is about a narrow set of constitutional choices, unconnected to discussion on the kind of society we want to live in.

This book aims to set out a very different prospectus – critiquing the conservative voices of Scotland – of left, right, nationalist, institutional and 'civic Scotland' persuasions. It argues that part of the change we have to go through needs to put our recent past into history, understanding not only the limits of British, but Scottish democracy, the blindsides of much of radical Scotland, and the need to understand the myths that we have created to tell ourselves how different and progressive we are, compared to the rest of the UK. Only by this self-reflection, honesty, and addressing the consequences of our cumulative choices, can we begin to understand where we are and where we might be going.

Scotland has not arrived in its present place solely by being inward looking and navel gazing, despite what some might say. It has been deeply affected by a host of historic and profound external factors. One such dimension is the long-term relative decline and crises of Britain and the British state. This has been aided and shaped in recent decades by the majority sentiment that Scotland rejected Thatcherism and instead remained steadfast in its commitment to what it saw as social democratic values.

But that is only one level and one that has become part of the 'official story' of modern Scotland which needs and demands a more rigorous critique than it has so far received. More crucial is a longer-term perspective which locates Scotland in the historical evolution of its administration, government, public services and state, from late Victorian times, and how this has altered Scotland both as a society and the voice and influence it has welded in the union.

This relates to the managed, ordered, closed society of 'high Scotland' whereby professional and institutional elites have dominated public life, often without any systematic scrutiny. One of the consequences of this state of affairs has been the development of a very weak, narrow public voice in society, and the interplay between domestic power dynamics in Scotland and the use of political voice by Scotland and its elites in the UK. This disequilibrium has shaped much of Scottish politics, society and culture, but is rarely commented upon let alone investigated, such are the power of some of the prevailing myths of modern Scotland: Labour, left, nationalist, and 'civic Scotland' being some of the most obvious.

One of the defining accounts of modern Scotland is one which emphasises our difference, uniqueness and the experience of this northern nation as progressive, social democratic and centre-left. This has come increasingly to the fore in the last 30 years since the election of the Thatcher Government (while drawing on earlier antecedents). Given the place in which Scotland now finds itself, it is time to ask whether the stories that we Scots tell ourselves are enough? Do we recognise ourselves in them? Do they reflect the diverse, contradictory, pluralist range that is modern Scotland, and do they aid mapping out and making sense of the future? The adequacy of the myths of modern Scotland is explored in the next chapter.

Then there is the important question of how the stories we tell inform and connect to our actions, values and practices. This book will attempt to explore this: the emergence of the modern Scotland we think we know and live in, the narrative of Scotland as more centre-left and progressive than the rest of the UK, and the quest for a different Scotland.

## A Diverse Assembly or Not?

The independence debate will naturally have sound and fury, adversarialism, insult and invective, but we have to make sure these are not the dominant, or worse, the only, voices which get heard.

Alistair Darling has talked of Scottish independence as 'serfdom' (*The Scotsman*, 17 November 2012). Gordon Brown similarly declared that the SNP's version of independence would be the equivalent of 'a form of self-imposed colonialism more reminiscent of the old empire than of the modern world' (*The Scotsman*, 4 November 2012). These are serious interventions by senior Labour Westminster politicians and display a deliberate decision to caricature and misunderstand the realities of Scottish independence and self-government. Darling, pouring scorn on the Scottish Government's White Paper on independence, on its day of publication, called it 'a work of fiction', not stopping to acknowledge the momentous nature of the day or that it might be a significant document (*BBC News*, 26 November 2013).

The late Baron Fraser of Carmyllie, a former Lord Advocate for Scotland, ruminated that a vote for independence may leave the rUK with no option but to take military action due to a military or security threat: 'If that were to happen what alternative would England have but to come and bomb the hell out of Glasgow airport and Edinburgh airport' (*The Herald*, 12 March 2012).

There is not a completely equivalent set of examples on the pro-independence side, but there are many examples of nationalist supporters making problematic statements. One prominent pro-independence blogger called *The Guardian*'s respected columnist Ian Jack an 'Uncle Tom', while the writer and pro-independence campaigner Alan Bissett stated at the November 2012 'Changin Scotland' weekend that our nation has been regularly wronged by 'the repeated English invasions, the Act of Union, Highland Clearances and Thatcherism – all violations of Scotland' (*National Collective*, 30 November 2012). This latter set of comments were meant to show the need for anger and indignation in Scotland, but instead painted a sense of victimhood, along with a subjective interpretation of history.

There is in much of this a politics of labelling, naming and tribalism which helps and motivates the most partisan voices but which does not help debate. In truth, such actions contribute to politics as a minority pastime which just sails past most people. This book has been written, and here I may incur the wrath of some of the voices of certainty, not from the perspective of any one tribe or set of labels, but as a direct challenge to them.

This stance proposes that the politics of seeing everything in terms of left versus right, nationalist versus unionist, or about anti-Tory, anti-Thatcherite values, or a simplistic interpretation of class politics as if the last 30 years have not happened, does not really deal with the realities and challenges of modern Scotland. Similarly, the constant use of the words 'separatism' and 'narrow nationalism' merely illustrate where the speaker is coming from, and in effect demonstrate their desire to close down debate by controlling language and definitions.

These actions, from whichever side they originate, are a kind of psychological crutch, a search for certainty and anchor in a world of flux and change. But this is increasingly a law of diminishing returns, as well as a counter-productive exercise. Rather than aid us formulating ideas for the future, such behaviours are nearly always about embracing a closed-minded attitude which regards sloganising and constant mantras as good enough. They have never really been adequate, even in some supposed golden era of left v. right and class politics. Increasingly, these labels talk and mobilise less and less people, for all the wider radical sentiments in parts of Scotland.

This book is not written from within the confines of the straightjacket of such labels and name calling, whether left or right, nationalist or unionist. Instead, it is motivated by trying to engage in a more open-minded conversation about ideas, values and ideologies, and the challenges and crises we face in Scotland and the West. As I make clear in Chapter Three, my own origins and politics come unambiguously from the left and being pro-self-government, traditions that have made immense contributions to our public life. But the future requires an understanding of their limits and that many of our future challenges – demographics, climate change and the ethical dilemmas science is posing for us, to take just three examples – cannot be fitted into this framework.

As things stand, we have a mainstream debate dominated by two rather conservative forces, both of which look like accountancy versions of Scotland; of a managerial, cost-focused, economic calculus notion of the world. That is a very narrow focus. It is also as a debate of two competing nationalisms, Scottish and British, with the latter seemingly unaware that unionism is a form of nationalism. Mainstream Scottish nationalism years ago became moderate, reasonable and sensible, perhaps too much for many of us. British nationalism, on the other hand, seems in places to be reverting to a politics of despair, repeating mantras about identity, and damning and diminishing Scotland's capacity to govern itself. This debate between two nationalisms has seen one 'out', self-reflective and mostly self-aware (Scottish), and one in denial, nearly completely lacking in self-knowledge and a sense of self-awareness (British). And this also illustrates the observation that nationalism of whatever kind was never going to be enough to offer adequate explanation to most people beyond some of the tribes.

Scottish society faces numerous constraints on how we debate, engage and listen to each other in public life. One of the most significant dimensions is that of gender, which still disfigures and diminishes too much of society – from representation in politics, business and the public realm, to the continuation of inequalities and discrimination, and the continued prevalence in places of misogyny and sexism.

There are so many layers to this. One is the over aggressiveness and combativeness of too much of political discussion, nearly always led by men. A couple of examples show the problem, which is not exclusive to any one party. Ian Davidson in August 2012 engaged in a bitter, acrimonious exchange with BBC Scotland presenter Isabel Fraser where he questioned her impartiality and that of the programme: the tone was menacing, drawing from a certain part of Scotland's past (*Newsnight Scotland*, 7 August 2012). More recently, in a debate in Orkney in September 2013, Davidson declared the independence vote won and that all that was left was that 'a large number of wounded still [had] to be bayoneted' (*The Times*, 18 October 2013).

These sorts of attitudes, evoking unreconstructed men and masculinities, can be seen at its worst in relation to domestic violence, an area in which women's and campaigning groups have done much work. Sadly, much more is needed. A terrible illustration of this was the recent revelation that with Rangers FC out of the Scottish top league, domestic violence levels in Glasgow have fallen. This had been widely suspected by the authorities but was given basis by St Andrews University research. The 'official' response from Celtic and Rangers was to deny the report and question its validity (*The Herald*, 21 September 2013). This problem goes deep into the psyche of our culture. Before the figures came out I discussed the above with a couple of Celtic fans – middle class, liberal, intelligent men – and what was their response? They dismissed it out of hand with what could only be called contempt. Clearly, we still have a lot of growing up to do.

Then there is the narrow spectrum of opinion put forward in public conversations and representation, one of which is male-only Scotland – a product of a middle-class self-preservation society, complacency and wider dimensions of power and exclusion. Recently a 'Thatcher and the Scots' panel discussion at the 'Previously' history festival in Edinburgh involved four males with the only woman involved being Margaret Thatcher. The examples of such discussions, panels and events are legion, but this is also about more than gender or 'diversity'. Widening the middle-class net of voices and representation is not enough. Instead, as this book explores and identifies, the missing voices of Scotland have to be noticed, and that means talking about power, class, race and age. All of this entails men, of all persuasions and backgrounds, reflecting on their positions, influence and status, acting in a different way and being open to change.

## Scotland and Voice, Loyalty and Exit

Scotland has been an imagined space, nation and place for several centuries, with a distinctive and autonomous public realm and public space. It has also, as this book explores, built up since the end of the 19th century territorial institutions and infrastructure of what can be seen as an embryonic state and greater self-government within the union of the United Kingdom.

Drawing on Albert O. Hirschman's influential *Exit, Voice and Loyalty* (1970) in relation to the Scottish dimension allows the development of a nuanced understanding of these dynamics, the tensions they embody, and Scotland's position and influence within the UK. From late Victorian times, we can note the evolution of a Scottish 'voice' leading to a period of conditional 'loyalty' in the union based on a more progressive expression of citizenship. Once this latter political settlement began to weaken and be challenged within British politics, a significant part of Scottish opinion began to move to the potential threat of 'exit' from the union and to a politics of more developed autonomy.

Whether the Scots embark on a formal embrace of 'exit' and independence, or a more partial, gradual 'exit' remains to be seen and may or may not be fully decided in the 2014 referendum. Hirschman argues that states can erect a high price for 'exit', and that this, along with the perceived price (and memories) of entry, can affect the balance between 'voice' and 'exit': 'the fact that one fully "belongs" by birthright may not nurture voice and thus compensate for the virtual unreliability of the threat of exit' (1970: 97–8). However, it is possible that 'the huge price of the "unthinkability" of exit may not only fail to repress voice but may stimulate it' (1970: 98).

This set of relationships – voice, loyalty and exit – within the UK can also be seen in the form of 'voice' at work historically within Scotland. This internal 'voice' matters in who is speaking, who they claim to speak for, and how they speak (along with who isn't speaking), and critically affects the relationship between the voice of Scotland's influence in the union, and this domestic voice and its components. The latter had self-interest in emphasising unity and consensus to be able to maximise the degree of Scottish opinion it claimed to represent, along with marginalising alternative, dissenting voices.

This is the politics of 'the Scottish lobby' in the union, and its institutionalised form in domestic life. This careful balancing act was articulated well by Scottish elites at the height of the union, in the increasing autonomy of Scottish public life, and in the 'high Scotland' of welfare state Britain, but post-Scottish Parliament, the tensions and divergent pressures in this have come increasingly to the fore.

The terminology of 'voice' used in this book explores both the domestic forces which have gained and claimed to speak for public opinion in Scotland, the summation of collective interests within the union, and the relationship between these. It is a useful and illuminating template for understanding Scotland's evolution, its public life and realm, the role of institutional opinion, and Scotland's position in the union, revealing much about Scottish society, power, democracy (lack thereof), and the nature of the UK.

## It's the Economy, Stupid

One of the other missing ingredients of most Scottish debates is an adequate discussion of the economy, and particularly the politics and dynamics of political economy, a subject Scotland gave to the modern world via the writings of Adam Smith (who was an enormous influence on Karl Marx). In the recent years of the Scottish Parliament, one of the main conventional explanations for the absence of the economy focused on two sources. The first was to blame the nature of the devolution settlement and the disjuncture between spending and taxation, and the fact that the Parliament had been devised with monies raised by Westminster. The second articulated a critique of the public sector, and bought into a right-wing argument that it had crowded out the private sector, encouraged a 'dependency culture' and suffocated innovation.

These explanations are not only superficial, but evidence of the lack of depth in economic arguments. A more serious contributory factor is the character of the Scottish economy, and studying an economy in which distinctive issues of ownership and control are even more problematic than your average capitalist economy. Basic questions abound, including: is there actually such a thing as a Scottish economy or an economy based in Scotland? How can we understand issues of capital and class without reverting to a caricatured Marxist analysis? And is there a substantial enough community prepared to engage in radical ideas of political economy which challenge existing orthodoxies and the biases found in mainstream opinion?

This brings us to *The Economist*'s infamous issue of two years ago, 'Skintland' (14 April 2012). This combined its cover with made up names for Scottish towns and areas to emphasise a world of no hope representing the future of the nation – 'Grumpians', 'Loanlands', 'Glasgone', 'Edinborrow' and more. Its editorial was entitled, 'It'll cost you: Scottish independence would come at a high price'. It took a dim view of the independence project, considering that it flew in the face of the magazine's vision of unfettered free markets. The editorial confidently proclaimed that Scots should decide on independence 'in the knowledge their country could end up as one of Europe's vulnerable, marginalised economies' and to underline this summed up an independent Scotland as 'a small, vulnerable barque'.

However, *The Economist*, for all its hyperbole and self-assuredness, isn't about small things such as facts. It is an ideological project committed to opening up the world to the liberating force of markets. Hence, in the last year on Scotland it has swung from 'Skintland' to acknowledging the numerous strengths of the Scottish economy. For example, it noted the Scottish success story of Foreign Direct Investment (FDI) in an Ernst and Young survey covering 2012. London with 22 per cent of UK GDP took 45 per cent of FDI, while Scotland has the highest figures for anywhere apart from London: taking, with 8.3 per cent of population, 16.1 per cent of FDI.

The Economist offers as part explanation that the Scots spend more government money per head than the neighbouring North East England on economic development: £191 per head versus £73, claiming that many think the 'Scots are offering more lavish subsidies to lure foreign firms' (31 August 2013). Another survey by the magazine the previous month explored why Scottish headline unemployment at 7.1 per cent was below the British average of 7.8 per cent, and found that the rate of private sector job growth north of the border in the last three years had been ahead of every part of the UK with the exception of London. The Economist tried to explain this by talking of its benefits from two industries – the oil and gas sector and food and drink – which have experienced strong growth through the recession. And it even tried to suggest that one reason for the robust figures was that 'that companies have been reading opinion polls' on independence. They did however, with grudging admiration, offer plaudits to the Scottish Government for its support of construction and investment in infrastructure (6 July 2013).

Yet of course it is easier to propagate the dismissive tone of 'Skintland' than to comprehend the facts cited in your own pages. This is because the worldview represented by The Economist is not the objective, calm, rational minded economic intelligence that it likes to present. It is the opposite: part of the market determinist, relentlessly privatising, outsourcing and undermining public services and goods dogma, representative of the neo-liberal project which has circled the globe.

Take again some uncomfortable facts – the first from The Economist about the British economy. The UK in terms of research and development is a staggering 159th out of 173 in the world; the 14 countries below include seven in sub-Saharan Africa. This was serious enough for even The Economist to worry declaring, 'Why being 159th best at investment is no way for a country to sustain a recovery'. If that was not bad enough, UK investment has dropped by a quarter in real terms in the last five years, and in the first quarter of 2013 stood at 13.5 per cent of UK GDP, compared to a global average of 24 per cent (6 July 2013).

Another uncomfortable fact has been the size of the 'real' British economy in relation to banking and finance. In 1960, the UK banking sector's balance sheets amounted to 32 per cent of GDP; in 1990 this had more than doubled to 75 per cent, and ten years later, it had nearly doubled again to 143 per cent. In 2010 the Bank of England estimated it was over 500 per cent and noted that, 'the UK banking system is second only to Switzerland among G20 economies and is an order of magnitude larger than the US system' (Martin, 2013: 212).

Then there is the silence in the mainstream media, politics and economic debate on the subject of economic democracy. Forty years ago, the UK and large parts of the Western world were filled with debates on workers' control, co-operatives and how to make accountable firms and the forces of capital, with radical ideas being seriously considered by governments, such as the Swedish Social Democratic wage earner funds (which were originally intended to slowly socialise and democratise private industry, and which were eventually implemented in a much watered down form).

The United Kingdom on any measurement of worker participation comes off appallingly. A survey by the European Participation Index studied the then 27 EU nations by a basket of indices: plant level participation, board level participation, collective bargaining coverage and trade union membership (European Trade Union Institute, 2010). The UK comes 26th out of 27 in this index, only exceeded in terms of economic autocracy by Lithuania. The top rated nations, Denmark, Sweden and Finland, all exceed the UK in terms of economic growth, GDP, competitiveness, and of course, on issues like poverty and inequality. But still there is an unshakable conviction on the part of British political and business elites in the superiority of the British way.

## The Masters of the Universe: From New Labour to the Neo-Lib Nats

The British bubble of the New Labour era produced a dramatic transformation of the party's attitudes to markets, globalisation, wealth and the City of London. Blair and Brown believed they were presiding over a 'British economic miracle' which in Brown's words had achieved 'the end of Boom and Bust': the reality was more prosaic, with New Labour's GDP annual growth averaging 1.6 per cent compared to 2.2 per cent over the post-war era 1948–98 (Toynbee and Walker, 2010: 72).

The mantra of New Labour constantly evoked the merits of entrepreneurship, deregulation, being pro-enterprise and pro-City of London and buying into corporate capitalist orthodoxy to justify it. Gordon Brown,

Tony Blair and Peter Mandelson, along with Mervyn King, Governor of the Bank of England from 2003–13, were unequivocal in this. The latter commented in 2003, '[T]he UK experienced a non-inflationary consistently-expansionary – or "nice" – decade' (Elliott and Atkinson, 2007: 94). There was a belief that these good times could just continue into the future, aided by Gordon Brown's blind faith that the Chairman of the American Federal Reserve, Alan Greenspan, understood the new dynamics of markets.

Pivotal to New Labour was two pillars: globalisation and the City of London. The former became an almost liberationary zeal of freedom, liberty and markets which would spread prosperity the world over and to which resistance was futile. Tony Blair encapsulated this at the 2005 Labour conference when he said, 'I hear people say we have to stop and debate globalisation. You might as well debate whether autumn should follow summer' (Finlayson, 2007: 42). This is a view of globalisation as an elemental force of nature which conjures up the idea of an economic whirlwind or tsunami, something which is useful imagery, but completely dangerous and wrong.

Peter Mandelson stated of New Labour's attitude to the City: 'There's almost nothing in the world to rival it. Of course, you have to support it. You want to advance it and you want to grow it' (Rawnsley, 2010: 480). This fed into a deeply reactionary, populist politics which spiralled right-wards on welfare, immigration and law and order. Peter Hyman, who worked for Blair in Downing Street, summarised his former master's credo: 'He also hates losers, hates impotence, hates meaningless protest' (2005: 94). That summary is an accurate description of the prejudices of the global elite who New Labour aligned themselves with.

Months before the collapse of Northern Rock, Gordon Brown, in his last Mansion House speech, proclaimed that thanks to the achievements of his ten year 'era', he could safely say that 'history will record [it] as the beginning of a new golden age for the City of London'. This had implications for the entire economy,

> I believe that the lesson we learn from the success of the City has ramifications beyond the City itself – that we are leading because we are first in putting to work exactly the set of qualities that is needed for global success.

Foremost among these was a 'deep and abiding belief in open markets' (Hassan and Barnett, 2009).

All of this was to come home to haunt New Labour as first Northern Rock had to be rescued, then RBS and HBOS had to be nationalised, forcing

Brown and others to eat the words of praise and the knighthood they had bestowed on Sir Fred Goodwin, who had trashed RBS by a series of colossal mistakes and over-expansion. One problem for Labour post-crash, which proved impossible for Brown as Prime Minister and Alistair Darling as Chancellor, was to satisfactorily offer any explanation of Labour's romance with the City, nor after the bubble burst to develop any convincing Labour position on the economy. But this was not just a problem for Labour.

The SNP's embrace of neo-liberalism followed a similar trajectory to New Labour. In the 1999 Scottish Parliament, Salmond and others approvingly cited the Laffer Curve, an analysis which had been used to justify Reaganite tax cuts in America, alongside their usual tax and spend pronouncements. Four years later, Salmond showed this was no exception when he said, 'Art Laffer's famous curve is alive and well, but for business rather than personal taxation' (*The Scotsman*, 25 February 2003).

When Salmond returned as leader in 2004 the party was affected by, and bought into, the great British bubble. Mike Russell, for example, co-wrote a book, *Grasping the Thistle*, which proposed shrinking the state by 40 per cent in the first four years of an independent Scotland: the kind of brutal shock therapy not even seen in scale in post-Communist Europe (MacLeod and Russell, 2006). Not surprisingly, he subsequently disowned it, with Salmond furious for the political flank it had exposed.

The election of the SNP as a minority government in 2007 brought the tensions between social democratic sentiment and buying into market determinism to the fore. Just before the election, in April 2007, Salmond spoke of the need under independence for 'light-touch regulation suitable to a Scottish financial sector with its outstanding reputation for probity' (*Daily Telegraph*, 16 October 2008). As the cracks began to appear in the British banking system, Salmond and the SNP, like New Labour, reacted by trying to offer reassurance and keep the show on the road. The Fred Goodwin inspired RBS purchase of Dutch bank ABN Amro was enthusiastically supported by Salmond (as it was by New Labour), who personally wrote to Goodwin to 'offer any assistance' with 'the bid' (*Sunday Herald*, 8 August 2010). Salmond seems at this point to have had a curious faith in the efficacy of the Financial Services Authority and UK regulation: a judgement which was to be proven spectacularly wrong (Fraser, 2014).

Then when Edinburgh based HBOS were forced into a merger with Lloyds TSB, Salmond at first condemned 'spivs and speculators' and called it a 'shotgun marriage' (*BBC News*, 17 September 2008). Things got more serious with the collapse of RBS and, as the UK government was planning nationalisation, Salmond, in a *Newsnight Scotland* interview, refused to condemn Goodwin and appeared politically to have lost his touch, declaring generally that there should be 'no scapegoats' (*Newsnight Scotland*, 13 October 2008).

Perhaps the most revealing comments of Salmond's attempt to point in two directions at the same time came in an interview with publisher Iain Dale. Talking about the SNP's opposition to Thatcherism, he commented, 'We didn't mind the economic side so much, but we didn't like the social side at all' (*Total Politics*, September 2008). Salmond and the SNP tried to explain and qualify the remarks, with Salmond having to take to the airwaves the next day to try and talk himself out his own remarks with little success.

A final example is the Scottish Government's current policy on corporation tax. Once the UK Government announced its intention to reduce the tax to 20 per cent by 2015, the Scottish Government declared that its policy would be to undercut this by three per cent whatever the UK/rUK rate (which Nobel Prize winning economist and Scottish Government Council of Economic Advisers member Joe Stiglitz has criticised [*The Herald*, 30 May 2013]). A discussion paper produced by the government claimed this could produce 27,000 new jobs and an extra 1.4 per cent economic growth over a 20-year period (*BBC News*, 9 September 2011). Similar to SNP policies on currency and monetary union after independence, this policy seemed to be trying to make a virtue out of the Treasury still controlling a large part of macro-economic and monetary policy post-independence.

The above remarks from Labour and SNP politicians show their similar views on banking, the economy and neo-liberalism, with little recalcitrance since the crash. This is not sufficiently talked about in Scotland. Instead, we have to witness a phoney war between Labour and SNP over such shibboleths as who most closely befriended Rupert Murdoch and his court, or ingratiated themselves with Fred Goodwin in his RBS reign of terror. This is displacement activity of the worst kind: both parties totally offered to acquiesce to the age of the self-defined masters of the universe. That is bad enough. Since the crash, this has all just been glossed over as if none of it had ever happened.

Scotland needs a meaningful debate to address the realities and compromises that politicians and informed opinion created with the mindset of 'Fantasyland Britain'. To do otherwise is to contribute to our very own 'fantasyland Scotland', kidding ourselves that we were not affected and tainted by the delusions of the bubble and neo-liberal orthodoxy. It contributes to collective thinking that Scotland's supposed social democratic consensus is enough; that we have resisted the market vandals who inhabit

Westminster, and that our choices, public services and outcomes already contribute to us being progressive, inclusive and different. If only that were the case, we would be living in a better country than today. But even if it were, we would still have to resist the Scots' propensity to want to close down debate and not interrogate too closely uncomfortable facts.

## How Do We Have A Different Tone of Debate?

In concluding, one of the characteristics this book sets out to value is empathy – the quality elucidated by Karyn McCluskey of the Violence Reduction Unit quoted at the outset of this chapter. Some simplistic accounts of the human condition state (following on from the Beatles) that 'all we need is love'. But this is transparently not the case. For love in too many circumstances can fall into loving too much, not being able to deal with the cavalcade of emotions, and in particular those who don't love what you love. Thus, there is a direct relationship between love and hate which can be seen too often in Scotland: in the Celtic/Rangers divide, religion and politics.

Empathy is different. It means emotionally moving beyond the limits of the idea of the self, to recognising and understanding the needs and interests of others. It requires engagement, listening, calm, quiet and reflection. It necessitates that we begin to consider that the world does not start from our own views and then to spread out in a linear way to views we must change or overcome.

A Scotland which valued empathy would look and feel dramatically different. It would have conversations where people did not talk past each other. It would recognise a range of responses and logic – from the rational to the emotional and a variety of impulses and influences which shape our views. And it would radically alter the contours of our society and debates – for example, assisting in getting us past the binary nature of Yes and No in the independence debate.

This book has been written in the spirit of empathy, of trying to under-stand the dynamics and motivations of people and different perspectives in contemporary Scotland. Whatever I have to say about any individual or group or any views, I have done so while trying to empathise and respect their views, and to recognise that they are trying to make a valu-able contribution. I am not claiming to have always succeeded in this, but I hope readers will feel I have at least tried.

In the forthcoming chapters, one important distinction is the funda-mental difference between the concepts of optimism and hope. These are often used interchangeably or in the same sentence complementarily, but are very different, even opposing, ideas.

Part of the allure of optimism is that it often makes the claim that everything will be alright and work out fine whatever the challenges or pressures. The mindset of hope much more often starts with an engagement or understanding of the real world. Barbara Ehrenreich, in her study of positive thinking, observed that in the US, optimism has become an 'ideology' and offered the following distinction between optimism and hope:

> Hope is an emotion, a yearning, the experience of which is not entirely within our control. Optimism is a cognitive stance, a conscious experience, which presumably anyone can develop through practice. (2009: 4)

Rabbi Jonathan Sacks, responding to Ehrenreich's book, observed that,

> Optimism is a passive virtue, hope an active one. It needs no courage, only a certain naiveté, to be an optimist. It needs a great deal of courage to have hope (*The Times*, 1 May 2010).

Capitalism by its nature has a culture of self-proclaimed optimism – linked to cycles of growth and recession, exuberance and retreat. This has an institutional optimism found in governments, banks and economic forecasting with a built-in bias to exaggeration and inflated predictions. This is combined with the rationale of linear optimism across the West pre-crash – an outlook centred on the idea of incremental growth and prosperity being a given. Taking this alongside the power given to measuring the world through numbers (growth, profit, loss) and mediated data, this legitimises instability, short-termism and a blinkered view of human behaviour. It is a perspective which was completely caught out by the global crash of 2008, and crisis of large parts of the international financial market.

If capitalist optimism illustrates the worst excesses of optimism, the idea of hope has to be differentiated and reclaimed. An important perspective in Ernst Bloch's *The Principle of Hope* makes the case that hope is a motivating force which lies at the very centre of humanity, and offers the prospect of animating actions and beliefs (1986). This outlook runs through significant parts of the arguments in this book, and offers part of the terrain for a radically different politics, culture and prospectus for social change.

This book has been influenced by a range of perspectives, eclectic, diverse and from far and wide. In terms of Scottish influences in recent years, one important contribution has been Carol Craig's *The Scots' Crisis of Confidence* (2003), a book I had the privilege of commissioning and publishing, and which has a special place in my heart. Craig's book acts as a lodestar to many, attracting many with its wide canvas and observations, while frustrating others for its deliberate failure to not stick to one predictable recipe. Then there are others, such as Lesley Riddoch's more recent *Blossom* (2013), which are deeply human and searching for a different kind of social change and Scotland of the future. Riddoch is also, in a way I admire, ever present as a dynamic force of positivity in her book, acknowledging her biases and motivations. Finally, in a very different style, there is Andy Wightman's *The Poor Had No Lawyers* (2010), which, as I explore later, offers an interrogation of power and the reclamation of lost history which both breaks new ground and taps into earlier radical traditions which need to be remembered and re-utilised.

From outwith Scotland, Fintan O'Toole's two critiques of Irish orthodoxies and the hubris of the 'Celtic Tiger' and its hangover, post-bubble, *Ship of Fools* (2009) and *Enough is Enough* (2010), offer a mix of polemical and informed thinking which takes on elites and asks public opinion to stop engaging in self-deception. O'Toole's prospectus is a call for taking on the myths of Irish society, and in particular, the notion that Ireland is a republic, calling for a 'second republic'. Then there was the writing of American academic and activist Stephen Duncombe who in *Dream: Re-imagining Progressive Politics in an Age of Fantasy* (2007), took on the constricted menu of too much of the left and radical opinion, and instead posed the importance of fun, play, irreverence and humour: an agenda with much relevance to Scotland.

Finally, this book is offered not as a final word or attempt at closing any debate, but as a call for an opening, and for more generous and wide-ranging public conversations. I have written it openly motivated by all the usual influences that people bring to such a project, thinking that their observations and insights may offer some inspiration to others. However, at the same time, a conscious personal strand runs through this book, and at several select points I reflect on my own experiences to connect this up to wider issues. I hope readers will find that this honesty and humanity aids the flow and case laid out in the book, for it is an approach I feel could facilitate a more genuine and engaging set of exchanges – ones which rise to the historic, challenging times we live in.

The environment in which we find ourselves is one of Scotland having changed and continuing to change, but many of our terms of reference, attitudes and habits do not reflect this. Many of the traditional institutions and ways of thinking about our nation and society are no longer adequate for the times we live in, while large sections of public opinion and what passed for commentary cling understandably to familiar and comforting truths.

The debate Scotland finds itself in during the year 2014 can only be understood in this historic perspective: reflecting on where we have come from, how we got here, and where we might be going. This dynamic – of a dramatically changing Scotland, the waning power of traditional authority but its inability to adapt or die, and the question of what kind of Scotland we collectively want to live in – will not be fully answered by the September 2014 vote. Instead, this is a debate without a final destination, which is reflective of a country trying to come to terms with what it is and what it wants to be. There can be no end point to that, but if we do it justice, we can begin to live in a country more attuned to the values and beliefs most of us aspire to.

CHAPTER TWO

# The Six Myths of Modern Scotland

When a country loses the dynamic of its own history the ability to develop on its own terms, its sense of its past can fragment and freeze into caricature. For a long time this was Scotland's fate...

A sense of continuity was difficult to grasp. This was the pop-up picture school of history. Oh, look, there's Bonnie Prince Charlie. Where did he come from? And that's Mary Queen of Scots. Somebody cut her head off. Wasn't it the English?

Moments of history isolated in this way from the qualifying details of context can be made to mean whatever we want them to mean. Our relationship to them tends to be impulsive and emotional rather than rational, since, there is so little for rationality to feed on. We see our past as a series of gestures rather than a sequence of events.

William McIlvanney, 'Freeing Ourselves from Inner Exile', *The Herald*, 6 March 1999

Modern Scotland is a land shaped by the power of myths and folklore. This is understandable as myths are fundamental to being human. But Scotland has arguably created a set of myths which tell a too cosy, comforting account of who we are, and which act as a kind of collective self-deception.

These myths have, for understandable reasons, differentiated us from the rest of the UK and England in particular, and externalised many of our problems by absolving us of responsibility for our situation. This is a kind of quasi-Brigadoon – a fictional political and social community which does not correspond to the reality of the country we live in. It bears a partial relationship to modern Scotland, in a way which aided us in the 1980s and 1990s, but which has now become increasingly problematic. Below, six myths of modern Scotland are outlined that need to be understood and transcended if we are ever to reinvent and reimagine our society in the future.

## One: The Myth of Scottish Democracy

Scottish people of all and no political persuasions profess the belief that they live in a democracy and country with proud, deep-rooted democratic credentials. Until they accept that this is not the case and understand that Scotland is not a fully-fledged political democracy, our chances of democratising our politics and society will prove impossible.

Scots cite as proof of their democratic traditions such tropes as the idea of popular sovereignty and the ancient idea that the monarch's authority sprang from the people, not God. Yet Scotland has not, and never has, been a real political democracy (as will be explored in more detail in Chapter Six). Our society has historically been run by elites; and the people are not, for all the rhetoric, genuinely active citizens in public life.

The so-called democratic realm of Scotland has been limited, heavily controlled and constrained. Today large parts of society are shaped by the notion of 'missing Scotland', which is defined in subsequent chapters. The 'high Scotland' which characterised public life for much of our history was more often than not a product of distinctive Scottish characteristics: of national and local elites operating to curtail debate, appropriate wealth and resources, and to incorporate people via a mix of patronage and preferment. Such a culture stifled challenges and dissent, and from the 19th-century Liberals to 20th-century Labour, the contemporary SNP and 'civic Scotland', forces of radical, progressive and left opinion have consistently avoided challenging this closed order. Instead they have used it for their own ends and to buttress their own nomenklatura.

## Two: The Myth of Egalitarianism

Many Scots people identify and see themselves in the traditional story of Scotland as egalitarian, inclusive, having a lack of deference and absence of class distinctions. The actual picture in modern Scotland and historically is rather different. Scotland is only slightly less unequal than England. In 2012 it was estimated that Scotland's wealthiest households were 273 times richer than its poorer households while Scotland's 100 richest men and women were calculated to be worth £21 billion – an increase from £18 billion the previous year (Oxfam Scotland, 2013: 27).

In some indicators, such as health inequalities, Scotland does not only rate much worse than England, it has the worst record of all Western Europe. A Save the Children report found a scandalous picture of life expectancy in modern Scotland: 'A child born in Lenzie North, a more affluent area of Glasgow can expect to live 28 years longer than a child born in Calton, a more deprived area of the same city' (Save the Children Scotland, 2013). An adaptation of Glasgow's railway network illustrates the relationship between nearby geographies across the city and huge health inequalities.

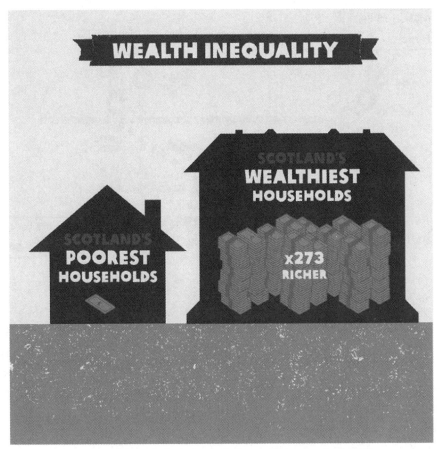

Fig. 1 Wealth Inequality in Scotland. *Source: Oxfam Scotland, 2013.*

The Scottish ideal of egalitarianism is deeply embedded in our culture through phrases such as 'Jock Tamson's Bairns', but what has been conspicuously absent has been a worked out, thorough idea of equality, and how it is to be understood and implemented. Instead, the egalitarian myth is more an attitude, aspiration and inspiration, a state of mind and belief in how people should act in relation to each other. This has made the Scots idea of equality profoundly meritocratic (in the modern sense of the word) and able to sit at ease with success, wealth and both extreme affluence and poverty.

Despite the power of this myth, less proscribed and more radical ideas of equality from the left and socialists have not been implemented. Scots have traditionally shown disdain towards the flaunting of wealth or being ostentatious, but this has historically not translated into a programme or a political will to redistribute power and wealth which has, until now, been seen as off the agenda.

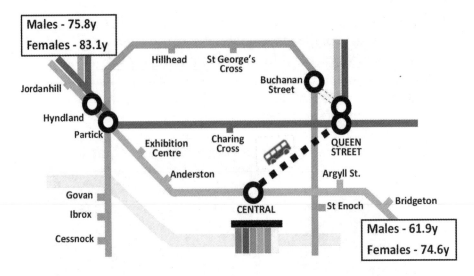

Life expectancy data refers to 2001-5 and was extracted from the GCPH community health and well-being profiles. Adapted from the SPT travel map by Gerry McCartney.

**Fig. 2** Health Inequalities in Glasgow.

There are contradictions and paradoxes in of all of this, and an element of Scots collectively not seeming to act to implement one of the central pillars of how they have defined and presented themselves. But this has been made possible by their attitude of not wishing to develop a more specific idea of equality which prioritises tackling inequality, privilege and poverty.

## Three: The Myth of Educational Opportunity

Related to egalitarianism is the conventional story of education – from the lad o' pairts, to the Kirriemuir career and the democratic intellect – which all emphasise the distinctive nature of how education has been seen north of the border.

Scotland is not the land of educational opportunity and advancement that it presents itself in folklore. In the age of international league tables on every conceivable subject, Scotland's educational inequalities (as well as the UK's) hold our overall ratings back, and should shock even the most cursory reader. At age 15, the richest quartile of pupils are at the level of Hong Kong overall (third in the Pisa tables of 2012), while the poorest quartile matches that of Turkey (44th in the Pisa tables) (*The Scotsman*, 21 November 2013).

It is true that Scotland sends more students to higher and further education than England (56 per cent to 49 per cent), but there is also a deep-seated social apartheid which disfigures every part of society. Take Scotland's universities and colleges. St Andrews University aspires for its latest intake to admit a mere 19 students of working-class background; Glasgow School of Art fairs even more poorly with seven students in its current year; both of these institutions have achieved these figures with the aid of significant access and participation programmes.

Scottish politicians may be able to repeat the mantra 'no tuition fees', but underneath the difference between the Scottish and English systems isn't as stark as presumed. For example, blogger Graeme Cowie looked at the debts that Scottish students in Scotland and English students in England build up; this produces a sizeable difference – £18k in Scotland, and £37.5k–£43k in England. But Scottish students start repaying at a lower threshold of income: £15,795 versus £21,000 in England at the end of 2012, which means that the Scottish system can be more regressive and punitive, particularly to those on lower incomes (Predictable Paradox, 9 December 2012).

Another issue that Scots shy away from is the role of private education. This has been described by one educational commentator as 'the elephant in the room', in relation to Edinburgh – where 24.7 per cent of secondary age school children go to private schools (Roberts, 2013: 121). This then affects some of Scotland's universities: 40 per cent of all entrants to St Andrews University and 30 per cent of Edinburgh are privately educated, and in Scotland as in elsewhere in the UK, these privileged groups disproportionately fill up middle-class professions such as accountancy, law and medicine.

Too many Scots do not want to confront difficult facts about the Scots and education, and prefer to find succour in the repetition of myth and cliché. There is the constant evoking by Scottish Government ministers of 'free tuition fees', and celebration of Scottish universities (and their world ratings), along with education at all levels, without beginning to face up to how they fall short. These accounts don't address how education lets too many Scots down, the barriers of exclusion in higher and further education making too many places exclusively the preserve of the middle class, and the question of where innovation and change comes from in the system.

## Four: The Myth of Holding Power to Account

Many Scots have a strange relationship to those with power in their land. Our radical sentiment about ourselves tells us that we scrutinise, challenge and cajole power and authority, but modern day Scotland offers a very different story. For most of the post-war era, Scots seem to have operated on the basis of a 'don't ask, don't tell' policy with those in power and positions of influence – being prepared to trust the faux people's stories of the public sector, various professions and those in business.

Only belatedly with the establishment of the Scottish Parliament has some of this begun to become apparent, but there is still a long way to go. For example, while in an area such as land ownership the huge concentrations of power have come more to the fore, this does not automatically equate with action. Scotland's 432 private estates own more than half the non-public land of Scotland (*The Independent*, 1 August 2013) – one of the most pronounced concentrations of ownership in all Europe – and bodies such as Scottish Lands and Estates (the lobby organisation for private estates) feel they are under scrutiny and pressure.

However, radical change requires a combination of political and popular will, along with an awareness that injustice needs to be rectified, and in land ownership, like other areas, this does not yet exist. How else can be explained the timid actions of the first Labour-Lib Dem Scottish Executive on land reform, or the even more cautious approach of the SNP Government, determined not to alienate big land owners, and presenting as action the setting up of a Land Reform Review Group under Alison Elliot (then chair of SCVO) which issued a report which gave the perception of change, but contained little substance.

Holding power to account involves the popular will wanting change and a political leadership having courage to take on vested interests and powerful voices which will resist and make life difficult. So far Scotland's politicians through the ages have chosen not to embark on this course, but this could change as deference continues to decline, and the pressures of continued austerity and public spending cuts start to hurt even more.

## Five: The Myth of Social Democracy

The most influential account of modern Scotland in recent years has been one that says we are the land that said no to Thatcherism, the Tories, the poll tax, and proved ourselves to have the credentials of 'radical Scotland'. This is supposedly because of the strength of Scotland's centre-left and progressive values. However, this is a strange kind of social democratic politics and settlement unlike anywhere else in the developed world.

What kind of social democracy is distorted by seismic inequalities, poverty and exclusion? For too many, the starting point in life and background a child comes from pre-determines their future life chances and outcomes; while the most powerful institutions and professions of the country seem to act as a mixture of a closed shop and self-preservation society, operating through multi-generational patterns of restricting social mobility and access.

Scotland's social democracy has been part sentiment, part romance, but has also offered a legitimising political story of the middle classes to validate their position in the system. The cumulative and distributional choices of politics has aided those with voice, assets and material resources, and not assisted those without these characteristics. This has been a social democracy for the middle class by the middle class, and Labour, SNP and 'civic Scotland' have played a contributory role in maintaining this.

If enough Scots want to live in a country known for its centre-left, progressive values, then a radical revision of how we think and act collectively is required. It would entail addressing the scale of poverty and exclusion, how the most vulnerable and marginalised are treated, and prioritising widening the life chances and opportunities of children to make sure that people are not left behind and written off from birth because of their background. This involves difficult choices and taking on those with the loudest, most articulate voices, and for this to happen, those who are currently failed by Scotland's supposed social democracy, need to speak up and say this is not good enough.

## Six: The Myth of Open Scotland

Finally, there is the myth of open Scotland. This states that we are a warm, welcoming place – for immigrants and visitors – and that our Scottish identity is inclusive, pluralist and comfortable with diversity.

There is truth in this account of Scotland: the lack of a popular base historically for the hard right, racist BNP; even the absence of support or any representation for Ukip so far. There are, however, also limitations. Scotland has within its multi-culturalism powerful monocultures and denials and antagonisms towards different cultures and identities.

Immigrants to Scotland face, just like elsewhere in the UK, racism, xenophobia and discrimination. And while most Scots have no issue with individual English people, there is a perfidious low-level anti-Englishness across large swathes of Scotland that should make us reflect on just how welcoming and inclusive we are as a society. English people are the largest national minority in Scotland (forming the largest group in the 417,000 non-Scots born elsewhere in the 2011 census), and yet there is amongst some the constant drip of 'Anyone But England' at football, and a host of similar attitudes which too many try to diminish as just being humour. This after all is how racism through the ages has been justified.

Scotland historically has had difficulty with immigration – witness the tensions around Irish immigration in the 19th and 20th centuries. This produced reactionary, prejudiced responses from large parts of the Scottish establishment, including widespread discrimination into the 1960s and 1970s. The Church of Scotland's infamous 1923 report on Irish immigration contained shocking attitudes and language, for which the church only apologised in recent years. In the inter-war years, Glasgow and Edinburgh politics were shaped by virulent Protestant, anti-Catholic parties which won mass support, with the leader in Edinburgh remaining on the council until 1962.

To this day, the Celtic and Rangers rivalry disfigures large parts of Scottish society, consumes too many football fans, and has led to what many see as problematic, flawed legislation – the Offensive Behaviour at Football and Threatening Communications (Scotland) Act 2012.

The Scottish Government's White Paper on independence identified that Scotland needs more immigrants to counter our aging population and meet future demographic challenges (Scottish Government, 2013). In this it inferred that Scotland is more welcoming and tolerant of immigration than England, but this is a dangerous assumption: only four per cent of Scots are of black and ethnic minority origin, compared to 14 per cent of England. Ian Jack, writing after the government paper was published, stated, 'Perhaps there is a little smugness here and elsewhere in the White Paper', and went on to say:

> The idea that Scotland is friendlier to foreigners or people of other ethnicities has proved remarkably stubborn, partly because the country has adopted such a bowdlerised version of its imperial history into which slaves, indentured labourers and massacres have only recently been admitted.
>
> *The Guardian*, 30 November 2013

A genuinely 'open Scotland' has to recognise some of the unattractive aspects of our past so as not to fall for a completely upbeat panglossian version of the present. It has to challenge the power and rationale of monocultural Scotland and within that, our very own exclusionists and deniers of the benefits of immigration and multi-culturalism.

# The Decline of the 'Too Small, Too Poor, Too Divided' Myth of Scotland

The combined effect of the six myths of modern society does not mean that Scotland is completely defined by negative characteristics. That would perpetuate another belittling Scottish myth which has had too much power through our history.

The account of Scottish inadequacy and lack of confidence is a well-known one. Most Scots have heard it, encountered it, and even know it in their own hearts. It states that as Scots we are too small, too poor, too divided, almost even too Scottish to take responsibility for ourselves and take charge of our own destiny. It has been a pernicious doctrine, one which has dwelt on the various setbacks and disasters of Scottish history – serious – Flodden, Darien and Culloden – and not so serious – Argentina 1978. It has been told by those who don't want the internal status quo and stasis of Scottish society to be changed, and who have much to lose from change. But the tragedy is that millions of Scots throughout history have believed it too.

Why the Scots should prove so susceptible to such a negative tale about themselves is seldom examined. Why should we as a nation through the centuries buy into a collective mindset which has strengthened political and cultural miserablism, and reinforced a sense of powerlessness and fatalism, both collectively and individually? The answers can only be found in our history and memories of the past.

For one, Scottish culture encompasses a profound, deeply embedded sense of loss, and because of this, of melancholy and pessimism. Think of the things Scotland has lost in its past – its statehood, millions of its people to emigration, and of course, in more recent times, the brutal deindustrialisation of the 1980s. Before the latter there was the loss of seismic societal and population changes: the Highland Clearances and the depopulation of huge areas of rural Scotland, and then the dislocation of rapid industrialisation with all the disorientation that entailed.

Second, the retention of Scotland as a political, legal and cultural community post-1707 – a society of autonomy in a stateless nation – was in Tom Nairn's words, 'a peculiarly patrician bargain between two ruling classes... a nationality which resigned statehood... a decapitated national state, as it were, rather than an ordinary 'assimilated nationality' (1975: 24). This produced a Scottish identity and public life which was depoliticised and about administration and bureaucracy, and where imagination, innovation and boldness were left to the numerous inventors or the Scottish imperialists who went off and ran the British Empire. The public life of the Scotland of the union while preserving our identity and distinctiveness did so in a way which reminded people of what was absent: power.

Third, there is the question of our relationship with England – historically Scotland's single most important external relationship. This has been one of relative harmony these last three centuries, but in the past blighted by many battles and spilt blood. To this day, Scots take perhaps a little too much umbrage at what they regard as English slights: from the constant referencing of 'England' when they mean 'United Kingdom', to Scottish football being denigrated by English opinion, and to Scotland's historic status as a nation often ignored.

This contributes to what Pierre Trudeau referred to as the 'in bed with the elephant' outlook (he was talking about Canada's relationship with the US), whereby Scots feel their identity and nation is fragile and under threat, and facing possible extinction at any time. The Thatcher years, for example, gave vent to this strand, with various Scots commentators worried that the right-wing policies of her Government could have led to the Anglicisation of Scots education, and ultimately, 'the Englishing of Scotland'. Of course, they didn't, but such fears are never far from the surface.

Finally, not all of this sense of loss can be translated into being about politics. Another dimension has been the elements of Scottish culture which have encouraged this pessimism. One factor has been the influence of religion, and in particular that of the Presbyterian tradition, with its belief in being damned or saved, and which has contributed to what many have seen as 'the divided self' theory of Scots identity – witnessed historically in the construction of the Caledonian Antisyzygy and in more recent times by R.D. Laing and Tom Nairn. This emasculated sense of self is seen as too enfeebled and in conflict to have voice, and has played a significant part in the too divided, too unsure and shaped by internal doubt and conflict argument which has so diminished Scottish confidence; at its worst this has played a part in the pathologising and problematising of identity.

These factors are a product of our history, and a mix of things Scots have done to themselves besides the impact of external influences and dynamics. The above menu of negativity has been reinforced by those who want Scottish society to remain as it is, and powerful forces outwith Scotland within the citadels of the British establishment.

These accounts of doubt, anxiety and fear have been with us for centuries, and will not disappear overnight, but in recent decades, have weakened dramatically. It is not hard to work out why. There have been the multiple crises and relative decline of Britain from the 1960s onward, the discovery of North Sea Oil in the 1960s, and the rightward drift of British politics over the same period. At the same time, the Scottish self-government movement has grown in status and confidence, and reshaped Scotland in politics, culture and identities.

The coming of the Scottish Parliament, the election of the first SNP Government in 2007 and the ongoing independence debate are all part of this gradual maturing of our society. All of this contributes to the erosion of those old negative stories but, as we can witness in the current referendum debate, they still have some traction, particularly from some of the older traditional Labour voices who feel they have much to lose from independence.

Beginning the process of being honest about some of the myths and folklores we have grown comfortable telling and are happy to believe about ourselves is not a negative act. It is not an act of collective national self-flagellation. Rather, continuing to define ourselves by holding as truths things which are self-evidently false, is a sign of doubt and defensiveness.

Understanding the above myths as this is an empowering act of being honest and truthful about where we are and who we are, the past choices we have made, and the future difficult debates we cannot afford to put off. This is, to put it bluntly, a moment for potential national renewal and mobilising our energies and talents, and for understanding the self-interest of Scots and British elites who have contributed these beliefs, while the facts on the ground were very different.

Confronting the myths of modern Scotland goes hand in hand with taking on the historic diminishing and belittling of Scotland. It is about embracing complexities, contradictions and ambiguities: that we have lots of things to be rightly proud of, and quite a few we should be ashamed of. We are a 'mongrel nation' and a mix of disparate characteristics and values, but one strand that we have progressed in recent times and need to encourage, is our maturing as a society and nation. That means understanding the myths which have shaped us and knowing them for what they are. We need to stop engaging in self-deception and reflect on what modern Scotland is and what we aspire it to be. Only by doing this can we begin charting an accurate path from where we are now to where we want to be in the future.

CHAPTER THREE

# The Personal is Political

How many times have I wondered if it is really possible to forge links with a mass of people when one has never had strong feelings for anyone, not even one's own parents: if it is possible to have a collectivity when one has not been deeply loved oneself by individual human creatures. Hasn't this had some effect on my life as a militant – has it not tended to make me sterile and reduce my quality as a revolutionary by making everything a matter of pure intellect, of pure mathematical calculation?

ANTONIO GRAMSCI, quoted in *Giuseppe Fiori*, Antonio Gramsci:
*Life of a Revolutionary*, New Left Books 1965

THERE IS A COMMON caricature prevalent in much of modern Scotland which is filled with an air of fatalism and pessimism. It says, amongst many things, the following sentiments: 'where are the stories of hope in Scotland?' and 'where is the hope which once defined much of society?'

These feelings can be sourced to a number of variants among the liberal professional classes in institutional Scotland and in wider cultural, social and political conversations. I will explore the first two groups and their sense of profound pessimism and its consequences later, but suffice to say, that the belief in the absence of hope, change and different realities, is depowering and limiting, and only of assistance to the maintenance of the status quo.

It is also wrong in its analysis. For what it ignores is the issue of the connection and disconnection between the individual and collective stories which animate our consciousness and that of wider society. So when various voices articulate the line of 'where is the hope?' – what we have to address is the rich, diverse, challenging realities of most peoples' lives in Scotland. Put it this way, before the current set of crises, before the pressures of the crash, the cuts and austerity, most of the lives of individual Scots from baby boomers and pre-baby boomers to Generations x (pre-1980) and y (post-1980), were shaped not by a lack of hope and disillusion, but a sense of possibilities, choices and hope.

Are not the accounts of most of our lives up until recent troubles shaped mostly by richness and possibility, and a belief that things would get better? At the same time, one of the emerging trends, even pre-crash, has been the growing disconnection between how people see their own lives and that of their families, and the collective sense of how they see wider society. This long-term divergence is one that needs close examination, and in these more difficult times, we need to explore the personal terrain of hope, anxiety and how we think of the future, and their relation to the collective stories that are told.

Our personal stories matter in this. They tell something of how we interpret and frame the world, and our formative influences and external environments have a huge impact on the values and ideas we choose. This is all obvious, but it is relevant to point out because too few of our political accounts in Scotland seem to acknowledge the role of the personal. Instead, they talk of the abstract, of theory, of events, history and people, with the role of the individual and the author's experience and background left unstated in the text, as if such areas can be 'neutral'.

There is an academic version of this, which, despite all the convulsion of university fashion and the fads of a debauched post-modernism and relativism, has posed 'knowledge' in an ideological vacuum, and in so doing, involved a retreat from politics, engagement and wider understanding. But that is only one strand. There is a widespread Scottish sensibility, which is a reticence about personal reflection and sharing, and while this has weakened across society, it can still be found in writing whether it is journalism, articles and books, and even much of everyday conversation.

A recent exception in this was Iain Macwhirter's *Road to Referendum* book (Macwhirter, 2013). At significant points the author is present in the text, without the book being about the author. Thus, we hear of Macwhirter's reflections on growing up in Edinburgh in the 1950s and 1960s, and his memory of how stuffy and oppressive the place was, his rejection of his parent's Scottish nationalism in the 1970s, and his constant lecturing of them on the superiority of a politics of internationalism, much to his embarrassment now.

## *The Road from Dundee*

A short exploration of my personal story is relevant to this. I grew up in Dundee, and my parents, Eddie and Jean, gave me, their only son, a secure, loving childhood. They both had decent employment, were socially and politically aware, and passionately and widely self-educated, my father having read Marx's three volume *Capital* in his teenage years, and my mother widely reading good fiction from Kafka and Woodhouse to Orwell and Greene.

My childhood was spent in the council estate of Ardler, built in the north-west corner of the city, where the city authorities had acquired the land of Downfield Golf Course, and built six tower blocks in an environment filled with green spaces, trees, and play areas. It was in many respects the perfect environment for a child, being defined by safety, trust and a sense of community, and against the backdrop of rising working-class living standards and increasing prosperity.

I can still recall elements of complexity in this generally uplifting, positive experience. We moved to Ardler in 1968 when our tower block, Edzell Court, was opened and for most of nearly the first decade we didn't know any male breadwinner who was unemployed. Then there was the planned new Secondary School for the area, which was never built and indefinitely shelved. And even as a teenager, I knew without knowing the details, that it signaled something of trouble ahead. That was the summer of 1976, and the Labour Government's IMF induced public spending cuts.

Then there was my father's employment. He worked at National Cash Register (NCR), the American based multinational, who along with Timex had a big employment presence in the city. His work there gave him pride, identity and a whole sense of male camaraderie. But in the 1970s as the economy hit trouble and unemployment rose, companies like NCR were engaged in major retrenchment in Dundee, and in 1978 they were offering generous packages of voluntary redundancy, one of which my father took.

This entailed a fundamental change in how my father saw himself, the extent to which I can only see now, decades later. He became unemployed, and I had never known anyone who this had happened to, with the exception of one friend's father who had a temporary period of unemployment and then became a bin man. It shames me now to recall that moment, but myself and my friends made fun of our pal because of his father taking such a job.

My father Edwin Hassan at home in Ardler, Dundee, 1978.

My father was unemployed for about six months in the summer and autumn of 1978, and I didn't tell any of my friends or teachers. I felt some kind of shame about it which I couldn't completely explain at the time, although now its reasoning looks obvious. In this period, my father went to the Manpower

Services Commission (MSC) retraining to aid him in his skills, and then got a job as a traffic warden, a job he completely and utterly despised. I do now see that my father's view of himself, and my mother's view of him, changed dramatically after this period, and never really completely recovered, eventually leading a couple of years later to their separation.

Throughout my childhood my parents had a fairly positive outlook on life, society and what opportunities they thought would be available to their son. My parents believed in Britain, the future, and the idea of the labour movement as a means of bringing about social change.

These were the three pillars of post-war Scotland and indeed post-war Britain, the powerful, potent account of 'Labour Britain' which had been given such foundation and form in the post-war Attlee Government. My father was in the 1970s working at NCR also a member of the Communist Party (CP), and active in the Shop Stewards' Combine Committee. My mother was involved in community politics, and contributed towards the running of the community centre and local newsletter.

There was a strange kind of tension between their politics and outlook to the world, which even though it was regularly played out in front of me, it took years for me to fully appreciate. My father, despite his shop steward role, for a period was mostly an armchair activist who liked to reflect on the world and challenge others from the comfort of his own living room (or if pushed, a neighbour's living room). That was apart for a brief period, the sum total of his commitment to bringing about revolution. My mother on the other hand just did things, got involved in planning, pushing and agitating across a range of issues. And to think for years into early adulthood, I thought my father was the political one; then it suddenly dawned on me, my mother was the real political activist.

My parents' worldviews influenced me in so many ways that it is difficult to list and do justice. On a general level, they gave me a deep seated belief that people collectively together can bring about social change, can shape and create the future, and the importance of a sense of optimism and hope. There are also more nuanced feelings. My father's membership of the CP always gave me from an early age an understanding that to be part of the wider labour movement, you didn't have to either be in the Labour Party or buy the 'official' Labour leadership line. Then there was an awareness of the tension between abstract politics informed by a sense of gesture and symbolism, which my father inhabited quite a bit of the time, and my mother's politics, of doing things and bringing people together.

Both of my parents were outgoing and at their best, energising and sociable people through most of my childhood years. We had a house full of people most weekends, and a constant supply of people coming to our door for a brief chat or going out entertaining. There is a small qualification I want to put to that. Part of my father's expression of this commitment to left politics was very different from the above qualities; it was shaped by a belief that he had the right to tell people off, correct them, and lecture them about the state of the world.

My mother Jean Hassan at home in Dundee in 1982.

Sizeable parts of my childhood are filled with memories of my parents having enjoyable times with friends, but with an underlying tension of my mother trying to keep my father off politics. Maybe this was a common experience in a period when there was a much stronger socialist public culture, but it was exacerbated with my parents, because a number of my mother's friends as well as relatives were middle class: owning their own homes, and even doing outrageous things like admitting they voted Tory and professing an admiration for Ted Heath or the early days of Margaret Thatcher!

My mother would succeed in this careful balancing act for most of an evening. Then one of our Tory inclined friends or relatives would observe that what was wrong with this country was that it was 'going to the dogs under this socialist government'. That would be an irresistible green light to my father, and he would be off, telling us all that 'what was wrong with Britain was that it had never had a socialist government', and all hell would break loose with the night defined by it. They were probably small incidents and arguments, as my father kept having them with the same people for years.

The other strand worth stating is my mother's interest in feminism and what was then women's liberation. She read widely on the subject, and was involved in women's politics. This was a kind of affront in the eyes of my father and the centrality of class politics. One question I remember my father asking my mother several times, and I can't imagine it was asked in that many Dundee working-class homes, was, 'why do women want a separate revolution? Why can't they be part of the general revolution?' I never remember my mother being given the time to answer, and I know my father wasn't really looking for one. Instead he was out to dismiss and diminish the notion of feminism; it was secondary compared to the real stuff of proper revolution.

One thing my parents did find common ground on politically was detesting the Tories. When Ted Heath first became Prime Minister, to begin with he adopted a markedly right-wing stance compared to his predecessors, and as unemployment rose, the Upper Clyde Shipbuilders (UCS) work-in took place, and the country was divided by the two miners' strikes of 1972 and 1974. My parents both expressed their disgust and hatred of Heath, calling him 'the most right-wing Tory leader you can imagine'. I know it sounds ridiculous now, but that was a widely held view then. Just as bad, as far as my parents were concerned, was my uncle Douglas, who lived in Carnoustie, and had three marks against his name. He was an estate agent, took part in Scottish country dancing, and was openly Tory. These were all major crimes in my parents' eyes, but I am not sure which counted as the most serious.

Another unifying cause my parents had was their dislike of what they saw as all things Scottish. They associated most things culturally Scottish with a sense of kitsch, old-fashionedness, the tacky and tawdry. So it was with my Uncle Douglas's love of Scottish country dancing. Proof if any were needed of his counter-revolutionary characteristics. Scottish things were about the past my parents felt, and invoked a feeling in them of the embarrassment of an awful Hogmanay party when a badly behaved relative does something which mars the entire evening. That was my parents' representation of Scotland when I was a child: something I can now understand as a very Scottish relationship with parts of our culture and traditions.

This was because they believed in Britain. They saw Britain as a society getting fairer, better and more prosperous, and the future as being about more of that. This is after all the nature of the post-war compact which united Britain and which all the parties and classes signed up to, at least until the 1970s. Britain was the means by which working people across the land, and in Scotland, were to be lifted up, liberated and their lives and that of their children enriched. It was a powerful and popular story, animating the vision of Labour Britain until the mid-1970s, and the trouble Labour in office hit in that period.

I can recall just that both of my parents voted against the Common Market as the embryonic European Union was called in the 1975 referendum. Their reasoning was that it was 'a capitalist club' and their faith in how Britain would look after working-class people. Then in 1979 came the first Scottish devolution referendum, and my parents voted against that, having, I can remember, a sense of incomprehension that they were being asked such a question; why would Scotland make some decisions better they thought, when Britain had and could deliver so much. These twin stands may seem idiosyncratic now, but they were representative then of a certain left and people's story of Britain.

The account of my parents above is in large measure a generational account: one of a whole spectrum of society who grew up with memories of the 1930s, mass unemployment, poverty and injustice, and collectively said 'never again'. My parents innately believed that the world, while imperfect, had permanently turned its back on such things, and that social change would make the world better. This is the post-war story of Britain and Scotland which lasted from about 1945–75, and appears now as a distant, long lost time, although still with huge lessons for today.

All of the above has had a huge impact on myself and how I understand the world. I learned at an early age to see politics as one of the main ways to change the world. I became imbued in a world of ideas, culture and discussion. I was intuitively taught to comprehend the fundamental difference between the labour movement and the Labour Party. I grasped somehow that there were inherent tensions in any kind of political thinking and project, and that, most of the time, it is better to not lecture or hector people, and ruin friends' social evenings.

I also understood that politics wasn't everything in how you live your life or make sense of the world. Even my father, who was a dogmatic Marxist and believed in the Soviet Union until the day of its collapse, had other passions, two of which have remained important in my life, Dundee United FC and the music of Frank Sinatra. So in the ensuing pages about politics, culture and ideas, the idea of politics isn't everything in how we understand and hopefully change Scotland and the world for the better.

Indeed, my argument will be that for a variety of historical and cultural reasons about Scotland and our society we have tended to construct a rather confined version of politics, centred on politicians and institutions, which is about a very restricted idea of top-down change that excludes the vast majority of the population. This treats the public as passive, inactive observers, while change is led by the flagbearers of enlightenment whether they are left, nationalist or the professional classes.

To break out of this we have to become aware of the nature of Scottish public life and limited democracy, and to do this we first have to understand what the United Kingdom is and has become, and how it increasingly poses problems for the people of Scotland and the majority of the UK.

CHAPTER FOUR

# The Global Kingdom: Britain after the Bubble

Too many things about this country turn out to be highly recommended because they are 'invisible'. There is the 'hidden hand' of the free market, the 'unwritten' Constitution, the 'invisible earnings' of the financial service sector, the 'magic' of monarchy, and the 'mystery' of the Church and its claim to the interpretation of revealed truth. When do we get as far as the visible or the palpable, too much of it is deemed secret.

CHRISTOPHER HITCHENS *The Monarchy: A Critique Favourite Fetish, of Britain's* Chatto and Windus 1990

I slightly bridle when the word 'democracy' is applied to the United Kingdom. Instead of that I say, 'we are a parliamentary nation'. If you… put us into the jar labeled 'democracy', I can't complain. I can only tell you that you have understood very little about the United Kingdom.

ENOCH POWELL, interview in *The Guardian*, 15 June 1982

THE UNITED KINGDOM – in how it presents and represents itself in its history, politics and culture – likes to stress its unparalled degree of continuity, lack of rupture and absence of conflict, claiming that this has characterised its evolution and development to the present.

This however is a partial and elite account of the UK – and one with enormous reach and resonance, from the forces of the old establishment to the new elites of privilege. It has significant popular purchase, including historically and contemporaneously in the labour and trade union movements who have consistently bought into this benign account of Britain.

This continuity willfully ignores and remakes the histories of the UK and the experience of the coming together, division and fragmentation of the four nations of the isles. To take one example, England's 'glorious revolution' of 1688 created a framework of a historic compromise between monarchy and Parliament; the significant shift this amounted to has been reincorporated in the dominant Whig account of seamless change and adaption.

This was followed by the union of Scotland with England (Wales at the time being legally subsumed in the concept of 'England') in 1707, which joined two different nations while preserving two distinct legal traditions.

Since then the narrative of British history has been presented as the adaptability and flexibility of the political system, yet this perspective ignores many inconvenient truths which jar with it.

For one, there is the English assimilationist perspective, which forgets that the union of 1707 was a historic compromise in the age of pre-democracy and between two equals. Whatever the rights and wrongs of 1707, it was a voluntary union unlike the previous conquest of Wales and the bitter, bloody conflict in Ireland. The British experience in Ireland showcased the brutal side of British imperialism, from the union of 1801 which brought into being the United Kingdom of Great Britain and Ireland, to the onset of Irish independence in 1922. Then there is the practice and legacy of Empire which has so shaped much of what Britain stands for and Britishness means. From administering over a quarter of the world's land mass to 'standing alone' against the threat of Nazi Germany in 1940–41, but with the support and resources of the Empire dominions and colonies, Britain was made by the material and psychic benefits of its imperialism.

These different facets of Britain, British interests and rule were manifest through what Andrew Gamble called the idea of 'England' as a 'world island' whereby it was placed at the centre of four intersecting circles: the worlds of union, Commonwealth, Europe and Anglo-America. These mirror Winston Churchill's historic grasp of post-war Britain within three worlds – Empire, Europe and Anglo-America – with the UK playing a role in all three, which allowed it to avoid having to make a decision about situating its role completely within one (Gamble, 2003: 30).

The British elite belief in the superiority and wisdom of itself, the system of administration and government and the British constitution, was a central pillar historically of these circles. Foreign observers who came to Britain marvelled at the British way of doing things and reflected back how the domestic establishment saw itself. In 1953 the American writer Edward Shils heard what he called 'an eminent man of the left' say that the British constitution was 'as nearly perfect as any human institution could be'; he reflected on his surprise that 'No one even thought it amusing to express such views' (Bogdanor, 2003: 689).

The stability of the British political system began to show stresses in the 1960s followed by cracks and crises in the 1970s. The Tory-Labour compact of what David Marquand has described as Whig imperialism and democratic collectivism, the first characterised by Burkean gentlemen, the second by Fabian technocrats, begin to shatter in the 1970s in a series of momentous challenges: the 1970–72 Heath 'Selsdon Man' right-wing lurch, the 1973 OPEC oil price rise, the 1974 'Who governs Britain?' election called by Heath which he lost, the 1976 IMF crisis and embracing of monetarism by Labour in office, and the 1979 'winter of discontent' and election of Thatcher (Marquand, 2008).

This decade and the political change which came after cannot be seen solely through the notion that there was a post-war consensus and then along came Thatcher who overthrew it. This simplistic view was promoted by some after the event, but chooses to ignore Heath's failed right-wing experiment which produced a Thatcherite backlash in the party, and the episodic and systematic crises of the 1970s. All of this cumulatively challenged the authority and legitimacy of the state itself, with questions being widely asked such as 'Is Britain governable?' and is it 'overloaded' in government?

There were by the end of the decade at least three coherent strategies on offer to resolve Britain's problems: Thatcherism, the Bennite new left-wing of Labour, and the pro-European viewpoint of what became the Social Democratic Party (SDP). There was no inevitability in the period 1979–81 that Thatcher would triumph with her government, initially massively unpopular, and public opinion first swinging behind Labour, then when it broke away from Labour, the SDP.

Thatcher sought to change Britain and the assumptions on which politics were based. The state and public spending were rethought and rebalanced, taxation reduced particularly on higher earners, and a programme of privatisation of public utilities proved exceeding popular. Internationally, Thatcher formed a close alliance with Reagan with their bond based on a common belief in free market capitalism and Cold War militarism against the Soviet threat.

This resulted, particularly after the British victory in the Falklands War of 1982 following the Argentinian invasion, in the emergence of a state with pretensions to 'world leadership' and which post-Falklands witnessed a hubris with such terms used as 'putting the great back into Britain'. Thatcher saw this as allowing her to stand shoulder to shoulder with the US. This practice was to continue post-Cold War under Blair and Brown and 'the war on terror', such was the allure and pull of Atlanticism in the British political elite.

How was this dramatic change possible in such a short time considering the Tories never won a majority of the popular vote in any of their four election victories post-1979, and the UK, on the evidence of the British Social Attitudes Surveys (from 1983), was stubbornly social democratic on many indicators and resistant to Thatcherite values? The answer to this is complex and involves the unpleasant truth that Britain has not and never has been a fully-fledged political democracy.

## The Slow Non-March of British Democracy

Think about the supposedly great events, tides and times of British political history from the 1688 English 'glorious revolution' to 1707 and then the successive reform acts, 1832, 1867, 1884, the coming of female franchise in 1918 and 1928, and the establishment of one person, one vote (with the abolition of plural voting and university seats) in 1948. These used to be told as the forward march of British liberty and democracy in school and constitutional textbooks, and compared favourably to other countries where revolution and rupture took place.

Unifying all of these measures is that it was the British ruling elite who controlled the entrance of new social groups into the public life of the country. It was not the people collectively forcing change – whether it was the Chartists in the 19th century or the Suffragettes in the early 20th century (women for example first got the vote in 1918 in response to their employment during the First World War).

The wider point is something which is implicit but left unstated in mainstream accounts of British history: the slow march of what passed for democracy never actually arrived at the point of making the UK a fully-fledged political democracy. The British establishment controlled the pace and entry points; the main changes between 1832 and 1918 happened within the elite, with a broadening out from an aristocratic and landed gentry to a more industrial and mercantile class.

The United Kingdom, much to the satisfaction of these elites, never had a democratising moment and never really came near to having one. Nineteenth-century Victorian politics were comprised of powerful caste groups with the great Reform Acts passed to maintain their position and rule. The powerful Liberal Party towards the end of the 19th century tried to accommodate the rising power of the working-class and organised labour, but failed too, and in the aftermath of the First World War, was replaced by Labour as the main opposition party to the Tories.

Labour's relationship to democracy has historically been a peculiar one. On first coming to office as a minority government in 1924, and then 1929, the party slowly began to embrace an uncritical attitude to the British state and the usages of state power. Labour's rise changed Westminster and British politics but Labour were at least as much if not more changed by their incorporation into Westminster. Pivotal in this was the rise of

Fabian gradualism which saw socialism come about by evolutionary methods, the power of reason (and reasonableness), and the knowledge of experts.

Despite all its radical and outsider roots, Labour was never a party of democratisation of British institutions, but instead of using them for progressive ends. The central instrument of change in this was the British state which was seen as neutral and benign. Along with the minority government moments of the 1920s, the crucial twin peaks of Labour incorporation were 1940, and 1945, which need to be understood together. In the first, nine months into the Second World War, Labour brought the Chamberlain government down by refusing to go into coalition, making it possible for Churchill to become Prime Minister in a coalition where Labour effectively ran the domestic 'people's war'. This aided the transformation of the British economy and the leftward swing of the electorate who saw the competence of Labour ministers. The famous 1945 election victory came after five years of Labour running large parts of the war effort, a contribution only broken by a short Churchill 'caretaker' administration pre-election.

The post-war efforts of Labour, whether in 1945, 1964, 1974 or 1997, have many positive achievements, but one thing the party was emphatically not interested in was greater democratisation of society. This is most obvious in what is universally seen as Labour's most successful government – the 1945–51 Attlee period which, while it had a string of achievements, showed in how it governed and did politics an unimaginative centralisation and command and control from Whitehall. Thus the NHS, public ownership of electricity, gas and the mines, and planning, were all about the insights of bureaucrats, civil servants and managers. This became so pronounced that the Scottish Tories campaigned on an anti-nationalisation ticket, portraying it as an attack on Scots industry and control.

To some this mattered less in the age of authority and deference such as the immediate post-war era and the means could be used to justify the ends of building a socialist Britain. The contradictions of trying to advance such a politics on the undemocratic institutions of the British state, and utilising them for the making of a 'New Jerusalem' were either not considered or seen of marginal importance in the wider scheme of things.

The problems of such a centralising politics became more manifest as society became less high bound to tradition in each period of Labour in office until the apex of this approach was reached with New Labour. Post-1997 Labour were shorn of their once proud socialist credentials but still committed to the politics of command and control as an end in itself, to maintain the power and reach of the centre, to engage in micro-management to the smallest degree, and for fear of letting go. All of this was while at the same time devolution happened to Scotland and Wales: two achievements which sat ill at ease with the above and for which New Labour seemed to have little time or insight.

The New Labour era of centralisation became one of unintended consequences as it sucked out the energies and drives of numerous intermediate bodies and civil society. At the same time the new post-imperial centre was oblivious to this and worried itself all the time about citizen and community empowerment and even worse, 'double devolution' while all its efforts pushed to undermining such concepts.

Why has the British state remained so resolutely immune to democracy? Firstly, this is a state whose modern formation dates back to 1688 and the aristocratic revolution which limited the powers of the monarch; seen as a fundamental shift at the time and heralding the epochal moments of 1776 and 1789 and the American and French revolutions, when what it actually did was to consolidate the power of the emerging elite. Secondly, this became the Empire State, a political centre which built the British system of governing and exploiting colonies and extracting resources. This form of state was a minimalist one at home and abroad, global in reach, but committed to *laissez faire* domestically, and running India with a couple of thousand British personnel in the 19th century.

Thirdly, British progressives, whether Whig, Liberal or Labour, did not challenge this as they were or became part of the establishment, seeing the state not in class or socio-economic terms, but as a neutral instrument. The high point of this is undoubtedly Labour's new social order of 1945, but other missed moments were late Gladstonian Liberalism and Lloyd George 'people's budget' and constitutional crisis of 1909–11. Fourthly, all of the above forces, with the exceptions of these two periods of radical Liberalism, were constitutional conservatives uninterested in nurturing voice in the political system. Finally, as the era of what Colin Crouch has called 'post-democracy' (2004) came into being due to the cumulative impact of Thatcherism and New Labour, it began with its courtier politics to look rather like the age of pre-democracy: a contest within elites. The tragedy in this was that the UK had passed from the pre to post stage of democracy, without pausing in the democratic age.

Today's British state is a byzantine creation owing many of its institutions and cultures to the previous era of pre-democracy. Thus only one pillar of the British constitution is elected – the House of Commons – while the House of Lords is, some estimate, the largest upper house anywhere in the world and growing ever larger as a result of hyperactive Prime

Ministerial patronage. Tony Benn calculated that the seven post-war Prime Ministers before Thatcher (Attlee to Callaghan) appointed 639 peers, making the point that this was more than the size of the Commons in 1979 (635 MPs) (Benn, 1979: 134). Wilson, in his two periods of being Prime Minister, appointed 226 peers – averaging 25 nominations per year in 1964–70 and 38 per year in 1974–76; Thatcher nominated 216 peers – a yearly average of 18, while Blair totalled 386 overall – 38 per year. In the 50 years since the introduction of life peers, 1,242 peers have been nominated to the Lords – 24 per year (Brocklehurst, 2008).

Such widespread patronage and preferment distorts and makes a mockery of Britain's claim to be a democracy. The Lords matters, not just as a revising but as an initiating chamber, and for its role as a forum in national life. The British Head of State as the monarch clearly has no direct democratic mandate but has managed to manufacture a popular legitimacy and affection which reveals much about the culture and psyche of the British body politic.

Thus the directly democratic component of what passes for national public life in the UK is narrow and constrained one. The expansion of the post-war state saw an explosion in the number and range of quangos and public bodies which has further complicated any notion of democratic accountability. Then in more recent years, there has been rise of the outsourced state and its myriad contractors – Serco, G4S, Capita, A4e – and the accountancy/consultancy class led by 'the Big Four' – Deloitte, Ernst and Young, KMPG and PWC – which has created new sources of power and authority and which has diluted still further any democratic input into the system.

The transformation of the character and culture of the British state by these processes is little understood. The fundamental change was never openly debated or voted upon and yet it marks something profound. The nature of what the British state is at its core, its principles and the values it chose in its relationships, has become very different from pre-Thatcher. Slowly the central state has become what can only be called a neo-liberal state: one which as its main purpose promotes the ideas of marketising, outsourcing, privatising and working in favour of corporate capitalist logic. The dynamism and mindset of the core centre in Downing Street and senior departments, which once were defined for decades by civil service impartiality, has now become over the period of Thatcherism and New Labour (and remains so under Cameron) one where the new class of neo-liberal agents and actors are embedded in the core with the consultant class having been granted permanent access and influence.

This has become so entrenched and the way of doing things that the British political elite no longer see the values and priorities of this world-view and class as an ideology. Instead it is seen as incontrovertible fact. This political and economic determinism has become regarded as how the world is mixing globalisation, the power of finance capital, hyper-competition and individualism, along with the weakening and dilution of the once powerful 'social contract'. George Osborne's ambition, revealed in his 2013 Autumn Statement of taking public spending back to 1948 levels in terms of health, education and infrastructure spending (excluding individual transfers such as pensions), is the logical endpoint of this base, anti-social, elite-focused mindset.

One of the less understood aspects of the historical development of the British state is the interconnection between it, the evolution of the Empire and the City of London; it is this which contributes one of the central pillars in the making of the British Empire state.

The rise of Empire and the City contributed to the rising class of the new wealth of the 19th century and the anti-industrial ethos of this elite which has characterised the economy and culture to this day. This may seem controversial to mainstream political thought, but was an argument explored a few years ago by the free market *Economist* in a 'Bagehot' column entitled 'The tiger under the table' (3 December 2009). This stated that one of the UK's central problems was 'the many ways in which Britain is living in the shadow of Empire' and that it is 'perhaps, increasingly – trapped by its imperial past'. 'Bagehot' went much further:

> If empire is the backdrop of Britain's foreign entanglements, it is also implicated in the country's exposure to another great debacle, the financial crash. The City and the empire grew up symbiotically. Imperial trade and investment made London a world financial centre; the City became vital to the British economy, while at the same time, preoccupied as it was with foreign deals, largely separate from the rest of it. The empire thus bequeathed commercial habits, and an overmighty financial sector, which British taxpayers now have cause to regret. (Some historians trace Britain's trouble with real engineering, as well as the financial type, to the empire too, arguing that protected trade inside it coddled British industry and left it uncompetitive.)

They observe, accurately, that every British Prime Minister post-Empire has struggled with the 'sense of thwartedness and decline' and attempted to address and reverse it. This has regularly invoked the grandiose, much trumpeted rise of a 'New Britain' which is meant to find a new purpose, international role, and to arrest the age of decline: from Wilson to Heath, Thatcher, Blair and Brown.

The British Empire state in its hyperbole, sense of its own importance and unreformed nature at the centre is with us to this day. Its characteristics are one of the main reasons why the neo-liberal transformation has proven so successful in the UK in the last 30 plus years. This is the Britain as 'a global kingdom' – a state at the centre of a series of transnational, multinational networks of power, privilege and wealth. There is the offshore, off the balance sheet Britain of tax avoidance and tax evasion on an industrial scale. There are the 'treasure islands' micro-states of the Isle of Man, Jersey and Guernsey which sit outside the UK, in what is called a 'partnership' – with the UK having responsibility for defence and international representation. This could be called 'a social union', with BBC services available, and UK postcodes and telephone numbers used. Jersey and Guernsey use the pound sterling, and the Isle of Man a Manx pound the equivalent of UK currency. It is no accident that these miniscule entities are some of the leading tax havens in the global economy, acting as virtual black holes sucking in economic activity and corporate tax activities for slashing their tax bills.

This world of offshore arrangements ran through the City of London, in the words of Nicholas Shaxson with its 'own private infrastructure and vision' to the three Crown Dependencies and 14 British Overseas Territories (BOTS), the latter under the jurisdiction and sovereignty of the UK and throwbacks and relics of Empire, conquest and Britain's global reach. The Isle of Man, Jersey and Guernsey would 'form the inner ring of the spider's web and would focus mostly on Europe', while the Caribbean territories such as the Cayman Islands and Bermuda 'would focus mostly on the Americas' (2011: 103). As well as this, there are other complex historic links and legacy such as the former colony of Hong Kong which became Chinese in 1997 and before had been run as a British exercise in minimal to no government, a project continued by the Chinese Special Administrative Zone.

What has made all this possible has been the continuing strength and adaptability of what has been called 'the conservative nation' – a version of the UK centred on power, privilege, money and its related institutions, and which Labour and many on the left have consistently underestimated (Gamble, 1974). This version of Britain has from the late 19th century become dominant, based on a concept of authority, the importance of the Crown as a political symbol, the value of deference, social duty and order, along with social reform, and which explains the endurance and success of the Conservative Party. This powerful anchoring and set of forces has marginalised Liberal and Labour opinion, and made it possible for the scale of transformation of society and state which has happened in recent decades, which has disorientated non-conservative Britain, and which they are still trying to fully comprehend.

## The Changing Face (or not) of the British Establishment

What has happened to the nature of the British establishment in recent times? The conventional view accounts for the decline of the old elites such as the landed gentry and the rise of a new class of self-made men and women, entrepreneurs, hustlers and City financers. The reality is somewhat more mixed with a coalescing and cross-fertilising between old and new; the former has never fully gone away, an observation fairly obvious in the most cursory analysis of Scotland's land ownership, while the latter is hardly made up of the self-starting, individually motivated buccaneers of BBC *Dragon's Den* fame.

For over 40 years – from the early 1960s to the first decade of this century, Anthony Sampson has charted the contours of Britain's establishment in his 'Anatomy of Britain' series. In the first books, published in 1962 and 1965, Britain was still emerging from a long Victorian overhang, with the post-war boom beginning to dramatically change both the working and middle-classes. New forms of power and knowledge were developing through mass media, TV, communications and popular culture, which articulated a belief and optimism in a more open society of wider opportunity and choice (Sampson, 1962; 1965).

Fast forward to the last book – *Who Runs This Place? The Anatomy of Britain in the 21st Century* (2004) – written just before Sampson died, for a very different mood. Instead of a fluid, dynamic opening up of society, Sampson found the emergence of a new set of concentrations of power around corporations and the City which limited and corroded politics, democracy and society. Gone was the positivity about Britain and the future found in earlier volumes. Post-Iraq war, in the slow degeneration of the Blair government, Sampson found reason for hope in some small parts of the media, NGOs and campaigning groups, but was far from confident whether these groups could stand up to or reclaim mainstream politics from the new elites.

Despite this there is still a panglossian mainstream story that everything is rosy in the state of Britain. It can be found in the TV don performances, interventions and books of right-wing revisionists such as

Niall Ferguson and David Starkey, who show impatience with any resistance or even questioning of what they see as the new realities, or more accurately orthodoxies, of our age – of the Britain as 'a global kingdom' competing in Cameron's 'global race'.

Then there are the more conventional and less ideologically loaded accounts of the liberal mainstream such as Andrew Marr's books, related TV programmes and pronouncements. In his *A History of Modern Britain*, Marr has articulated a post-war account of Britain, from Attlee to Thatcher and Blair and Brown, which is still sanguine and confident about Britain, articulating the modern version of Whig history and believing in the innate wisdom of Britain's institutions and elites. He concludes his study with the observation, 'in the years since 1945, having escaped nuclear devastation, tyranny and economic collapse, we British have no reason to despair, or emigrate. In global terms, to be born British remains a wonderful stroke of luck' (2007: 602). This was of course written at the end of the Blair bubble, and just before the banking crash, but somehow the effortless faith of the liberal classes that everything will be alright has continued irrespective of uncomfortable facts on the ground.

Another perspective provided by the political commentator Peter Oborne has been coruscating in his damning of the behaviour, morals and ethics of the British political elite. He has widened this in his book, *The Triumph of the Political Classes* (2007), into a savaging of the new elites of contemporary Britain across public life, whether politics, business or civic life. Oborne powerfully critiqued the deceptions of the Blair years, from Iraq to 'the war on terror' and the expanding database state, along with the collusion of Blair, Brown and Cameron (in what I used to call 'the BBC consensus') with the Murdoch empire.

Oborne charged our political elite with selling out British democracy via getting too close to Murdoch and his apparatchiks. In this he was undoubtedly correct, as public standards were debased and trashed by the cumulative actions of Blair, Brown and Cameron. This of course all concluded in the phone hacking scandal and the public exposure of Cameron's 'Chipping Norton set' of political and media connections.

Oborne has been a persuasive voice, but a voice of doubt has to be raised in relation to where he believes the origins of our current crisis began. Oborne is rightly damning of New Labour, but he believes they are the main originators of this malaise, and exonerates the Thatcher Government of any part of the blame. More, in his savaging of the 'new' establishment, Oborne shows a hankering, even yearning, for the supposed codes of behaviour of the 'old' establishment. This is in short a traditional high Tory view of Britain: of believing in the importance of gentleman, decency and deference – a world long gone from contemporary times.

## From the Neo-Liberal State to Culture and the Remaking of the Self

Britain has changed in dramatic ways in the last three decades. The political centre of government has altered beyond any imaginings. One way of charting this is the transition from *Yes Minister* to *The Thick of It*. Both see some ministers as child-like simpletons deceived and controlled by those around them in the system, and both take a cynical, world-weary view of politics and government.

Beyond that there are huge differences. In the first, advisors were part of a well-oiled, supremely confident mandarin class of civil servants which believed in itself and its place at the centre of power along with the protection and maintenance of its privileges. In the second, the advisers now come from a more diverse set of backgrounds with some outsiders present in the inner fulcrums of power; now they represent a hyper-active, micro-controlling, constantly crisis managing system of omnipotent authority which has to strategise, fire-fight, make and break alliances, manage news headlines, and all the while recognising that all power is relational. This latter elite believe that all that matters is the politics of power, of access, influence and status, and take the view that personal positioning, advancement and cosying up to those who possess these is what makes the world go round. They have little time for reflecting on whether this 'business of politics' approach is an ideology; clearly to many observers outside this is a post-democratic, neo-liberal mindset.

This is part of the transformation of politics, government and administration. Parliament is no longer the debating chamber of the UK or where crucial decisions take place. It is now commonplace for Prime Ministers to treat the place with disdain and scorn, only regularly attending for the once weekly theatre of Prime Minister's Question Time. How policy-making and formulation is undertaken has altered perhaps even more. There has been the denigration and diminution of the civil service, and the emergence of what has been called by US political advisor Joe Klein a sprawling 'pollster-consultant-industrial complex' at the heart of government, with the rise of political consultancies, public affairs and a dense network of think tanks, pseudo and real. All of this has aided the validation of power lying in the new elites of post-democracy in the corporate and business world. Related to this the language and style of politics has changed – defined in words and manner by a business ethos, which has led to technocratic sounding politicians, advisers and an insider class, all of which then reinforces the corporate capitalist predilections of government and its decisions.

None of this can be fully understood without referencing the role of the press in the transformation of British politics and society. Central to this for more than 40 years has been Rupert Murdoch, who bought the *News of the World* in 1969 and *The Sun* in 1970. His control of the latter gave him a popular and populist bridgehead (as well as a profitable cash cow) to push British politics rightwards, to challenge what he saw as the old tarnished establishment, and to support his global expansion. *The Sun*, from its origins as a Labour supporting paper, became a leading advocate for savaging left-wing values, public spending, the welfare state, trade unions and immigration. It exploited the arrogances of liberal elitism to promote a base consumerism, sexism and xenophobia, presenting this as a popular people's agenda.

In 1981, Murdoch gained control of *The Times* and *Sunday Times* with the connivance of the Thatcher Government (avoiding a reference to the Monopolies and Mergers Commission), and in 1983 installed Andrew Neil as editor of the Sunday paper. From this a more concerted assault on the values of collectivism and the labour movement began, with Neil leading debates on the notions of 'the underclass' and 'welfare dependency', importing these from the US right. Neil later reflected in his autobiography, *Full Disclosure*, that Murdoch's politics were 'a combination of right-wing Republicanism from America mixed with undiluted Thatcherism from Britain and stirred with some anti-British establishment sentiments as befits his colonial heritage' (Neil, 1996: 165).

Neil explained that working for Murdoch and News International involved understanding the opinions, desires and whims of 'the Sun King', meaning Murdoch, and that, 'All life revolves around the Sun King: all authority comes from him' (1996: 160). From the early 1980s Murdoch's influence over British politics grew: the right-wing nature of the Thatcher administration, the Reagan-Thatcher alliance, the miners' strike and Wapping conflict, and then after Labour lost its fourth election in a row in 1992, with the emergence of Blair and New Labour, the charming of Murdoch pre-1997.

Labour in office got even closer than Thatcher to Murdoch, a style of politics and understanding of power which contributed to the dilution of progressive credentials in the party: the equivocation on Europe and the euro, the populist hard line on law and order and immigration, the Blair-

Bush axis on 'the war on terror' and Afghan and Iraq wars. Post-2010, this incestuous network which had developed under Blair, Brown and Cameron came into public view with the phone hacking scandal and subsequent Leveson inquiry, revealing the scale of court politics and connections between the political elite and Murdoch empire (see McKnight, 2013).

The rightwards shift of Britain of course is not just restricted to the world of politics. The market fundamentalist revolution has affected nearly every aspect of our lives – from culture, to football, to our very ideas of the self and who we are. Popular culture has been bent out of shape in recent years by a mix of dumbing down of TV and radio, instrumentalisation on terms of arts and culture, and in the wider world, a constant daily drip of celebrity, consumption, and celebrating success and the allure of the self-made individual. This is a world which judges what achievement is constantly and narrowly: a culture of winners and losers, haves and have nots, where those who strive, manoeuvre and calculate to win are hailed as being personally vindicated, while those who don't are judged harshly as dinosaurs, not being flexible and 'with the times', and as failures. All of this is undertaken by the most remorseless economic calculus, which delegitimises and marginalises other ways of judging worth and value.

This culture of neo-liberalism, as the shift from an ideology to an all-pervasive social order can be witnessed in the dramatic alteration of the nature of 'the self'. How people see themselves, act and live their lives has been dramatically altered by this ideological re-configuration whereby all that concerns mankind is a very constrained, constricted set of needs. Individual aspiration and self-actualisation are the mantras of this change, shown in how people think of work and careers to property, the media, talent shows and reality TV programmes. It can also be seen in the rise of psychotherapy terms, which have attained such common currency that there is now popular psychobabble in everyday usage ('can I share?' 'we need to get closure'). The rise of psychology matches a zeitgeist about the individual as a sovereign, self-governing object running his or her own life – the logical end point of this is a dystopia – the equivalent of Adam Curtis's *Century of the Self*.

Without aspiring to sound like some doomsayer such as Neil Postman, who wrote a pessimistic tract (*Amusing Ourselves to Death*) about the insidious, inescapable dumbing down of media (and which inspired former Pink Floyd lead singer Roger Waters to pen an entire album), this is a fundamental shift in how we understand ourselves, engage with others, and lead our lives. It is a transformative change which many observers and commentators have struggled to fully comprehend, in particular the connections between a neo-liberal politics and state, and the making of a neo-liberal culture and self.

There has been much time spent worrying about the corrosive effect of materialism and hyper-individualism, but much of it, from the likes of Oliver James and others, has no real recognition of the importance of an ideological dimension (James, 2007). There is in Scotland and the UK a middle-class guilt about materialism which acknowledges its damaging effects as an end in itself and how it presents a distorted version of human nature, yet such perspectives expressly do not talk about who has power and voice and who does not, and the role of neo-liberalism in all of this (while this does not mean that is only guilt as centre-left ideas have also been based on economic determinism as we shall explore later).

This unedifying world is not thankfully how many of us choose to live most of the time: it is not how we choose partners, friends, jobs, and pastimes. It is not the values we prioritise and celebrate when we raise children and grandchildren, or look after aging relatives. Thus, there is a deep and widening chasm between the values most people wish to nurture and use as guiding life principles, and the 'official world' of government, corporates, culture and the media. Many of the external agencies do not even see that the consequences of their actions are ideological, anti-social, and reinforcing a winner takes all view of the world.

One arena of popular culture which has been totally transformed is the world of football. Once a reservoir of working-class culture and values, it has now at its top level become part of a global brand and elite. The most advanced example of this in the world is the English Premiership which has now been running for 22 years (since season 1992–93). More than half of its 20 clubs are foreign owned and have offshore tax arrangements; at the onset of the 2012–13 season only seven of the 20 clubs were UK owned (FootballFansCast.Com, 16 September 2012). Clubs such as Manchester United (owned by the US Glazer brothers) or Manchester City (owned by the Abu Dhabi United Group) are as far removed from being community owned and run, as it is possible to imagine.

The English Premiership is a direct offshoot of the casino economics of the City of London, but so far has weathered the harsh storm which has blown through the rest of the economy aided by the monies from SKY TV sponsorship (and now BT Vision). One calculation a few years ago had it that more than half (56 per cent) of all European football club debt was accounted for by the 20 clubs of the English Premiership, totalling £3.5 billion (*The Guardian*, 23 February 2010).

Such a culture creates ripples at every level: individual, community, national and international. Many football fans across the world now choose to support global winners such as Manchester United or City, Chelsea or Arsenal in England (or Barcelona or Real Madrid in Spain) to the detriment of their local team. At some of the leading Premiership clubs each Saturday, rows of 'football tourists' can be seen, who have flown in on expensive, exclusive packages to see their far-flung heroes.

The Scottish football world pales into insignificance, both in terms of its monetary value and global footprint, compared to England. Our domestic clubs cannot match the transfer fees and wage bills of the English Premiership, or dream of the related TV deals. But it is also true that despite this, Celtic and Rangers are significant global brands, and that Scottish football, aided by the diaspora and the history and traditions of the game, has a bigger audience than many would at first assume. Yet, the world of marketeering, corporate orthodoxy has not been immune to Scotland, seen in the David Murray free spending days at Rangers, and the MBA mindsets of Stewart Regan and Neil Doncaster, heads respectively of the Scottish Football Association (SFA) and Scottish Professional Football League (SPFL), more of whom latter.

Football matters far beyond the world of football. It is one of the ways in which the ideas of 'the global kingdom' reach out with its message to a largely apolitical world. It tells football fans that all that matters is winning, that massive rewards, celebrity, selfishness and inequality are all a price worth paying for success, and with its model of foreign ownership and little to no real fan power, promotes a culture of widespread powerlessness which is the epitome of the global economy. There are significant gender dimensions to this: of how young men perceive what makes them adult and attractive, and consequences for many young women, which sees 'bagging' a footballer as an avenue to a meaningful life in the world of WAGS (wives and girlfriends). Such a corrosive, narcissistic culture has seeped out from football into other sports and nearly every aspect of society.

The debasement of much of public language and discourse has been mirrored by, at least pre-crash, the triumphalism of our political classes. There was, emerging in the 1980s and New Labour era, a near-certain belief in 'the end of decline' from the political elite. They were convinced that Britain was no longer 'the sick man of Europe' as it had been labelled in the 1960s and 1970s. Instead, the UK had become revitalised by 'the great British economic miracle' which had 'put the great back into Britain' (see for example, Brivati, 2007).

This was not just a Thatcherite project and rhetoric but one embracing

New Labour and, post-crash, the Cameron Conservatives. Tony Blair and Gordon Brown appropriated this Great Britishness for their project of neo-liberal economic orthodoxy combined with progressive social justice policies which amounted to an attempt at a new configuration within the elite – of neo-liberalism with a social conscience. What continued and accelerated was the faith in British exceptionalism and great powerism, shamelessly and endlessly lecturing Europe and the world about the merits of deregulation, privatisation and encouraging enterprise and innovation.

This attitude reflected something deeply embedded in the British psyche, which the political elite believed gave them permission to act in this manner. Gordon Brown, to take one example, dared to lecture the Germans and French on the over-rigidity and pitfalls of 'the European social model'. Historic roots which contribute to this will be explored below, but in the shorter-term, the Britain of Thatcher, post-Falklands and post-miners' strike, felt in its political classes that it had gained the right to lecture the world on the vivacity and vigour of British ideas and economics.

The longer account of where such attitudes come from entails understanding the importance and evolution of what has been called 'the Anglosphere', namely, the English speaking democracies of the developed world. These comprise six countries: the UK, Republic of Ireland, USA, Canada, Australia and New Zealand. The idea of 'the Anglosphere' has its origins in part in Empire, Dominion status and the so-called 'special relationship' which emerged between the UK and US in World War Two.

'The Anglosphere' can be seen as an expression of Winston Churchill's idea of 'the English speaking peoples' and of the notion of 'England' as a 'world island', touched upon earlier. It is not an accident that the six countries of 'the Anglosphere' have had the most comprehensive and harsh neo-liberal experiments unleashed anywhere in the West; nowhere else has had a comparable experience from central Europe to the Nordics and Japan.

The reasons for this go beyond the immediate impact of Thatcher and Reagan in the UK or US, or Paul Keating and John Howard in Australia and 'Rogernomics' in New Zealand, but have deeper roots in the cultural values, politics and ideas of each of the individual nations, and where these came from. This has included a common notion of political economy, an emphasis on the free market and a culture of individualism, and liberty being seen foremost as an economic idea and a social concept secondarily. It has also evolved emphasising a distinct notion of business, corporate governance and responsibilities that has a bias towards short-termism, shareholder interests and defines stakeholders in a restricted manner; at the same time the idea of the state and role of government is not seen as one of a developmental state as emerged in France and Germany in post-war times.

Many of the most radical neo-liberal transformations were undertaken by supposedly centre-left parties in government. The New Labour of Blair and Brown is not an exception but part of an 'Anglosphere' phenomenon which also included Bill Clinton's New Democrats, Bob Hawke and Paul Keating's Australian Labour, and the 'Rogernomics' of New Zealand Labour under Finance Minister Roger Douglas. This became so pronounced in the Blair-Clinton period that some commentators switched from talking of a politics of 'the left' or 'centre-left' to what they saw as 'the near-left'.

This 'Anglosphere' model is one whose roots and origins can be traced back to the UK, and in particular to the genesis and ferment of ideas in 'the Scottish Enlightenment', and such thinkers as Adam Smith, David Hume and William Robertson. In recent years, writers such as Arthur Herman have tried to claim that 'the Scottish Enlightenment' contributed to 'the Scots' invention of the modern world', but a more relevant observation would be to acknowledge Britain's role (and thus that of Scotland) in making 'the Anglosphere' (Herman, 2002).

It is not an accident that at this point in the UK's history, the idea of 'the Anglosphere' has returned on the centre-right, amongst such Euro-sceptics as Daniel Hannan, Tory MEP. He utilises it to propose a modern reading of a very old story: the British account of liberty, the rule of law and free trade, which he believes are at odds with the bureaucratic behemoth of the European Union. A revived 'Anglosphere' is the answer to the UK's problems and the challenge of creeping 'uniformity, centralisation, high taxation, and state control' across the core six English speaking countries (Hannan, 2013: 370). This is another politics of 'exit' (from the European Union), and one which for all the qualifications is profoundly English, and oblivious to very different Scots, Welsh and Northern Irish agendas.

The current political crises of the UK are thus multiple, overlapping and with long-term historic origins: economic, social, democratic, and about Britain's international role and profile in the world. They are about how the UK nurtures and supports the commonweal of Britain's populace, and whether it has any interest in being a country which is democratic, modern, forward looking and progressive. As the next chapter will describe, in one of these key characteristics – whether the UK sees itself as a modern country – there are gathering doubts.

This is, in short, an existential crisis of the UK as a geopolitical entity and one which at its roots is a crisis of 'the Anglosphere' model, which an increasing number of voices believe has to go back to its origins and first principles. All of this poses significant pressures on the dominant British political class answer to this situation which has been until now a near-uniform one – from Tory to Lib Dem to most of Labour – seeing it as 'restoration' and 'Back to the Future' in 'Fantasyland Britain'. Yet, outwith the corridors of power in Westminster and Whitehall, a growing number of people realise the inadequacy of such an outlook.

CHAPTER FIVE

# Back in the Old Country: The Power of the Past

A nation is a soul, a spiritual principle. Two things, which in truth are but one, constitute this soul or spiritual principle. One lies in the past, one in the present. One is the possession in common of a rich legacy of memories: the other is present day consent, the desire to live together... Where national memories are concerned, griefs are of more value than triumphs, for they impose duties, and require a common effort... A nation's existence is, if you will pardon the metaphor, a daily plebiscite, just as an individual's existence is a perpetual affirmation of life.

ERNEST RENAN, *What is a Nation?*, 1882

PART OF THE EMERGING Scottish consensus in the 1980s was based on a critique of what was seen as increasing flaws in the Westminster parliamentary sovereignty and the existing practices of the British state. This informed the approach and philosophy of such key documents in the evolution of devolution as 1988s *A Claim of Right for Scotland* (reprinted in Dudley Edwards, 1989).

This was not wrong, but did not go far enough. For example, it did not recognise the limits of democracy in Scotland itself, aided and reinforced by our historical experience, as well as in the wider context of the UK.

The United Kingdom is not a modern country. It is not now or ever has been a fully-fledged democracy. This isn't some left-wing fanatical or conspiratorial view, but based on a level-headed analysis of history and the facts.

The UK is a state increasingly defined and imprisoned by its past; and in a constant, never-ending cycle of marking and celebrating its past military battles and triumphs. There is an impressive procession of significant moments in British history which would make Michael Gove, Tory education minister, proud with his commitment to a Ladybird version of the history of these isles. In recent years, we have seen celebrations of the 1805 Battle of Trafalgar (which was enacted out again) and 1940, Dunkirk and the Battle of Britain, but all this seems to be preparation for the year to end all years: 2014.

This year will see commemoration of the start of World War One (the 100th anniversary on 28 July), the onset of World War Two (the 75th of that on 1 September if you take the German invasion of Poland and 3 September if you take Chamberlain's reluctant declaration of war on Germany), and if that weren't enough, there is the 70th anniversary of D Day (6 June). Then the following year, if we have any energies left and depending on the state of the UK, George Osborne, UK Chancellor, has announced a series of special events to mark the 200th anniversary of the Battle of Waterloo where Wellington, with Prussian assistance, defeated Napoleon.

Scotland is not completely immune from this. There is the Bannock-burn-'Braveheart' strand of Scottish identity and the 700th anniversary of the former later in 2014. But I don't think Scotland marking this episode tells us the same as the serial activities of the British state. Scotland isn't shaped in a living, breathing way by 1314, Wallace and Bruce and the Wars of Independence. Those myths are not the foundation stories which inform and shape modern, present day Scotland. That is not to say that they don't matter as story and folklore as they do in some profound sense, but it is in a very different, background way.

Let me put the divergence between Scotland and the UK and the power of the past this way. In the UK, the rise of the power of the past and a mythical sense about dead generations has increasingly come to the fore in public life. And that this happened in recent decades is not an accident or coincidence. This has occurred because it gives legitimacy to the economic and social order and values of the last 30 or so years. As the UK has become more unequal and its elites more self-interested and brazen, they have used these stories as the glue which supposedly bind us together. The same could not be said of modern Scotland to the same extent.

## Why does the Past of Britain Matter So Much Now?

Part of the 'official' account of the UK put forward by its political classes is that this union offers the protection, security and shared risk, which being a smaller, self-governing entity just doesn't offer. The language of, in particular, Labour and Lib Dem politicians, invokes that the pulling together of resources and the supposedly effective redistribution from the haves to those who are in more need. Michael Moore, then Lib Dem Secretary of State of Scotland, actually dared to talk of 'a generous British welfare state' (House of Commons, 11 January 2012), which clearly shows little knowledge in how it comes off in international comparisons.

While this version of Britain is articulated by politicians and has an element of self-deception, the real instinctual stories which hold Britain together have moved into another realm: the construction from history of a fabled, magical, unique past. This is evident in the mantra of the Westminster political classes and how they talk about the UK in relation to the Scottish dimension. Michael Moore, for example, said in the Commons of the UK, 'For over 300 years our country has brought people together in the most successful multinational state the world has known' (*Huffington Post*, 10 January 2012). This is from the same lexicon as the Gordon Brown-Douglas Alexander perspective from the early days of New Labour in office; it is present in the evoking by Brown and Cameron of the Britain that fought the Nazis, abolished slavery, and won the Cold War.

This emergence of the past as a powerful political weapon in the present is directly related to the demise of the real 'we are all in it together' Britain which the political class still like to hanker for, whether they be Michael Moore or the left version in Ken Loach's *The Spirit of '45*. It has become a populist, celebratory window dressing for the age of insecurity, anxiety, doubt and worry, and the rise of inequality, a fragmented society and the emergence of the new plutocratic class.

What can Britain offer the populace as feel good, common stories of connection? The UK can still put on events, gatherings and happenings, as media and business types and politicians constantly tell us. These include ceremonies and celebrations such as the London Olympics of 2012, which drew on powerful images of current and historical social capital and evocative pop music, mostly from the 1960s and 1970s.

It may be then that all the UK seems to have left is its past – a rich, varied past – which seems nearly inexhaustible in its supply of anniversaries and military victories and achievements, which isn't surprising given the power of the British Empire. Yet in this there is not just diversion and the re-making of the past, but a deep sense of loss and failure, for the UK has in a sense given up on the future. Once upon a time the UK was about promising its people a better, fairer collective future; but no more. All the UK can offer now is the recycling of our glorious past, and the marking of various victories over a whole host of foreigners.

It is an argument previously explored about the UK nearly 30 years ago in Patrick Wright's *On Living in an Old Country* (1985) and Tom Nairn's *The Enchanted Glass* (1988), the latter of which explored 'the glamour of backwardness'. What is often ignored in contemporary British debates, and both Wright and Nairn address, has been the historic complicity and incorporation of the British left in the dominant 'island stories', the state of non-democracy, and the rising power of the past (see Colley, 2014, for an alternative take).

The left has traditionally taken one of two positions on this. One has been that all of the concerns about pageantry, tradition and even past excesses are now marginal, just artifice and flummery which can be bypassed, or pushed well and truly into the past. The other perspective has been to believe that at its heart the British state is democratic or capable of democratic change, altered at its core by the slow march and cumulative power of the Chartists, Suffragettes and radicals.

In short, this is the Whig Labour view of British history. It has informed and imbued Labour's idea of Britain and where it has wanted to go for most of its history. This drew on socialist thinker G.D.H. Cole's idea of 'the common people' gathering power and confidence to slowly break down the feudal and privilege constraints of the establishment, and was seen in 'the forward march of labour' idea, of a disciplined, almost militaristic, collective force, inexorably advancing with the weight of history behind it. There was almost something determinist in these ideas, which used to influence the sense of socialist optimism that tomorrow was theirs to be taken and remade; events proved to work out in a very different direction.

In Whig Labour Britain, democracy either doesn't matter, or it can be used in the small public sphere permitted by the British political system. It has proven over the long arc of 20th and 21st century Britain to be a historically and politically disastrous strategy. It has aligned Labour with a British state which never embraced democracy, and which still in its psyche, believes in its global pretensions, and hasn't shorn itself of its imperial characteristics – as it has morphed from the British Empire state into 'the global kingdom' which has become a leading advocate for national and transnational elites.

What this perspective failed to take into consideration as seen in Chapter Four is that the UK has not and never has been a fully-fledged political democracy, and shows no intentions of becoming one in the near future. The rest of the UK is characterised by the feudal relics of the age of pre-democracy, privilege and elite power.

The monarchy has long been explained by its advocates as only having symbolic power. But now we know that there is a potentially real Royal veto over legislation where bills which might be seen as affecting Prince Charles' private interests are given to him pre-assent for his comment and approval. This was revealed by *The Guardian* in 2011 in what they called a 'secretive government loophole', which had seen 12 bills subjected to this process in the previous six years, including bills on road safety, gambling and the London Olympic (*The Guardian*, 30 October 2011). This represents much more real power over legislation than the Queen's symbolic Royal Assent to bills.

Then there are the activities of Prince Charles, his parallel state and active advocacy and lobbying of numerous government ministers and departments. There are also the 'voluntary' arrangements of the Royal Family on tax (since 1992 and the Queen's annus horribilis), and the Duchy of Cornwall's avoidance of corporation tax, refusing to designate their business interests as a 'corporation'. It has emerged that in his capacity as the Duke of Cornwall, his estate gathered monies from people who died without leaving wills or any family. This amounted to £450,000 in 2012 and in May 2013 he was sitting on £3.3 million gathered intestate (*The Guardian*, 1 May 2013). This latter revelation could only be described as the 21st-century equivalent of feudal lordship and serfdom.

Of course to some all of this is insubstantial tittle-tattle compared to the decoration, grandeur and gaiety which is contributed to British life and traditions, as well as being a huge pull in terms of tourist numbers. The constitutional authority, Vernon Bogdanor (not without relevance, David Cameron's tutor at Oxford University), showed the establishment's irritation at this continued criticism, writing that, 'There is much confusion, to which the *Guardian* has contributed, concerning the Prince of Wales's constitutional role'.

He then presented a false analogy to knock down, arguing that Prince Charles did not become involved in party politics, 'Where a matter has become party political after the prince has raised it, for example GM crops, he has refrained from mentioning it in public, again'. This is the sound of a British elite, annoyed at having to explain itself; none of this matters, it argues, don't concern yourself, as you have a vote once every four or five years for one bit of the British constitution, the Commons. Bogdanor even goes as far as to dare to argue that Prince Charles' lobbying isn't really worthy of the name, as 'the key feature of a lobbyist is that he has a vested interest. The prince has no vested interests on such matters as Shakespeare or modern architecture' (which he has 'lobbied' ministers on) (*The Guardian*, 4 September 2013). This really won't do. Bogdanor's world is the logic that has ruled Britain for centuries, but today it can be exposed for the *Alice in Wonderland* thinking which has always characterised its establishment.

## Britain as Disneyland

Kirstie Allsopp, Tory property developer and craft promoter, showed a similar set of thoughts when she said at the time of the birth of William and Kate's royal child, George, 'what is wrong with Britain being a Disneyland?' (*Channel Four News*, 23 July 2013). She believed this was a cost-free, entertaining addition to the collective joy of the people. But to reduce the UK to a giant fantasy playground and to infantilise the people, culture and public life, has to have, to put it mildly, implications. Allsopp's position is that of the new super-rich, who aren't that different in many respects from the old elites, her social place being gained not just through the meritocratic world of property development TV programmes, but through her aristocratic connections, her father being the 6th Baron Hindlip, and a former chair of Christie's. Why would dismissing a central part of the affairs of state as 'Disneyland' be of any concern to such people as Allsopp, because tradition and privilege are what they have known, and the idea of a different Britain which is democratic, is an alien thought to them?

The British version of itself as a modern day Disneyland, a kind of amalgamation of newfound privilege, with modern day leisure and tourism, and a small amount of play, cannot just be dismissed out of hand. Christopher Hitchens, writing about the impact of the monarchy on identity and the national psyche over 20 years ago, put it in the following terms:

> The British monarchy inculcates unthinking credulity and servility. It forms a heavy layer on the general encrustation of our unreformed political institutions. It is the gilded peg from which our unlovely system of social distinction and hierarchy depends... It contributes to what sometimes looks like an enfeeblement of the national intelligence, drawing from our press and even from some of our poets the sort of degrading and abnegating propaganda that would arouse contempt if displayed in Zaire or Romania. (1990: 19)

This has become much more serious in the intervening years. 'Disneyland Britain' and the diminishing of the public as a direct consequence of the monarchy is connected to the contemporary version of Tory Britain, which takes from the rich, potent past of imperialism and continuity, and wraps it up in a language of self-importance, self-delusion and self-deceit.

David Cameron gave a revealing exposition of the Tory Britain story at the G20 summit in St Petersburg in September 2013. Clearly riled by Russian government remarks after the UK Parliament's vote for non-intervention in Syria in which they dismissed the UK as 'just a small island... no one pays any attention to them', Cameron launched into a rhapsodic eulogy of the UK which has been called his 'Hugh Grant moment', declaring:

Britain may be a small island, but I would challenge anyone to find a country with a prouder history, a bigger heart or greater resilience.

Britain is an island that has helped to clear the European continent of fascism – and was resolute in doing that throughout World War Two.

Britain is an island that helped to abolish slavery, that has invented most of the things worth inventing, including every sport currently played around the world, that still today is responsible for art, literature and music that delights the entire world.

We are very proud of everything we do as a small island – a small island that has the sixth-largest economy, the fourth best-funded military, some of the most effective diplomats, the proudest history, one of the best records for art and literature and contribution to philosophy and world civilisation.

For the people who live in Northern Ireland, I should say we are not just an island, we are a collection of islands. I don't want anyone in Shetland or Orkney to feel left out by this.

I'm thinking of setting this to music... (*The Guardian*, 6 September 2013)

Cameron's vision is fascinating, as coming from the Tories and his upper-class background, he has the effortless élan and arrogance which Blair or Brown never had in their numerous rebranding and repackaging exercises about the UK. Some of the elements remain the same: creative Britain of the Blair era is still present and correct if a lot less bombastic, as is elements of progressive Britain such as the fight against slavery, so often cited by Brown.

The overall meaning of the statement is captured in the Hugh Grant comparison: this is a country led by not too bright privileged men, who feel in the culture of our age that it is time for them to stop apologising about their pasts, and instead, to start exercising their right to govern and utilise their age old privilege. 'Traditional values in a modern setting' might be one way of putting it, to paraphrase John Prescott on New Labour.

All countries have comforting stories and foundation myths, but the chasm between the Cameron modern version and the reality of the UK for most people is stark. And this gap is aided every day by the wilful acts of the Cameron-led government – diminishing welfare and social provision, and diluting or privatising the public nature of public services and public goods. All of these actions can be disguised and even more powerfully, legitimised, by this make believe account of Britain.

Not surprisingly this isn't the only prevailing mythic version of the UK. Even in these difficult times of austerity, cuts and popular anxiety, there is still in places beyond Labour politicians, the occasional articulation of the vision of an inclusive, progressive Britain, which draws on a host of Labour, Liberal and radical voices.

This is one interpretation of Danny Boyle's opening ceremony for the London Olympics in July 2012. This stunning performance presented the continuous lineage of that other version of Britain. It ranged from the 'green Olde England' to the land which saw the industrial revolution and tamed it, humanising and alleviating its worst effects, the Britain of invention and creativity in science and ideas, the country that made the welfare state and NHS after the war, and of course, the power of British pop music from the 1960s onwards. Boyle's audacious seizure of the Olympic platform to tell this version of Britain surprised most people at the time. It pleasantly surprised lots of left-wingers and liberals, and even parts of conservative England.

Charlotte Higgins of *The Guardian* wrote that the opening ceremony offered an 'impassioned poem of praise to the country [Boyle] would most like to believe in... tolerant, multicultural, fair and gay friendly [with] the principles of the welfare state stoutly at its heart' (*The Guardian*, 28 July 2012). From a very different place, the *Daily Mail*'s Jan Moir articulated similar sentiments, calling it 'a vision of Britain, past and present, which was touching and special, without being pious or grandiose' (*Daily Mail*, 28 July 2012). But it also shocked some right-wing opinion, the most famous example being Tory MP Aidan Burley who slammed it as 'multicultural crap' and 'the most leftie opening ceremony I have ever seen', declaring, 'Bring back Red Arrows, Shakespeare and the Stones' (*The Guardian*, 28 July 2012).

What is interesting in this context is the resonance of this account of Britain and its near absence from contemporary British politics. Its popular appeal should not be that much of a surprise given the existence of significant communities of left and centre-left opinion in Britain, and there is a natural appeal to part of this story: of portraying Britain as the moral guardians of universal human values, and the good guys remaking their own country, civilising it over the centuries, and standing for such values internationally.

The main trouble with this is twofold. The first is the reality of modern Britain as one of the most unequal countries in the developed world, and related to this, the retreat of any such progressive British account in the last 30 years or so. It is one thing, as Danny Boyle did, to present a theatrical artistic and cultural intervention, but it is another to remake a country's politics and society. Maybe the Olympic opening showed that there is still a significant yearning for a different Britain to today, which draws on past progressive Britains. In this Boyle has something in common with Ken Loach's *The Spirit of '45*, but presented in a much more cool, hip and seemingly relevant way. But both are at the moment rooted in nostalgia, lack of reality and disconnection from present challenges.

Therefore, it is not surprising that David Cameron can feel he can dare to get away with his Hugh Grant vision of Britain. The St Petersburg declaration was a revealing moment about the state of Britain, and one which shows how confident today's ruling elite are, and how sanguine they feel about their place and privileges.

The rising power of the past, and the use that historical military expeditions, moments and previous generations are increasingly being appropriated for, tell us much about the state of Britain's elites. The once powerful, popular strands of Britishness – which had potent Tory and Labour stories – have given way to a much more threadbare account which offers little positive and optimistic about the future.

Instead, the Britain on offer from our political classes is a deeply unattractive, unpleasant one, of an increasing parsimonious, punitive state and public realm, and political environment defined by populism and authoritarianism on a host of issues from welfare to law and order and immigration.

It is not an accident that in this environment the rising tide of a mythical past should move centre stage – a kind of regressive collective set of imagined memories. This then carries huge consequences for progressive and left strands in Britain, whether inside or outside Labour. Once there had been a powerful Labour and labour movement vision of the future that was intertwined with a story of Britain. No longer can that be said with any credibility. This then brings us to a profound crossroads which has to ask: are there any viable roads back from the 'fantasyland Britain' which has been constructed these last three decades, and if not, what alternative routes are available that can challenge this state of affairs? This brings us to the Scottish debate and context which we now turn to.

CHAPTER SIX

# Scotland is not a Democracy

A democracy ignorant of the past is not qualified either to analyse the present or to shape the future; and so, in the interests of High Priests of Politics and the Lordy Money-Changers of Society, great care has been taken to offer us stories of useless pageantry, chronicles of the birth and death of Kings, annals of Court intrigue and international war, while withheld from us were the real facts and narratives of moment, the loss of our ancient freedom, the rape of our common lands and the shameless and dastardly methods by which a few selected stocks matched the patrimony of the people.

TOM JOHNSTON, *Our Scots Noble Families*, Forward Publishing 1909

THERE IS A POTENT sense in parts of Scotland that all or most of the frailties and limitations of our democracy and society are external. This focuses on the dysfunctional nature of what passes for British democracy and politics and lays almost exclusively the responsibilities for its shortcomings south of the border. This is deeply grained in parts of Scottish nationalism and the left, and is increasingly problematic, denying some of the less edifying characteristics of Scottish public life and our collective role in creating them.

## The Problems and Importance of Sovereignty

This can be seen in the eulogising of the notion of Scottish popular sovereignty over what is often posed as the English idea of parliamentary sovereignty. This is based on a number of historic sources and arguments such as the Declaration of Arbroath of 1320 and the idea that the legitimacy of the Scots monarch was located in a very different kind of authority, based on the people, compared to England. This latter point is seen as validated by the titles – Mary, Queen of Scots and Queen Elizabeth of England.

None of the above beliefs have any substantive foundation. Popular sovereignty is not a legally binding concept. It is not even a practical notion in the public life of Scotland either now or in the past. If popular sovereignty had legal power behind it, Scots would have, for example, stopped the poll tax and a whole host of other measures. If Scottish public life were shaped by such a notion, in practice Scotland would not have

been administered for decades by Labour (and before that Liberal) paternalism. Sovereignty itself is a problematic term in the modern world, with
its origins in the age of absolutism, 'the Divine Right of kings' and
authority which monarchs claimed emanated directly from God.

With all these qualifications, popular sovereignty does matter in Scotland and that is at the level of folklore and mythology. It tells something
about who we are as a people, about political community, our values, and
our understandings and connections to a sense of past, which is idealised
and in part an imagined sense of our shared histories and ourselves. It
reveals some powerful indicators about how the Scottish people see themselves, aspire to be, and in what ways they differentiate themselves from
others. This is part of the construction of who historically and contemporaneously 'we' are.

But so far Scotland has not used this resonance of popular sovereignty
to democratise and empower people and to develop a vision of society
markedly different from the status quo. This is not entirely surprising as
not one country in the world has yet had its politics and institutions
shaped by such a principle becoming practice. Even the USA and France,
both formed in revolutionary republican periods, have invoked the principle, and have used it as part of their national mythology, but despite this
their political systems are not shaped by it.

Scotland then is not a fully-fledged political democracy. It has never
had a democratic moment which has brought its elites to account, defined
public institutions and seen the people as a historic collective agency of
change. At the time of the Acts of Union, Scotland clearly was not democratic and the negotiated autonomy which the nation retained post-union
was defined in 'the holy trinity' of the Kirk, law and education. These
carried with them the seeds of institutional memory of what was Scottish
identity, tradition and practice and a culture of distinctiveness through the
high tide of unionist Scotland (see Paterson, 1994; Mitchell, 1996).

Thus as Scottish administrative institutions grew and developed later
in the union, a profoundly apolitical sense of Scots identity began to
emerge: one of experts, elites and benign paternalism, believing they had
the skills and knowledge to act and think in what they thought were the
best interests of the people. This came to take the form in late Victorian
Scotland of an emergent Fabian enlightened authority, which was even
less challenging to the conservative modes of society than the explicit
Fabianism of the Webbs and Shaws south of the border.

The zenith of this 'high Scotland' was 1945–75: the managed society
on which the welfare state and post-war consensus were built (see Roy,

2013). There is a particular Scottish account of this period, of this settlement being a coalescing of the old order, institutions and elites with an optimistic belief in planning, modernism and the future. There was, at times of its greatest strength with this outlook, a seemingly endless spirit of goodwill and identification with this 'high Scotland'. It was engaged in enormously productive activities: building huge numbers of council houses, the Forth and Tay Road Bridges, and the powerful Hydro Electric schemes of the Highlands. This was a period when government bodies and the state rose to some of the great challenges, but in a manner which was not about democratising Scotland or the instruments of power. The main means of delivery of this era of social progress and transformation was centralisation and control both at a British and Scottish level (see Maxwell, 2012).

There were voices at the time which challenged the remorseless logic of authority and central government knows best attitude but these were not heeded. James A. Bowie's *The Future of Scotland*, published just before war broke out in 1939, forewarned that major advance was not possible without 'vision' and 'a reawakened popular consciousness' (1939: 256–7). The Scottish Labour Party were still notionally committed to home rule when the Attlee government was elected in 1945, but did nothing to progress or even examine the issue. Eventually when Labour went into opposition in 1951, it dropped even tokenistic support for devolution in 1958 (Keating and Bleiman, 1979). Calls for decentralisation, wider participation and devolution were to remain marginal until the 1960s, when the rise of the SNP and the limits of centralism in such measures as slum clearance and town planning began to become apparent.

Scotland's public institutions and public realm have grown more distinct and autonomous from late Victorian times – and more centralised and standardised (see Bort, McAlpine and Morgan, 2012). These two factors are intrinsically linked. At the start of the 20th century, there were over 1,000 councils – 869 parish councils, 33 county councils and 200 burgh councils. This was reduced in 1929 to just over 400 – 21 large burghs, 176 smaller burghs, 33 county councils and 196 district councils. In 1973 this was reduced to nine regions, three island authorities and 53 district councils, and in 1995 this became 32 local authorities – the current situation (McConnell, 2004). Today groups such as the Reform Scotland think tank have called for the number of councils to be cut further – from 32 to 19 (Thomson, Mawdsley and Payne, 2012).

These dynamics can be seen across public services. Once there was 13 water boards, then three, and now only one body: Scottish Water. Once there were 12 fire boards, now there is only one: Scottish Fire and Rescue Service; there used to be 20 police boards and now there is just one: Police Scotland.

This inexorable centralisation was in the past about the forward march of progress, sweeping away the cobwebs of the old boards and what was seen as pre-democratic Scotland. But now it is only motivated by supposed claims of efficiency and a bogus version of modernity – defined by top down processes and consultancy logic.

A complex inter-relationship of three factors is at work here. First, the expansion of Scottish administration and government which can be seen in the exponential increase in public bodies and services from the late Victorian era onwards, much of it mirroring changes across the UK. Second, a more Scottish dimension took form both institutionally and also in popular sentiment with each reinforcing the other; increasing autonomy and public bodies drove even more public expectations for democratic control and scrutiny. Third, this widening Scottish public space and set of institutions took power into its own hands within society, centralising and standardising public services, in so doing usurping and frustrating some of the democratic pressures.

This set of trends have been powerfully at work from the end of the 19th century, from the first days of the Scottish Office, the ebbs and flows of the home rule movement, and the Scottish Parliament era under both Labour and SNP. This we can gauge, is directly related to the form of voice within Scottish society and how it has articulated itself in the UK, and contributed to the maintenance of a limited, controlled form of democracy in domestic Scottish public life.

It is not surprising that the Scotland of centralisation and standardisation which has defined our society for so long has accelerated under the Scottish Parliament, and that people should intuitively notice and feel this burgeoning democratic deficit in domestic public life. A recent survey found that only 22 per cent of Scots said they felt they could influence decisions affecting their local area; 36 per cent wanted to have a greater involvement while only 23 per cent though their local council was good at listening (Scottish Government, 2012).

## The State of Control: 'Undemocracy' and 'Unspace'

This brings us to the current state of affairs whereby a Scottish Parliament has been established, more or less sitting on top of this culture and legacy but which has never been democratic.

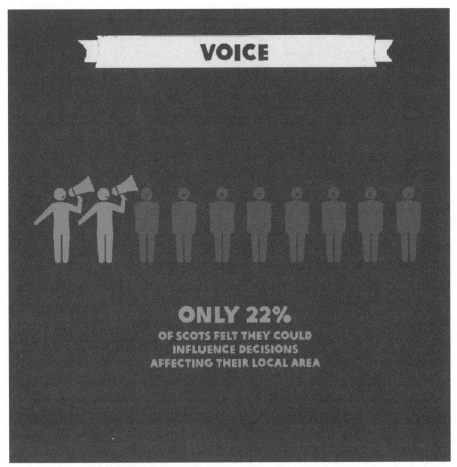

**Fig. 3** Scotland's Lack of Democracy and Voice. *Source: Oxfam Scotland, 2013.*

Scottish political life and practice is informed by what I call 'undemocracy' – meaning a state of affairs which has never been defined by a democratic evolution or maturing. It has the superficial appearance of a modern political democracy – contested elections, free parties, public debate – but lacks the substantive characteristics. This is part of a wider condition in Scottish public life which is defined by what I call 'unspace', meaning the prioritisation of official voices and interests, and the marginalisation of dissenting, non-conformist opinions.

Some would argue that this same situation exists across the developed world and, in particular, in small nation states, but the culture of unspace is very different in Scotland because of this backdrop of undemocracy. Unspace is a deliberate, conscious system of social control, conformity and legitimacy in public discussions, places and places. It aids the legitimisation of official voices and perspectives, which then dominate and shape discussion, and thus by so doing, perpetuate this existing state of affairs. Many people are, as a result, wary of crossing the tangible barriers and codes which inform the official spaces and discussions, which dissent would entail. All of this reinforces the official story of Scotland, the institutional biases and focuses in public life, and the tendency to collective groupthink and orthodoxies.

There are some alternative, messy, fuzzy spaces, but there are not numerous, well-funded or imbued with authority and a formal sense of power. Instead, the alternative spaces which can be identified exhibit a sense of informality, and often combine politics or current affairs discussion and intervention, with culture, music, and a civic activist ethos.

There has been, as later chapters will note, some movement in this alternative Scotland associated with the independence referendum, but for it to have a long term influence, it will have to take on these deeply imbedded cultures of undemocracy and unspace. Part of this trend can be seen as a delayed attempt to democratise the Scottish public sphere, but to transform this in the short period between the 2011 election and 2014 independence vote is unlikely if not impossible. Instead, such a project would be a generational one.

## The 'Missing Scotland'

An examination of the state of Scotland's current limited democracy should be a salutary shot in the arm compared to the rhetoric of 'the new politics' and illusions of 'civic Scotland'.

The 'missing Scotland' from our supposedly democratic national life, even measured at the most minimal level of political participation of voting in Scottish Parliament or UK general elections, comes to just under one million adult Scots. If one looks at the last Scottish Parliament (2011) and Westminster (2010) and assesses their turnouts by the UK turnout of just over 20 years in the UK general election of 1992 (75.4 per cent Scotland), we can map the burgeoning gap of political disconnection.

In the 2011 Scottish Parliament elections, in figures estimated by the Electoral Commission Scotland, 989,540 voters are missing, compared to the turnout of 1992. For Westminster, the figures are significantly lower, but still stark: 446,954 voters are missing compared to the turnout levels of 1992. The lowest turnout in Scotland in 2011 was the constituency of Glasgow Provan in the city's north east with 34.5 per cent. This is a set of communities which contain a mixture of socio-economic characteristics, people and places; it would be wrong to just portray all of it as deprivation, unemployment and poverty – instead it ranges from what was the council estate of Easterhouse which has seen massive regeneration, to Alexandra Park and Dennistoun, with significant parts of affluence. Despite this mixture it produces the lowest turnout of all Scotland, and one which sees 16,809 voters missing compared to the turnouts of just over 20 years ago.

The 'missing Scotland' has grown as our society has become less collectivist, more individualised and fragmented, resulting in political parties (the SNP apart) retreating in membership and activity. Places like Glasgow Provan once thrived with political and civic activity, from parties, trade unions and churches, which connected people and gave them a sense of anchorage. It is also true that Glasgow's East End seats often caused Labour a problem, with party officials warning as long ago as the late 1950s that they were atrophying, inactive and getting smaller (Hassan and Shaw, 2012).

Without doubt Glasgow Provan's local Labour Party with all these caveats would have been much more active in the 1950s, and one of the drivers of this, along with class and party identification, was greater party competition. It was a completely different political world then as one of Glasgow's Provan's previous incarnations, Glasgow Camlachie, saw the Tories win the seat in a 1948 by-election, admittedly on a split Labour-Independent Labour Party ticket.

This was not a freak result, for in the 1951 and 1955 UK general elections, Glasgow's 15 constituencies split nearly 50:50, seven Conservative and eight Labour. This competition meant there were relatively few completely safe seats, and even where one party knew it would be re-elected, the other had a very respectable vote. Glasgow's turnout in 1951 was an impressive 81 per cent – and the variance across the 15 constituencies was relatively modest ranging from Glasgow Central at 74.3 per cent to Scotstoun at 85.1 per cent: a difference between lowest and highest of 10.8 per cent. Central was the only seat with a turnout below 75 per cent, while ten of the 15 constituencies had a turnout at or higher than 80 per cent.

If we fast-forward from the era of 1951 to the Scottish Parliament elections of 2011, Glasgow's turnout fell from 81 per cent to 41 per cent. This produces a much shrunken electorate on two counts. First, the city's population had fallen by nearly half over the 60 years, and turnout by almost half, producing an electorate who actually made it the polls in 2011 which was almost one quarter of its size in 1951. Charting actual votes over the period, the Tory vote in the city of 1951 has collapsed, falling from 272,155 to 12,749 in 2011: meaning that the Tory vote in actual numbers is a mere 4.7 per cent of its 1951 level. Tory Glasgow has literally just disappeared: either it walked away, died or changed its mind.

Labour have not exactly prospered either. In 1951 they polled 305,922 votes across the city, and in 2011 this had fallen to 73,031: 23.9 per cent of its previous high. Both Labour and the Tories have seen long-term decline in their votes and organisations, but it also continued recently, with both their actual votes falling across the city consistently since the first Scottish Parliament elections of 1999. And of course, the Scottish Nationalists have gained, who were not present in the 1951 elections in the city, but who outpolled Labour in 2011 with 83,109 votes. There is also the impact of the Liberal Democrats, who as the Liberals did not contest any 1951 seats; and the rise and fall of the various versions of the Scottish Socialist Party (who polled impressively in Glasgow in 2003, nearly challenging the SNP for second place in votes). Each of these latter forces has contributed to a more diverse, fragmented politics in recent times, compared to the 1950s.

The difference in turnout between seats in 2011 in Glasgow is not that more dramatic than 60 years ago. The lowest turnout was Provan with 34.5 per cent and the highest Rutherglen on 47.7 per cent: a gap of 13.2 per cent which isn't much larger than 1951. Turnout across constituencies has fallen uniformly with, in 2011 not one seat above 50 per cent turnout, which in some electoral systems would have been a trigger for a recall or recontest, and five of the nine below 40 per cent.

Where we can identify an even more alarming collapse in turnout and marked differentiation is at the level of local government ward. In the 2012 local elections the lowest ten turnouts all produced rates of under 30 per cent, and while most of these were in Glasgow (six), three were in Aberdeen and one in Dundee (see Table below). The lowest two turnouts were in Aberdeen: with George Street/Harbour with 20.5 per cent and Tillydrone/Seaton/Old Aberdeen at 22.0 per cent.

## Table 4.1  Scotland's Geography Of Political Disconnection 2012

| Place | Council | Ward | 2012 per cent turnout |
|-------|---------|------|-----------------------|
| 1 | Aberdeen | George St/Harbour | 20.5 |
| 2 | Aberdeen | Tillydrone/Seaton/Old Aberdeen | 22.0 |
| 3 | Glasgow | Anderston/City | 23.6 |
| 4 | Glasgow | Calton | 26.0 |
| 5 | Glasgow | Springburn | 27.1 |
| 6 | Glasgow | North East | 27.5 |

| Place | Council | Ward | 2012 per cent turnout |
|---|---|---|---|
| 7 | Glasgow | Canal | 27.7 |
| 8 | Glasgow | Hillhead | 28.1 |
| 9 | Aberdeen | Torry/Ferryhill | 29.3 |
| 10 | Dundee | Maryfield | 29.7 |

*Source: Electoral Commission Scotland, 2013.*

Aberdeen's George Street/Harbour, with the lowest turnout in Scotland, is not an area of abject deprivation. It is part of the city centre, and although part of its shocking turnout may be due to voters moving from the previous electoral register, something has gone wrong. STV *News* profiled the ward in the run-up to polling day, taking about the challenges of city regeneration, of 'breathing new life into the heart of Aberdeen', the problem of 'increasing numbers of empty retail units and the poor state of some buildings on Union Street', and the opportunities of 'Aberdeen Business Improvement District' which had invested millions in the area (STV *News*, 27 April 2012). The ward was even significantly competitive, with the SNP winning 33.7 per cent to Labour's 31.5 per cent, and Labour two to the SNP's one councillors, but none of this could improve the turnout.

The third lowest was Anderston/City with 23.6 per cent, the lowest rate in Glasgow. This coincidently turns out, in a city-wide contest which was presented as a key (if not the key) struggle between Labour and SNP, to be the ward of Glasgow City Council Labour leader Gordon Matheson. Labour won 50.3 per cent of the vote to the SNP's 29.6 per cent and Greens 10.5 per cent, producing two Labour, one SNP and one Green councillors.

Such low turnouts to a massive extent make a farce of democratic elections, outcomes and the notion of 'mandate'. Never mind the concept of differential turnout, and winning by getting more of your voters out; with these sort of derisory turnouts, you win by getting any of your vote out. And yet both Labour and the SNP and large sections of the media, saw the struggle for Glasgow as critical in assessing future politics.

This 'missing Scotland' disfigures and diminishes the public life of Scotland and makes a sham of our democratic pretensions. It is something that is not talked about or conceded in polite society, let alone the root causes examined and what it might say about politics and engagement.

We know who are the 'missing Scotland'. They are disproportionately the voices of younger, poorer people, who are more likely to live in social housing and have less financial 'assets', and while they can be found every-where, they are more pronounced and concentrated in the West of

Scotland. These are our fellow citizens, our friends, family members, work colleagues and more, and on a political level we have just chosen to ignore that they are not engaged in or present in our supposed democracy.

Why is this 'missing Scotland' so missing that we fail to even acknowledge it? One reason is that it jars with the nice, comfortable story of 'civic Scotland' that we are this land of inclusion and warmth, which has just never been completely true. Another is that the voters who no longer turn up at polling booths have no voice or weight in these supposed great political contests, whether it be the Labour v. SNP Glasgow struggle or the independence referendum. If both sides contest existing voters there is little incentive to try and draw from the gathering group of discontents who don't vote; this of course makes even less sense if this group is increasing, but more often than not parties think they can win mobilise existing voters.

Then there is the public and cultural representations of this 'missing Scotland' which exasperates the problem. How often do we see BBC or STV head off into a disadvantaged part of Glasgow or another urban setting and frame it in a way filled with cliché, boarded up housing and wasteground? Such items are often then shown with various voters offering vox pops with such laminations as 'all politicians are the same', 'they don't do anything for people like me', or 'there are no jobs about'. This caricature of disadvantage and a fragmented society helps no one. It provides the media with cheap copy, but does not offer any understanding or empathy, and leaves people reduced to passive, cynical whingers, waiting either for the politicians to do something, or for the economic upturn to reach Springburn.

A revealing example of this was the 2008 Glasgow East Westminster by-election, which was fought at a critical time for the then prime ministership of Gordon Brown, and in the lexicon of the SNP-Labour struggle, post-the Nationalists winning office the previous year. The contest came at the end of Wendy Alexander's Scottish Labour leadership, and saw Labour go through several prospective candidates, before Margaret Curran (already an MSP) emerged as the party's standard-bearer. The SNP's John Mason won by the narrow margin of 365 votes (with Curran winning it back at the 2010 UK election). This was, as I pointed out at the time, the first by-election in Glasgow's East End in modern times. The one before it was the Camlachie contest of 1948. Thus, it was the first contest of the media age covering this area of Glasgow.

Not surprisingly it produced cliché after cliché about Glasgow, Glaswegians, areas of deprivation and the changes undergone. One BBC *Daily Politics* item saw Fraser Nelson, now editor of *The Spectator*, visit the

The Missing Voices of Scotland by Greg Moodie.

constituency and describe the older, aspirational working-class culture which had produced his father, and by implication, himself. What was illuminating was that to draw together this thesis, Fraser stood outside his father's former council house and observed that it had now been bought and transformed – both potentially powerful and potent stories – but sadly did not speak to a single local resident or voter (*The House Magazine*, 21 July 2008). This example could be multiplied numerous times, with Fraser's film hardly the worst example as at least he did not stigmatise and demonise the people of the area. But what he did not do was give voice to, or explain the lifestories of, people in the area. He felt he had the authority and status to interpret and assume through his narrative their stories. And that is what happens every day to 'the missing Scotland'.

Some of this is the political and wider civic engagement equivalent of what is called 'the Glasgow effect' in public health inequalities. We will explore this perspective, one of professional Scotland later, suffice to say at the moment, that this analysis while having much to commend in it, does not make the connections between public health inequalities and the wider inequalities in the city and elsewhere, and the cost in democratic, political and civic engagement. And that is a significant omission, because all of these factors are inter-related.

The 'missing Scotland' is our version of truncated democracy, a phenomenon that is seen across large parts of the West and developed countries. This has produced across numerous nations, a hollowed out, atrophied political debate, narrow engagement and because of that a constrained set of political possibilities. The truncated democracy means that the voters becomes increasingly unrepresentative of the electorate per se, as older voters turn out and younger people don't, while the more affluent vote and the poor increasingly don't. The 2010 UK election saw 44 per cent of 18–24 year olds vote compared to 76 per cent of the over-65s (Ipsos MORI, 2010). The US political system has increasingly been dominated by the politics of truncated democracy which has contributed towards handicapping the Democrats and driving politics more rightward.

One manifestation of this truncated democracy is the rise of Ukip who are made up disproportionately in voters and members of older people. Their concerns over Europe, immigration and welfare are reflected in Ukip and its rise has been both a product of this truncated democracy and exaggerated by it further.

Just because Scotland does not at the moment have a significant Ukip presence does not mean we are immune to such trends. Scotland's limited democracy and atrophied participation constricts even more how politics, politicians and political change are perceived. It becomes more seen as synonymous with the political class and elite, closed conversations in which most of the public are spectators, not active agents. This set of perceptions then aids a cycle which reinforces the above, squeezes the parameters of politics and the realm of what it is permissible and viable to talk about, change and challenge.

If you think Scotland is that different from the above and that such a critique is misplaced, just ask yourself why have all the main parties subscribed to the idea of the council tax freeze for so long? Not because it has effectively targeted hard-pressed voters. The council tax freeze aids the well-off and those with the biggest, most costly properties. Research by Unison has shown that those in the highest property band (H) gain an average £441 per year, while those in the lowest property band gain £147. That's a redistribution away from the poorest and towards the most affluent.

The reason Scotland has a political consensus on the council tax freeze is because of our truncated democracy, and the power and influence of older, more affluent voters. These people matter more and more to the political parties, because they vote, and not surprisingly are quite attached to the idea of retaining benefits targeted at them, such as the state pension and free care for the elderly.

The cost of Scotland's limited democracy can be gauged in many ways but perhaps the biggest damage it does is to our individual and collective belief that change can come about. This is what American psychologist Martin Seligman has called 'learned helplessness', by which he means the way in which people internalise and come to believe they are powerless, voiceless and lacking in the capacity to alter this (Peterson, Maier and Seligman, 1995).

'Learned helplessness' means that people don't see themselves in the political discussions of our nation, and any conventional methods used to reach them fail, as people just don't see themselves reflected in the language, talk and culture of the system. Instead, 'learned helplessness' is a culmination of decades of economic and social change, which have literally left hundreds of thousands of Scots disempowered and bewildered at how they make sense of the modern world.

This is a result of huge upheaval which all of us are still trying to make sense of but which in its deindustrialisation, economic dislocation and social change, has turned many people's lives upside down. Its effects have been unevenly distributed and experienced, with older working-class men in particular thrown out of a whole host of industries. This structural and cultural change has had an equally damning psychological impact, with people internalising a sense of personal powerlessness and helplessness, and from this believing that they have a lack of personal and collective voice.

If we are going to change this, a small but fundamental start would be to begin to notice it. The 'civic Scotland' account of our nation has been conspicuously silent on all of this, and there is a sense that after Labour Scotland's collusion in such a state of affairs, Nationalist Scotland and the mainstream argument of independence could go down the same route, as they choose to believe that their own bubble version of the country is the whole reality, and that their 'official story' amounts to the real Scotland when it isn't, and in actual fact, is a central part of the problem.

Recognising 'the missing Scotland', the people, their voices, hopes and dreams, and the damage it has done not just to them individually as well as our society, would be a start. But that is not enough. We also need to notice the wider ramifications and limitations in our public life, and the potent sounds of silence which inhabit so many aspects of society.

There are numerous reasons for this pervading conformity and closure in public life, many of them historic, and originating in the power of the Kirk and authority. As these forces have declined in Scotland, the collective memories of them have become mixed up in the modern version of our constricted public realm. Clearly the culture and overhang of Presbyterianism and Calvinism to some play a contributory part in all of this today, but these are not the main drivers of contemporary Scotland.

Instead, what can be witnessed today is a strange hybrid between the institutional practices of 'high Scotland' and the world of enlightened, omnipotent authority, which at its zenith believed that it could remake Scotland in a progressive way, and the orthodoxies of the modern Western world, and in particular the UK, its politics, culture and state, and the characteristics of 'the global kingdom'.

The prevailing mainstream account of Scotland is that it has resisted the worst excesses of the neo-liberal revolution, but that does not mean that it has not affected and changed Scotland. The combination of the practices and legacy of 'high Scotland' taken with the current age of managerial orthodoxies, aids a powerful sense of groupthink in what passes for our public debates and conversations.

This is what the Norwegian sociologist Thomas Mathiesen calls the process of being 'silently silenced', by which the parameters of what it is feasible to talk about in public are filtered and negotiated (Mathiesen, 2004). In Scotland, this produces a political culture which portrays itself as progressive and even in places radical, but is actually deeply conservative, insular and insecure, and which is wary of change, wherever it comes from. Later chapters will explore some specific examples, but it massively reinforces the psyche, politics and cultures of status quo Scotland.

Understanding this would be a seismic shift in how we understand 'missing Scotland'. But this as well is not enough on its own. Instead, addressing this stain and shame on our claims to be a modern, inclusive democracy has to entail addressing the fundamentals of power and voice, which I will turn to in later chapters.

CHAPTER SEVEN

# The Rise and Fall of 'Civic Scotland'

Clearly, people on the street are not civil society, only the organised are; nor is civil society completely separate from the state or necessarily any less politically partisan. Civil society does not even necessarily promote democracy, such that the more civil society there is the more democracy there is. Civil society (and civil societies) pursue political and often partisan objectives and can promote socially and exclusive behaviour.

JEAN BARR, *The Stranger Within*, Sense Publishers 2008

## *The Difference Debate*

SCOTLAND IS DIFFERENT in many regards, partly because it sees and thinks itself so, and partly because the language and discourse of politics and public life is very different.

But different from what you might think? The unstated or sometimes stated assumption in this is 'different from the rest of the UK', which implies that the UK is some kind of norm to be judged against. This is a mindset prevalent in the 'policy divergence' school of thought, where Scotland is seen as departing from the model of a standardised British welfare state; but what if it is the British government and policy-makers who are abandoning such ideas and Scotland in a small way taking an informed stand in favour of such principles?

The difference debate is often posed as about either/or but is really about emphasis and nuance. There used to be an element of defensiveness in explaining this; a 1980s academic sociological paper was titled, 'Scotland is Different, OK?', which gave the impression that, at least to fellow British academics, this was a case which had to be made on tentative grounds, challenging as it did what had been known as 'the homogenisation of Britain' thesis which had been very persuasive until the mid-1970s (Dickson, 1989).

None of this means that the idea of difference should be taken at face value. There is both in Scotland a narrative of difference which has increasingly become part of 'the official story', which at its most extreme version becomes a fetishisation of the most miniscule or imagined difference. There is also a counter-trend in academic circles which seeks to talk about how small the difference is between Scotland and England, and draws from Scottish Social Attitudes Surveys to make this case. A quick summary of the data can establish the pro and anti-difference camps. The anti-difference perspective cite a number of public policy preferences which show Scotland is only at most marginally more left-wing than England: 78 per cent of Scots voters compared to 74 per cent of English voters said that the gap between high and low incomes was too large; at the same time 43 per cent of Scots support governments adopting redistributive policies versus 34 per cent in England (Curtice and Ormston, 2011).

The pro-difference argument can point out that Scotland has a very different political system and culture to England, seen in the dominance of centre-left parties pre- and post-devolution, the absence of right-wing electoral forces and ideas, and the divergence between Scots and English voting behaviour which markedly parted company post-1979. Two factors can be seen in this latter phenomenon, first, the weakness of the Conservative vote in Scotland compared to England, and the difference between the Labour/Conservative lead between the two countries. On this last measurement, the two nations gap rose to 20.6 per cent in 1979, then a historic post-war high, before rising to 35.1 per cent in 1987, falling back to 18.2 per cent in 1997, and producing a record 36.8 per cent gap in 2010.

Different figures highlight a significant set of public policy preferences for Scotland compared to the rest of Britain. Fifty-eight percent of Scots in a May 2013 Ipsos MORI Scotland survey believed that 'publically' owned and run public services would be more professional and reliable, against 19 per cent who chose 'privately' owned and run. In England and Wales, the respective figures are 30 per cent for 'publically' owned, and 29 per cent for 'privately' run in the public sector. Similarly, 50 per cent of Scots believe that the public sector provides better value for money, with 17 per cent saying the private sector; in England and Wales, the figures are 27 per cent private and 25 per cent public (Diffley, 2013: 16).

The above figures and arguments demonstrate that both cases have validity but also contain elements of over-reach. Scotland is different, but not that different from England and the rest of the UK. It is both a different nation, with its own traditions, practices and institutions, but also shares a whole set of common experiences with the other nations of the union. The narrative of difference has become imbued in the collective ether of Scotland's public life, particularly post-1979 and the election of the Thatcher Government, and in this it is part myth, part fact, but one which has shaped how the leading political, cultural and civic bodies interpret society. At the same time, the critique of any sense of difference has become the default academic and empirical counter-story, and it is both true to an extent and partial. Scotland's politics and public life are much more nuanced and varied than Scottish Social Attitudes Surveys, and on numerous other figures and evidence, there is both a measurable and real difference.

## The Strange Story of 'Civic Scotland'

The manifestation of Scottish difference can be certainly observed in the articulation of ideas in the public sphere, the importance given to the notion of civil society and from this the Scottish idea of 'civic Scotland'. To be precise, there are three different terms in usage, nearly always used inter-changeably and without differentiation – civil society, civic society and 'civic Scotland'. In the context I want to look more closely at one of those, namely, 'civic Scotland'.

'Civic Scotland' came to prominence as a term in the 1980s to denote the public life, institutions and networks of society. It implicitly states that Scottish society is very different from English society. It is an idea based on an explicit rejection of Thatcherite individualism, which infers that this part of society is imbued with an egalitarian, compassionate ethos.

In the course of writing this book I asked over a dozen public figures their thoughts on what 'civic Scotland' meant, why it became important, and where it is today. These ranged from a number of people associated with the term, academics and journalists, some well-disposed to the notion and some critical. One individual synonymous with the term in the 1980s and 1990s, when asked to define it responded, 'I think Civic Scotland is "the rest of us"!!! The non-professional politicians who take an interest/involvement in how the country is run and how we live.'

Another similarly defined voice offered an element of criticism calling it 'a substitute establishment' with 'a certain cosiness and complacency in Scottish civil society'. This person refused to use the term 'civic Scotland', instead plumping for civil society, and only invoked the latter when asked too. They did offer the following prospectus of who sat outside 'civic Scotland':

> Typically excluded are the old mainstream media who resist social accountability, the rich and big corporate players who tend to lobby government directly and avoid social dialogue, and the 'voiceless' – i.e. those too poor, depressed etc. to organise themselves even in small community groups, and who typically allow 'professionals' to speak for them.

A more institutional voice associated with 'civic Scotland' reflected that, 'I never use the term Civic Scotland. I think it is confusing and, in particular, has municipal overtones...', part of the reason being that they said their work was 'to patrol the boundary between independent citizen action and the state...'

There was in these perspectives a nervousness and tetchiness about being asked to think about definitions and who was in and who was out of this group. For example, a leading Scottish academic associated with this strand and thinking posed the following rather defensive explanation:

> I don't engage in grand theories, but that is a matter of academic caution, not of 'civic Scotland'. You can thus find relevant definitions in many places, each time I use the term 'civil society'... 'Civic Scotland' I have only ever used in specific contexts where I have been involved in some kind of debate, since I don't much like it either.

Some of the more detached voices from the term offered a perspective informed by this distance. One commented:

> Who can and cannot be a member is never examined; can, for example, a bank as an institution or an individual banker be a member of 'civic Scotland'? What about businesses or business membership organisations? This lack of clarity shows an element of confusion between whether the notion of social location or individual views are the main determinant for consideration.

An academic offered the following criterion for 'civic Scotland' – stating that it was made up of 'non-state and non-economic actors though [I] recognise that there is a lot of grey areas (so much of third sector is state supported/funded for example)'. One prominent journalist reflected that 'civic Scotland' was made up of:

> STUC and many trades unionists. Politicians from all parties (except perhaps Tories, but since a Tory PM launched the devolution debate in 1968 you can't exclude them), Charities individually and through the SCVO, NGOs ditto. Individual businessmen and organisations like the Federation of Small Businesses are very much part of civic Scotland today... Churches... the General Assembly Church and Nation committee is now almost the civic Scotland at prayer... Writers, academics and journalists. McIlvanney, Gray, McMillan, Harvie etc. Anyone else who knows me.

The language of 'civic Scotland' came to the fore in the 1980s and 1990s and the experience of the Thatcher and Major governments. Its usage implied that there was already in existence a progressive Scotland with the potential to resist Tory rule and embark if it chose on a different political direction. Post-1999 the term became associated in the era of devolution in such controversies as Clause 28 with the implication that this nascent progressive Scotland had lost its voice or somehow been silenced compared to its past golden era.

There is a peculiar trajectory in the above. The emergence of 'civic Scotland' can be seen as a product of two very different trends. One was the decline of socialist and radical thinking. Pre-1979 a significant part of Scotland, in the labour movement, Scottish Trades Union Congress (STUC) and Communist Party, gave voice to a socialist culture and radical politics, which many in these groups saw as a viable political agenda in Scotland. Its gradual dwindling away post-1979 opened up a clearing in the political scene which others sought to fill. After the mythologies of a socialist Scotland came the idea of 'civic Scotland' which spoke for a less overtly oppositional, more respectable politics but which differentiated itself with the options available in British politics.

The second dynamic was that the Thatcher Government's agenda challenged the negotiated, managed order of post-war society, the 'high Scotland' of 1945–75, and was a direct affront to the professional, middle-class groups who had become the officers and lieutenants of this settlement. The idea of 'civic Scotland' gave this group a vehicle for describing their social ideology, drawing others into alliance, and pulling a veil over their own self-interest in all of this.

The narrow characteristics of this group were seldom if ever seriously examined or questioned as was the possibility that this might be a problematic term, Janus-faced, both inclusionary to its core insiders, but exclusionary to most of the population. This is polite, respectable Scotland, nearly entirely middle-class, professional, and overwhelming urban, white and connected; and their experience of working and serving the managed society made them value compromise and dialogue, thus, they prioritised the notion of consensus.

'Civic Scotland' in the 1980s was a key component in the growing belief that Scotland was different, its politics more progressive and centre-left than the rest of the UK, and from this sprang a desire for what became known as 'the new politics'. This rejected Westminster adversarialism and absolutism, and instead embraced the idea of being participatory, consultative and consensual. This set of assumptions fed into the creation of the Scottish Constitutional Convention, but also the ideas behind the Civic Assembly and Civic Forum, and post-1997, the Consultative Steering Group on the Scottish Parliament. All were centred on the idea of a more inclusive politics and set of processes – a proportional representative Parliament, how it did politics and Scotland engaged with it.

Behind this is an ideology or set of beliefs that processes, structures and developing the right systems of consultation and engagement, are what matter most. This is a politics without conflict; certainly without class or conventional ideological conflict; ideology as anti-ideology which does not take account of the clash of ideas, values and social groups. Its underlying mindset thinks that all will be alright in 'the big tent' of 'consensual politics' if we just gather people together and get them talking because ultimately people are reasonable and reason will prevail.

As 'civic Scotland' has become perceived over time with a certain kind of politics and view of the world, more critical opinions have emerged. One senior journalist stated:

> 'Civic Scotland' sounds much better than 'Unelected Scotland' doesn't it? But that, these days, is what it is. At least that's part of it. It's a conglomeration of STUC, COSLA, Quango types and their media cheerleaders (Ruth Wishart, Joyce McMillan, Lesley Riddoch etc.). Membership is by invitation only. The 'establishment' isn't the Duke of Argyll or the New Club membership; it's Civic Scotland.

They concluded that, 'One of Civic Scotland's characteristics, however, is that it denies being the Establishment'. Another stated that, 'Above all though civic society doesn't represent the country's excluded people – fine if no-one claims it does but dangerous since it's often implied it does'.

One journalist who has contributed to public debates for the last four decades had a very definite view of what it was:

> Attendance at conferences organised by *Holyrood* magazine. Patting each other on the back at awards ceremonies. Appearances on '*Newsnight Scotland*' – they count them like trophies. A whole set of sentimental illusions about Scotland. A tendency to speak in jargon about things like outcomes and stakeholders.

Another prominent commentator of the last few decades put a similar view stating that, 'Civic Scotland is the Fight Club of polite society. It draws on vestigial historical ideas of 'estates'... There is no shortage of presumption'. One characteristic of some of civic Scotland is that believing they are the embodiment of the 'good society' doing their good, who don't take kindly to criticism, scrutiny or being held to account. In this they are the modern day supposedly progressive expression of 'the committees of the great and the good'.

One voice identified with 'civic Scotland' reflected back to myself in this enquiry, 'I know you like to think that Scotland is weird, dysfunctional and different...' It may be the case then that part of 'civic Scotland' does not want to get into difficult debates about our inequalities, how we fall short, why this is, and how we can change it, for to do so would draw attention to their own position and shortcomings.

One example of the limitations of 'civic Scotland' was provided by the Clause 28 episode. At its height one of the leading figures in the Scottish Civic Forum said to me, 'If only we can get the pro and anti-Clause 28 supporters in the same room and get them talking, we will be able to solve this and get agreement'. This seems hopelessly naïve, and to miss the fundamental conflict between those who were pro-equality and those who were anti-equality. This attitude can be found across parts of self-declared and self-defined 'civic Scotland' with a kind of 'Kumbaya Scotland' outlook that if we all hold hands and are nice to each other things will work out. This optimistic understanding of human nature proposes that we are all intrinsically co-operative and social; but as previously suggested, ignores or downplays completely the role of ideology, competing interests and power.

The notion of 'civic Scotland' can also be seen as articulating the managed society of 'high Scotland' that saw its period of peak influence between 1945–75. The positioning and evolution of 'civic Scotland' here is critical to understand, for post-1979 its advocates understood it relative to what they believed to be the onslaught of the radical ideas of the new right who had become so influential in the Thatcher Government and were driving the sensibilities of British politics south of the border. Thus, 'civic Scotland' supporters called for a moral agenda for a 'good society' against the ideas of the right, but in so doing seemed content to embrace the current status quo in society, and to reject radical ideas wherever they originated.

'Civic Scotland' believes in the notion of public good and public service which are noble goals, but at the same time buys into the idea of professional society where institutions, interests and elites which declare that they are acting in the public good or progressive are taken at face value. This ignores conflicts of interest, bureaucratic creep, and the possibility that any institution of a certain size or history has a propensity to become self-perpetuating, and to be driven by internal rather than external dynamics.

There is little engagement from this perspective with notions such as producer capture which, while they stem from new right thinking and became an obsession of New Labour, offer a profound insight into organisational dynamics and cultures (with neither of these groups being prepared to accept the equally problematic and growing problem of corporate capture).

Any civil society should be characterised by evolution, creative innovation and destruction, with institutions rising, becoming successful and influential, and once they have begun to decline, fading away and dying. This cycle of institutional growth and withering seems to be something with which the idea of 'civic Scotland' feels uncomfortable, preferring a public culture littered with organisations which have long past their sell by-date, but which struggle on, failing to adapt or die. One example of this would be Scottish Council for Development and Industry (SCDI) set up in 1931 to aid a tripartite approach to industry and in post-war times to attract inward investment. Since the creation of the Scottish Development Agency (SDA) in 1975 (which subsequently became Scottish Enterprise) which has, for example, taken formal responsibility on inward investment, SCDI has become a business member organisation in a crowded field, struggling to find or justify any real role.

'Civic Scotland' then is a partial account of modern Scotland, that came to the fore in the 1980s as the voice of respectable society taking a stand against what it perceived as the onslaught of Thatcherism. In this it could claim to speak for mainstream majority Scottish opinion, but in placing itself against the ideas of the new right, it gave voice and legitimacy to a conservative, cautious culture, and became an elite account, which believed it spoke for most of the people. It was as much as Thatcherite opinion, a one-dimensional view of human nature, public life and institutional power, which didn't address how vested interests and bureaucracies collude and corrode their professed values and mandates, and thus, need to be scrutinised and challenged.

Scottish society has been defined for decades by a closed order of the managed, deferential ethos previously outlined, and the emergence of 'civic Scotland' in the 1980s can be seen as a way by which power groups have attempted to maintain their position and importance. It is illustrative of its hold, and the nature of society, that in the early decades of the 21st century it still holds significant sway.

'Civic Scotland' came to the fore at a certain point when Scotland needed alternative accounts of power and social change. There was an understandable logic to its rise under Thatcherism but it quickly became not just a substitute for social change, but an impediment. Post-2011, 'civic Scotland' ran into the ground on the issue of whether to have a two question referendum; already in decline after the establishment of the Parliament and abolition of the Civic Forum, it tried in association with the SNP to stage one last hurrah and it all blew up resulting in the current one question vote in September 2014.

One of Scotland's most respected journalists describes where 'civic Scotland' is as a result, 'Its role today is much diminished, symbolised by the failure of Alison Elliot [then chair of scvo] and the scvo's 'Future of Scotland' group.' They continued, 'It's lost an empire and not yet found a role, to paraphrase Dean Acheson'.

A leading social media blogger observes that, 'Is it just my imagination, or are we hearing less and less about "civic Scotland" these days?' They then stated that, 'the idea of "civic Scotland" belongs in a museum… nostalgia for an age when things were simple, and well-ordered, and fixed up behind the scenes'.

Where this takes us is a fascinating question. A political system such as Scotland will always have insiders and those looking for access, patronage and validation. It is a time-honoured way of how the Scottish nomenklatura has worked, in particular since the expansion of the state in Victorian times. One academic, critical of the Scottish Nationalist project takes the view that:

> Given the highly managerial stance of the SNP and its success in obliging much of civic Scotland to operate on its terms, the supreme insiders are bodies prepared to perform government service while still proclaiming their neutrality.

> This kind of politics will continue into the future independent or not and irrespective of whether we call it civic Scotland or not. But we have to manage to bring in an element of self-criticalness and self-awareness: that all unelected groups and elites eventually become tainted by their entitlement culture, patronage and power.

Importantly, we need to put the rise and fall of 'civic Scotland' in a historical setting – of the emergence of a sizeable Scottish system of administration, the 'high Scotland' of order and deference, and the reaction of these elites to Thatcherism. Slowly, a process of democratisation and challenging power is emerging in Scotland, not quickly or systematically enough for many, but it is there and probably irreversible. Later chapters will address the power, coherence and form of this set of trends, but it is suffice to say for the moment that the old elite Scotland – whether Tory, Labour, civic-minded or notionally progressive, is waning and in decline. That means we need to identify and embrace different ways of thinking about, explaining and organising society which will be fully explored later.

CHAPTER EIGHT

# The Stories of Radical Scotland

Why do Scots still place their faith in a bureaucratic corporatism which manages a greater part of our national resources than in any country outside the Soviet bloc? The answer, in brief, is: poverty, castration, fear of freedom, distrust of our leaders and doubts about our capacity for self-government.

COLIN KIRKWOOD, *Vulgar Eloquence*, Polygon 1990

ONE DEFINING FEATURE of Scotland in the last century and more has been that of the appeal of socialism and social democracy, and of left and centre-left politics.

This persuasive version of Scotland has emphasised its socialist credentials, left-wing characteristics, and capacity and potential for a radical political future. This has been a very Scottish story, stressing distinctive national characteristics, and one which has drawn on a rich pedigree and traditions of radical Scotland from the Covenanters and 1820 rising to World War One rent strikes and 'Red Clydeside', Independent Labour Party (ILP) activism, the Upper Clyde Shipworkers (UCS) work-in, and the non-payment campaign against the poll tax in the 1980s. If there is a 'civic Scotland' somewhere, this then is 'uncivil Scotland': protesting, being difficult, challenging authority and injustice.

Many of us know well this account of ourselves. Iain McLean, author of a revisionist account of 'Red Clydeside', stated that, in that era and today, 'it has now been commonplace to argue that Scottish socialism as well to the left of British socialism' (2004: 148). The sociologist David McCrone commented that 'Scotland's history can largely be written in terms of class conflict and class politics' (2001: 78); academic Alice Brown writing just after Labour's 1997 UK victory wrote that 'some even speak of the country as a class in and of itself... Scotland and class seem to go together... (1998: 138).

From a conservative political perspective, viewing the influence of the Scottish left, historian Michael Fry commented that:

The Scots began to believe the myths preached to them for 50 years: since socialism was inevitable, its supremacy was actual and inevitable. The mythology was so powerful as to obscure the profound conservatism into which Labour had in fact fallen. (1987: 227)

This is part of how a large section of Scotland has portrayed itself in the past, and in recent times such as the 1980s and the contemporary independence debate. There have been the occasional questioning and dissenting voices, often from the radical left or isolated radical right, pointing out similar arguments to Fry in addressing the deep seated, all-pervasive conservatism which has defined so much of Scotland and in particular, the Scottish left and Labour.

This chapter aims to look at cultures of the Scottish left, what they were and what they gave permission to, examines its shortcomings and omissions, and what implications this has for present day Scotland. Despite there being a small scale industry of academics and writers who have studied the history of the left, there has been scant analysis of the origins of Scottish socialism, its roots and influences in society and the impact this has had.

## The Rich Traditions of Previous Radical Scotlands

The Scottish socialist tradition drew on religious, evangelical and radical dissenting lineages which long predate it. There was the power of Presbyterian oratory with its Calvinist belief in being saved or damned; there was Catholic social idealism which later influenced liberation theology; and there was a Gladstonian Liberal inheritance which provided Scottish Labour in its early days with much of its ethos, as well as with prominent figures (Ramsay MacDonald for example having first been Liberal before joining Labour). For example, home rule, land reform and temperance were all stances Labour adopted directly from the Liberals.

The Scottish radical tradition has a longer and more diverse history than that of socialism north of the border, including over the years numerous dissenters and non-conformists. For most of the 19th century the Liberal Party, which won nearly every election in Scotland between 1832–85 was the primary vehicle for mainstream progressive political change. A central debate for radicals at the close of the 19th century was whether to work inside or outside the Liberals. In this context, how to advance working-class representation and to challenge vested interests such as land, and in this the cross-class nature of the Liberals became, live topics. The Liberals, despite their progressive credentials, were also a party of industrial interests and land, as well as economic laissez-faire, and this was a factor in how Lib-Lab joint candidates to promote labour interests saw their chances of success and influence.

Scottish socialism's origins can be found in the early 19th century and in Robert Owen's social experiment in New Lanark, whereupon the British establishment rejected his ideas for factory reform which made him realise the need to embrace socialist ideas. Owen, a Welshman, who took over and ran New Lanark from his father-in-law Robert Dale, remarked, 'Even the Scotch peasantry and working-class possess the habit of making observations and reasoning with great acuteness' (Fry, 1987: 149).

Throughout the 19th century, Scottish trade unionism, Chartism and Highland radicalism, contributed to this radical tradition, but the development of a socialist politics in this was at the margins. This began to change as industrialisation accelerated, the working-classes grew, and Scotland's population increased from 1,608,420 in 1801 to 4,472,103 in 1901. All of this related to intense industrialisation, which saw Glasgow become 'the second city of Empire' and a place of huge wealth, commerce and poverty.

Such vast change brought economic and social transformation and dislocation, making Scotland at the start of the 20th century one of the richest nations in the world by GDP per head (a point Alex Salmond has liked to make on many occasions), but one of the most unequal with grinding absolute poverty (a point he does not make in conjunction with the above).

This was fertile ground for anti-capitalist agitation and socialist politics, and from the late 19th century the expansion of the electoral franchise with the 1885 Reform Act brought politics out of an exclusive upper and middle-class embrace and into sections of the male working-classes. Keir Hardie stood in the now famous Mid-Lanark by-election of April 1888 under a Labour banner, and though he finished a distant third behind the Liberals and Unionists, and only won a paltry 617 votes (8.4 per cent), a marker had been put down. Later that year the Scottish Labour Party was born under Hardie's leadership, and although it did not win parliamentary representation, the previous pattern of politics was now under strain. In the 1892 election, Hardie won West Ham South, and in 1893 the Independent Labour Party was formed, leading to the creation of the modern Labour Party in 1900.

Scotland contributed many of the most influential politicians to Labour in its formative years. Besides Hardie, there was Ramsay MacDonald, who twice became Prime Minister of minority Labour Governments in 1924 and 1929–31 (before he defected to lead a Tory led administration and become a byword for treachery), John Wheatley (Housing Minister in the 1924 government), James Maxton, and Tom Johnston, more of whom later. Yet not all of Scotland's radicals and left-wingers found a berth in the broad church of Labour. The Communist Party had significant support in parts of Scotland and in particular the coalfields. Then there were other influential revolutionary leaders such as John Maclean and James Connolly, the latter who gave his life for the cause of Irish liberation.

These 'Red Clydeside' traditions to the left of Labour have been debated and discussed endlessly, but the Scots dissenting strand went much further and was much more diverse. Many of these seem to have been airbrushed out of history by the dominant strands of Clydesidism and workerism. One example was the creation and success of the Crofters' Party which grew out of the Highland Land League and managed to elect five MPs in the 1885 general election. This emerged from Highland agitation and disappointment about Liberal identification with landed interests, and resulted in the Crofters' Holdings (Scotland) Act 1886 which gave real security to existing crofters and set up the first Crofters' Commission with rent fixing powers.

Another is the even less known Scottish Prohibition Party which, first won seats on Dundee Town Council in 1908. Its most notable figure, Edwin Scrymgeour, was returned to Parliament in 1922 for Dundee, defeating the sitting Liberal MP, Winston Churchill, and remaining MP for the city until 1931. My father, Edwin, was named after Scrymgeour, and when I was growing up in Dundee there was a radical memory that the city had rejected Churchill and elected the iconoclastic Scrymgeour. However, by the 1970s how this was recalled was lost in the midst of time. It become a collective act of Dundonian oppositionalism to 'Toryism' and part of the anti-Tory ethos of the city (even though Churchill had been a Liberal).

Both these parties appealed to specialist interests, were short-lived and never likely to become permanent national parties. They also emerged at a time when class, politics and representation were in major flux, as the Liberals tried to adapt to the mass franchise, alongside the rise of Labour and numerous socialist organisations. Today we live in a very different age, but there are some similarities in that traditional Westminster politics are in a crisis of trust and legitimacy, the main parties are in retreat, and new political spaces are opening up, witness the rise of Ukip in England.

The early decades of the 20th century saw in Scotland, as in the rest of the UK, a radical ethical socialism with its base in the ILP. This provided a significant part of Scottish Labour's grassroots and many of its first generation of national leaders. Notable in this group was Tom Johnston, founding editor of the ILP paper 'Forward' and author of two bestselling books, *Our Scots Noble Families* (1909) and *The History of the Working Classes in Scotland* (1923).

*Our Scots Noble Families* was a link between the late Victorian radicalism of liberals and crofters and the early socialists, before the Fabian
centralisers became dominant intellectually in British Labour. It dealt with
the history and ownership of land, the power of aristocracy and offered
detailed research and polemic as weapons against the powerful and privileged. It did all of this with anger and indignation:

> Generation after generation, these few families of tax gathers, have
> sucked the life-blood of our nation; in their prides and lusts they have
> sent us to war, family against family, clan against clan, race against race;
> that they have might live in idleness and luxury, the laboring mass have
> sweated and starved; they have pruned the creeds of our church and
> stolen its revenues; their mailed fists have crushed the newer thought, and
> their vanities the arts. In their vandalisms they buried and destroyed our
> national records.

He continued in the same vein, 'they have barred us by barbed wire fences
from the bens and the glens; the peasant has been ruthlessly swept aside
to make room for the pheasant... Time and time again they have sold our
land to the invader' (1909: viii).

This is Johnston the campaigning journalist and writer, historian,
socialist and nationalist (as the last line shows) in a way that some of the
Labour pioneers felt free to be, contrasting with those of the present. This
had political as well as commercial impact, contributing to debates around
Lloyd George's 'People's Budget' and the resulting 'People versus the Peers'
constitutional crisis, as well as Labour land reform debates. A corollary
is that in Johnston's rise up Labour's hierarchy he openly repudiated the
book, writing in his *Memories* in 1952 that it was 'historically one-sided
and unjust and quite unnecessarily wounding' (1952: 35). This comment
tells much about the journey of Scottish Labour socialism over 40 years,
from principles to collusion with elites.

The story of the defeat of ethical socialism is complex but one key
factor was the disaffiliation of the ILP from Labour in 1932, following its
disappointment at the party in office and its clinging to economic orthodoxies and fiscal discipline as a response to the Great Depression. This
robbed Scottish Labour of a whole generation of activists, campaigners
and idealists, and condemned the ILP and some of its most notable figures
(James Maxton, John McGovern) to the margins of political influence.
Equally important were the consequences of Labour coming to office in
1924 and 1929, becoming a party of the British state and seeing it as the
main institution from which to advance progressive politics. Labour under
the influence of Fabianism, became a party of centralisation, planning,

technocrats and experts, and in so doing became a vehicle of administration and bureaucracy.

This shift produced many notable achievements from the Attlee Government with the setting up of the NHS, the welfare state, nationalisation of key utilities, and achieving full employment, but at a price. The language and values of earlier socialists – of emphasising freedom, liberation of mankind's potential, and decentralisation – were pushed to the side. This allowed the right to claim the mantle of freedom and portray socialism as crushing individualism, liberty and freedom and being authoritarian. The eventual consequence of this was Mrs Thatcher's election victory in 1979 under a libertarian banner and her portrayal of Labour and the trade union movement as the problem holding the country back, and as a virtual establishment.

Today Scottish left-wing culture still has numerous adherents, some of a long standing nature and some galvinised by the independence referendum. Yet Scottish leftism, despite its rich traditions, has some fundamental weaknesses. There is the Cinderella-like outlook that a natural socialist majority in the electorate is just there waiting to be reawakened by the right kind of leadership and rhetoric. This is an untenable position to take and not grounded in any analysis of facts.

Where is any evidence of a Scottish socialist majority? The answer is nowhere. Therefore this argument must rest on a mixture of belief in a widespread false consciousness which can somehow be overcome, and faith in the transforming power of correct left leadership. How this all-persuasive leadership is going to develop the powerful vehicles and channels of communication bypassing the capitalist media to transmit this politics is another question. But the more basic problem is that Scotland has never on any occasion now or in the past shown itself a majority socialist country. The only means by which this could be claimed of past times is to count the Labour Party vote as a socialist vote, producing left majorities in the country in 1945 (including ILP and Communists) and 1966 (including Communists). But that would be a gross distortion given the nature of Labour and the Labour vote.

## The Lost World of Scottish Communism

Numerous other factors have impacted on the decline of the left beyond the changing industrial base, wider economy, increased individualism, and ideological environment which has seen the rise of a radical right in Britain and elsewhere. One important contribution has been the demise of the

Communist Party, which played a disproportionate role in the politics of the Scots left until its demise in 1991. Although there remain Communist splinters and fragments, the Communist Party of Great Britain (CPGB) despite never having a large British or Scottish membership (peak UK membership was 56,000 in 1942 at the height of the battle of Stalingrad), was for decades the dominant force to the left of Labour. It had significant industrial influence in shop stewards groups, and in Scotland, a presence in the coalfields in Fife and Ayrshire, in the miners' union, the NUM, and in trades councils and the STUC and in places such as Dundee. It produced an impressive production line of self-educated working-class men from Jimmy Airlie and Jimmy Reid who led the UCS work-in, to Mick McGahey and George Bolton in the NUM, and Jimmy Milne who became General Secretary of the STUC.

The Communist Party's influence in the STUC was one of the many ways in which 'the labour movement' was broader and often more radical than the 'official' Labour Party. It also made the STUC a different beast from the TUC down south. A good example of this was the relationship of Labour and the labour movement to the perennial tricky issue of home rule. Scottish Labour had turned its back on the issue post-1945, formally repudiating it at Scottish conference in 1958, and the rise of the SNP from the mid-1960s posed it all sorts of problems.

Labour's initial reaction after hesitancy was to be dismissive, even more centralist and articulate even more loudly the benefits of being in Britain. The most prominent advocate in this was Willie Ross, Wilson's Secretary of State for Scotland from 1964–70 and 1974–76, who many credit with the phrase 'tartan Tories' and using it as a sobriquet in relation to the SNP. This is not in fact the case; the alliteration was always in the popular lexicon, and was just given prominence by Ross. Will Marshall, Scottish Labour General Secretary told the party's 1968 conference that the SNP 'created interest among young people by hammering away at nothing but idealism', as if this was a negative (*The Herald*, 23 March 1968).

As Labour clung to its centralism and anti-devolution stand, the STUC, aided by the influence of the Communist Party, began to move to a more subtle position, debating the issue at 1968 Congress in the aftermath of Winnie Ewing winning Hamilton. The STUC debated both a pro- and anti-devolution motion, the former moved by McGahey who laid out the difference between a 'healthy' nationalism centred on 'love of one's own country, love of one's own people, and pride in their traditional militancy and progressiveness' and chauvinism. He took on what he saw as the false dichotomy of nationalism and internationalism, cited old Labour heroes such as Keir Hardie, and claimed, 'The best nationalists in Scotland are represented in the STUC and the Scottish labour movement' (Aitken, 1997: 218–19).

Both resolutions were remitted but within a year the STUC had unanimously reached a consensus on a Scottish Parliament with legislative powers. It was typical of STUC internal politics that even such a divisive issue could be dealt with in this manner (unlike Labour), while the language was completely different: from the earliest days of this debate it was always a Parliament and never an Assembly (except when dealing with Labour's 1970s plans).

The Communist influence in the STUC and other forums was one which combined principle, idealism and a willingness to embrace broad fronts. This is not a eulogy to everything the CP did; for most of its existence the party toed a pro-Moscow line, famously over the 1939 Molotov-Ribbentrop pact where it dismissed the Second World War until the Nazi invasion of the Soviet Union as a 'imperialist war', to the trails and tribulations of the Soviet invasions of Hungary in 1956 and Czechoslovakia in 1968.

I grew up knowing of these epochal moments from my father, who was in favour of both the above Soviet invasions, and even as late as the invasion of Afghanistan in 1979 would take the Moscow line. There was a generation of numerous leftists who grew up admiring the Soviet Union for its achievements, being 'the first workers' state' (or so it claimed), and defeating Hitler. There was in many places in Scotland an innate working-class identification or sympathy with the Soviet Union with different gradations: from my dad's Stalinism to 'fellow travellers' to a more general class solidarity. My dad used to say until the last day of the Soviet Union, 'why do workers need to strike in a workers' state?' with an air of bafflement to which I would reply 'because it isn't a workers' state'.

We did however have these conversations with a gentleness and my understanding of this generational divide of the left: my dad had grown up in the Second World War whereas all my politics came after Hungary and the Prague Spring. He did at least, when the Soviet Union collapsed, reconsider his politics while remaining of the left, and said to me quietly one day, 'so you were right all along on the Soviet Union', which was a big thing for him. Many other conversations weren't filled with that grace.

Despite this the CP's influence in Scotland provided a positive counterweight for much of the post-war era to the increasing deadweight of a Scottish Labour committed to a politics of anti-pluralism and what Ken Livingstone memorably described talking of British Labour as its 'Stabian' characteristics – meaning a combination of Fabianism and Stalinism. McGahey in a 1987 interview phrased the CP in the following terms:

> ... the Communist Party in Scotland is a good proletarian-based party. From the days of Gallacher the party in Scotland was always well established in industry and made a contribution to the trade union movement. If you look at the role of the Communist Party... there was always the amalgam, their political work associated with their trade union work. There was no question of one or the other. They were part of that broad Scottish people's movement, so that others were not able to isolate the party in Scotland as they could in other places. (*Scottish Trade Union Review*, Spring 1987)

In the 1980s, internal factionalism, the slow attrition of membership, and its supplanting on the left by groups such as the Socialist Workers' Party (SWP), all contributed to the decline of the party's influence. It played a role in STUC support of the miners' strike of 1984–85 and the campaign for a Scottish Parliament, particularly after the 1987 third Thatcher victory. Yet it was now battling against the global tide of history, as Gorbachev attempted to reform the Soviet Union, the Eastern European countries threw off Communism in 1989, and two years later in December 1991, after an ill-fated hardline Communist coup against Gorbachev, the Soviet Union ceased to exist.

The British Communist Party ceased to exist at the end of 1991, transforming itself into the even smaller, less influential Democratic Left which lasted for a decade (although still existing as a Scottish group). Whatever the balance sheet of British Communism something had been lost by its slow decline and then sudden departure which affected the vibrancy of the left. No more is this true than in relation to Scotland. Raphael Samuel wrote a study looking at 'the lost world of British communism', but no one yet has taken the time to examine 'the lost world of Scottish communism' for they would tell a fascinating picture (Samuel, 2006). It would be one of idealism along with the taints of Stalinism and being at points pro-Moscow, but it offered shelter for a different politics to Labour – less careerist, more theoretical, and partly due to the party's size, more outward looking and focused on alliances.

The Scottish left after the CP's demise more than 20 years ago has been a less dynamic environment (at least until recently), clearly missing something. The age of the CP produced 'men of iron' and 'men of steel' (the name of famous Polish films about life under Communism), along with a cadre of women activists and campaigners (see Rafeek, 2008). Men such as Jimmy Reid and Mick McGahey didn't appear out of nowhere; they came from a movement which, however small, hothoused them, sent them on courses of intellectual and political study, and gave them the opportunity to travel internationally.

It made these individuals and made them part of something bigger: giving them self-discipline, a focus and understanding of ideas, history and politics. The demise of the CP in Scotland led to the emergence of a different left politics and politician, and is probably in some way a contributory factor in the emergence of George Galloway and Tommy Sheridan. These post-Communist left-wingers had many qualities: the power of oratory, striking self-confidence and the tenacity to take a stand on an issue often at personal cost. But neither of them were movement builders; indeed Sheridan presided over the rise and destruction of the Scottish Socialist Party.

Galloway and Sheridan have admirers and detractors, but have proven to be individual populists and serial political entrepreneurs who operate most effectively on their own. This has seen some notable gains such as Sheridan's first term in the Scottish Parliament and the Abolition of Poindings and Warrant Sales Act 2001. But both seem to have little wider discipline or self-awareness of how individual ego has to be compromised to the demands of the wider cause. Such an approach would have been less possible in the age of a more potent CP; either in it or out of it, there is the prospect the CP's existence would have offered a different frame for left politics. It would also have been much less possible in an age of greater class solidarity, for the Galloways and Sheridans are as much a product of the culture of individualism as any venture capitalist.

## Cultures and Rituals of the Left

As critical as the shortcomings of any left politicians and the end of the CP, has been the limited style, means and iconography of what has traditionally past for left politics. This is seen in the rituals of a typical left campaign: protesting, demonstrations, marching through streets shouting slogans, signing petitions, and listening to endless top-down speakers.

There is a quasi-religious element to this litany: of reciting, salvation, certainty and control but often without understanding it – a sense of biblical inflexibility without a bible. The endless list of speakers haranguing an audience with no place for discussion, questions and a space for conversation is a well-known tactic.

I once went in the aftermath of the Scottish Socialist Party implosion in 2006 to a 'Save the Sheridan Seven' rally (these being the original number charged with perjury by the authorities following the first trial in 2004) out of curiosity only to find the audience faced with a platform containing nine people, all male. I left after an hour, less than half their way through the speakers, as several of them openly made comparisons between this supposedly persecuted group and the genuine state injustices of 'the Birmingham Six' and 'Guildford Four' (including speakers from these groups). It was a completely inappropriate comparison, belittling and demeaning what had been horrendous miscarriages of justice by the British state and a prime example of part of the left talking to itself and divorcing itself from reality.

There are other tropes which reveal the limits of left politics. Take the example of the September 2013 independence rally at Calton Hill, Edinburgh. Dennis Canavan, former MP and MSP and Chair of 'Yes Scotland' addressed the crowd and told them that 'the people need to be persuaded' and that 'we need to take our argument to the people'.

These are typical left rhetorical flourishes and ones which have been used so often they are left unexplored, but this makes them even the worthy of study. First, the people are posed in this perspective as external and 'other'. There are two types of individuals: the people needing convinced and woken up, and those who know the truth and will show the way. This is a world for left rhetoric of creating new hierarchies: of the political elect and everyone else. Second, the mass of the population outside the left is posed as passive, inactive and apolitical. They are sitting waiting to be convinced and to become aware of the state of the world as it has revealed itself to a small elite.

Then there is the endless repeating of familiar mantras in place of strategy or understanding issues. Speaker after speaker at the 2013 Calton Hill independence rally offered the prospect of a left future and independence along the lines of, 'Equality, Fairness, No Trident, No Bedroom Tax'. These are all complex issues, the first two philosophical concepts with different interpretations and trade-offs in which progress has been mixed over the course of 30 years of post-war Labour Governments. This list of familiar left mantras mixed with predicable rhetoric made the blogger Kate Higgins's father complain of the dominance of 'too many shouty socialists' at the rally (Burdz Eye View, 20 October 2013). It is a menu with a limited palette and appeal; and one which parts of the left feel revitalised to use in relation to independence, but which has been, up until this point, played to diminishing audiences for several decades.

There is in this an often prevalent mindset of feeling secure in political outlook, values and how those who are allies and opponents are defined through a series of beliefs of what the left is against. Thus to be left in the late 20th and early 21st century is often defined by a series of negative characteristics: anti-war, anti-imperialist, anti-cuts, anti-welfare cuts, anti-nuclear weapons, anti-Trident and more.

What this shopping list of terms does not make explicit is what being left is positively for. That isn't an accident because implicit in being, say, anti-welfare cuts, is to pose as the unstated, undefined alternative that we can all collectively envisage and agree what our ideal welfare state would be. The thorny fact that this is seldom defined, and that crucial choices and trade-offs are often left unexplored, leaves all of this as a kind of fantasy politics rarely questioned. Nor that this kind of mindset facilitates a continual cycle of left disappointment and failure, which contributes to disillusion and resignation for many.

## No More Heroes Anymore: The Importance of Thatcher and Blair

The uncomfortable fact is that the politics of left retreat over the last 30 years has encouraged in some a triumphalist re-affirmation of the same old hymn sheets preaching to a declining congregation (except at special moments such as Christmas for churches, which in this case would be the Blair march to war with Iraq and other such moments of moral outrage).

The eras of Thatcher and Blair gave enormous vindication of this approach; first there was the politics of opposition of 'Defending Jobs and Services' which even acknowledged that it was fighting not for the people public services provide for, but the actual services, and conceding that the struggle was a defensive one. No army no matter how skilled and dexterous has ever in human history won a defensive war; the best you can ever hope for is the chance of a stalemate and these are rare occasions.

Then there came the Blair years. New Labour had already incurred the disappointment of a large part of the left before the 1997 Labour election victory, even before the folly of the Iraq adventure. Iraq brought many casualties: hundreds of thousands of innocent Iraqis killed, many more displaced, and British and US military deaths and injuries. As well as all of this, there has been the corrosion of the truth by the Blair and Bush administrations, without a hint of regret or insight into the damage they have caused to politics and Iraq.

However, bearing all this in mind there is something equally unattractive in the left anger against Blair (and similarly in the US towards George W. Bush or on the right against Barack Obama). This isn't in any way an argument for their actions or an apology for them, but for a morally informed politics. Iraq allowed people to march with banners saying 'Bliar' and 'Indict Blair and Bush as War Criminals' and to think this was enough. It represented a politics of moral indignation, of seeing the world in black and white, the absolutes of good and evil with no ambiguity in between. It made people feel good, but it was bad politics and inherently limited because all it offered was hate and caricature of political opponents.

Strangely, this left evangelicalism with its sense of certainty met its match in the manner in which Blair and Bush, neo-conservatives and liberal interventionists, saw the world. They believed in a principled crusade for what they believed to be democracy and against a distorted version of Islam. Blair has kept to this line post-office, coming close to invoking 'a war of civilisations' between the West and radical Islam, and calling for military intervention against Iran. But nowhere did the left protestors note their strange relationship and similarities with Blair; or he with them.

The Thatcher and Blair years offered a left politics what some imagined were their ideal political opponents: zealots and ideologues who operated on a terrain the left thought it understood. But people consistently misrepresented and misunderstood both politicians and the political ages they represented. They were a mixture of pragmatism and conviction and each built successful alliances with both winning three consecutive terms.

Post-Thatcher and Blair, myths have grown up about both leaders from supporters and detractors, seen in the controversial debates about Thatcher's influence after her death. To her supporters, she had won the Cold War, saved Britain from socialism, and put 'the Great back in the country' reversing decades of economic decline. To opponents, she had created mass unemployment, poverty and inequality, closed traditional industries such as mining and steelmaking, and let communities the length of Britain be starved into submission. These simplistic myths of Thatcher bore little connection to the more complex record of her 11 years in office.

Of course the left indignation about Thatcher was more potent in Scotland seen as it was through the collective folklore of Scots not voting Tory or for Thatcher: both points which happen to be true but don't tell everything. What Scotland were we remembering or mourning when the supposedly revolutionary Thatcher was being invoked after her death? Indeed, the wider truth is that the anger and outpourings of a left on Thatcher and Blair was partly an expression of a much more widespread left powerlessness over the last 30 years.

Thatcher and Blair were successful on their terms; they remade the political weather in a way the left used to think was its business. The world turned out a very different place from that which any left-winger thought at the end of the 1970s. Then the future was still 'ours'. It might have not been progressive enough, or socialist, but the forces of reaction and privilege were supposedly in retreat the world over. The future didn't turn out to look like that.

There is a pain of loss and cognitive dissonance in all of this; what happened to the heroes and heroines of the left, to the expected triumphs and continued progress? Why in recent decades, this perspective asks, has it come about that more and more, we are talking about retreats, defining ourselves by our opponents and enemies, and searching to find villains? Could it be that that in the pining for golden eras and the past, that large elements of radical Scotland have become the very embodiment of conservatism they profess they detest with every fibre in their body? These are questions we have to begin to understand and to formulate answers.

# CHAPTER NINE

# A Different Kind of Politics is Possible: The Left, Laughter and Imagination

The market is king. So what aboot this parliament of oors? It's like we fought our way tae the bar just in time for the barman tae tell us he's stopped serving.

'No,' Mike protested. 'I don't feel that. We're at the start of something new and different. It can't be like it was before.'

JAMES ROBERTSON, *And the Land Lay Still*, Hamish Hamilton 2010

THERE ARE MANY more fundamental weaknesses inherent in parts of the left than what people felt about Thatcher or Blair. These attitudes are indicative of deeper views. George Orwell in his influential essay 'Inside the Whale', first published in the Second World War, used the metaphor of being 'inside the whale' to understand the detachment of the masses from current affairs and their enclosure in a world of safety and familiarity (Orwell, 1940).

Twenty years later, as the new left began to emerge, the historian E.P. Thompson wrote a reply, 'Outside the Whale', which attempted to challenge this thesis and the post-war belief that affluence was strengthening the hold of popular inwardness (Thompson, 1960). Thompson called 'Inside the Whale', 'an apology for quietism', while Raymond Williams wrote that Orwell's description of an apolitical masses 'created the conditions for defeat and despair' (1971: 79).

More than 50 years after Thompson's essay, the original Orwell thesis still has relevance, with its argument validated by constant misrepresentations by Thompson, Williams and Salman Rushdie. Orwell's moral voice and the uncomfortable complexities he investigated, decades on, proved strangely discomforting to the post-war British new left. These reactions, challenged by the likes of Christopher Hitchens, make Orwell's 'Inside the Whale' thesis still resonate today: that the apolitical nature of the masses is reinforced by the mutual comfort zones and safety of the left (see Hitchens, 2002). These have been the characteristics of too much of the left for too long and come at high cost.

The left has also had a complex relationship with the past and nostalgia, and what Alastair Bonnett has called 'radical nostalgia' (2010). While a significant part of the left has imagined a progressive future, another element has consistently yearned for the past. This latter expression can be seen in the pastoral communist utopias of William Morris with their sense of loss at industrial and social change. As the right has advanced in the last few decades, this notion of 'radical nostalgia' has become more widespread on the left, hankering after a supposed 'golden age' of more socially responsible capitalism in the West.

There are also significant shortcomings to how large parts of the left have done their politics – culturally, organisationally and in their styles of leadership. Dennis Tourish has written extensively of the self-destructive tendencies of many of the revolutionary left's archetypes of leadership – authoritarian, heroic, masculinist and hyper-active (2013), pointing out the similarities between different kinds of transformational leadership, from the left, business leaders and religious groups, and in particular, the dysfunctional similarities between the mindsets and activities of left and religious sects.

## Where is Scotland's Left?

In contemporary Scotland, various voices hope to utilise the prospect of the independence referendum debate to revitalise the left, its politics and influence. Numerous initiatives have arisen in the immediate period between the election of a majority SNP administration between May 2011 and the vote in September 2014. Whether this small but significant upsurge can be of lasting impact is yet too early to tell, but it is noteworthy, and against the trend of left retreat and defeat of recent decades in Scotland, the UK and elsewhere.

Two examples from very different lefts give some insight. First is the book, *Scotland's Road to Socialism: Time to Choose*, published by Scottish Left Review, and itself a follow-up to *Is There a Scottish Road to Socialism?* (Gall, 2013; Gall, 2007). Across 22 chapters there is a near total lack of concern for the crisis of socialism domestically or internationally, along with a complete conflation of social justice and socialism. There also seems to be an abiding faith amongst those of a pro-independence persuasion that Scotland could do what no other country in the world has achieved and become the first ever democratic socialist nation. In other words, something none of the Nordics, Allende's Chile or Chavez's Venezuela has yet managed.

The most noteworthy exception to this overall direction in the book is Robin McAlpine, director of the Jimmy Reid Foundation's contribution, 'We have to stop complaining and up our game', which sits at odds in tone and in its energy and self-criticism of the left compared to other chapters. McAlpine weighs in to the Scots left for its propensity to miserablism, sanctimoniousness, believing its own hype and propaganda, and generally being rather poor at how it does politics, culture and campaigning (2013). It is a stimulating counterblast to the sentiment of the Scottish left, and one of which more is desperately needed.

The next example comes from the collection, *Class, Nation and Socialism*, put together by the Labour inclined Red Paper Collective (Bryan and Kane, 2013). This collection contains powerful chapters analysing the state of the Scottish economy from John Foster and Richard Leonard (two of seven contributors shared between the books despite the different politics), but has a difficulty navigating the politics of modern Scotland. For one there is no analysis of what has gone wrong in Scottish Labour and how it might be realistically put right to advance the agenda of the book. Second, there is a near-complete silence and lack of engagement of the SNP and wider self-government and independence movement and arguments.

This gives the book, despite its introductory chapters, the air of existing in a parallel universe Scotland: one where the left just talks to itself, doesn't acknowledge the arguments of people it disagrees with and feels more comfortable just pretending they don't exist. This is truly Orwell's 'Inside the Whale' Scottish left circa today. Revealingly, when some of the chapters look to identifying appropriate models of change in 21st century Scotland they go back into the past. The decade of the 1970s and UCS work-in are offered as the salutary examples for today, ignoring the state of trade union membership then and now, falling rate of profit then, and lower levels of unemployment all of which contributed to greater confidence in organised labour – instead invoking a nostalgia for workerism and Clydesidism which is increasingly out of touch with an economy becoming more feminised and with greater rates of women's employment.

The more outward focused parts of the left: National Collective, the Radical Independence Campaign (RIC) and the Jimmy Reid Foundation and its Common Weal project ('to build more we must share more'), have been previously identified as having the shared characteristics of what I have called 'the third Scotland' (explored more fully in Chapter Thirteen). They have shown a greater capacity for imagination, creativity and sheer drive and energy (see Foley and Ramand, 2014). However, they also illustrate for all this the grip of an unreflective socialist modernisation which has hitched its wagon onto the independence project.

Their activities have many positive qualities but there is also an air of ignoring some inconvenient truths. So for example one of the growing sentiments on parts of the pro-independence left is for Scotland to become a Nordic, northern social democratic country; this can be found in the Common Weal project and in the Nordic Horizons network. But it is near-nigh, impossible for Scotland to become a completely Nordic social democracy. Scotland has contributed to and been shaped by Anglo-American capitalism; indeed, many of the ideas which have spanned the world, on political economy, the division of labour, and role of business, originated in Scotland in the writings of Adam Smith, David Hume and others.

Scotland is always going to be influenced by its legacy and impact of Anglo-American capitalism. The Nordic model is a complex creation of historical, economic, cultural and political factors, along with climate and geography; its vision of capitalism and solidarity state has evolved over centuries, and has in Norway, Sweden and elsewhere begun to, in the eyes of many citizens, erode and retreat in ways similar to us: the rise of inequality, outsourcing and privatisation, along with challenge of immigration. This is not to deny that Scotland could learn from our Nordic neighbours, or break with the orthodoxies of Anglo-American capitalism and its resultant market vandalism. That would be a big enough challenge, but we are building unrealistic expectations if we think we can become completely and effortlessly Nordic.

Similarly, the Radical Independence Campaign (RIC) have developed in the course of the last two years an impressive network of activism, campaigning and brought together a previously disparate group of left-wingers drawing in new younger voices. This has been all the more surprising considering RIC originated from a split of mostly twentysomething pro-independence activists from the Socialist Workers' Party (SWP), who have years practiced the politics of vanguardism and left posturing; and most recently embarked on strategic alliances with the Sheridan era SSP and George Galloway's Respect, both of which ended up in tears.

The RIC network has been widely seen as a hugely positive development, but have yet to contribute many original ideas to the politics of the Scottish left – beyond campaigning and creating new spaces. This is not to diminish the contributions of these groups, merely to warn against people believing the world can be changed overnight, and feeling a sense of disappointment and disillusion when that doesn't happen.

National Collective, the Jimmy Reid Foundation's Common Weal project, RIC, Nordic Horizons and numerous others are part of something interesting, namely, the search for a different kind of Scotland and society. This points to dissatisfaction with the narrow bandwidth of conventional politics on offer whether in Scotland or Westminster, and how this has translated into the absence of real debate between the forces of Yes and No in the independence referendum. Then there is the growing political and ethical bankruptcy of the UK and British politics, which now seems stuck in a trajectory under the Cameron government post-crash, of restoration of the financial and property bubble. This poses a crisis of progressive Britain for British Labour and pro-union centre-left Scotland, all of which acts as a catalyst for the groups described above.

Scotland along with the rest of the UK is part of what Andrew Roberts and others have called 'the Anglosphere' following on from Churchill, meaning the six English speaking developed countries (UK, Ireland, US, Canada, Australia, New Zealand). It isn't an accident that the six have been the site from the 1980s on of the most concerted market determinism, vandalism and assault on social privilege. This is because there was something in British (and Scots) ideas of economy, business and the role of government from the beginnings of industrialisation which gave the counter-revolution of recent times, roots and validity. Then there is the cross-fertilisation of a shared legacy and language, particular in the London-Washington axis of seeing the world.

A Scotland that even subtly shifts its geopolitical positioning and values has to address this context. Robin McAlpine talking of the Common Weal project described one of its core aims thus, 'We are a disconnected society in the most literal sense – we never look east and we never look north. We have a frame of reference that sketches only from Washington to London' (LRB Blog, 21 October 2013).

## The Pulpit and the Prophet: The Left and Religion

There are in too many strands of the left an absence of humour, play, fun and irreverence and grasping their centrality to a politics of radical imagination. The Scottish left has had a well-established pedigree of not embracing lightness, the power of letting go, and celebrating what Barbara Ehrenreich has called 'collective joy' (Ehrenreich, 2007).

A major reason for this has been the contribution of religiousness in the origins of Scottish left: of the power of evangelicism, preaching and believing in a moral code and order. Most of the Scottish left was predominantly influenced by one of two strands: the Presbyterian tradition and the Catholic Church. The former gave us the men of mission and purpose, and being saved or damned which reinforces a black and white judgemental world and generated a whole swathe of Scottish Labour politicians from Keir Hardie and Ramsay MacDonald to Willie Ross and Gordon Brown.

The Catholic tradition invoked at times a more charismatic, energising, but also bordering on demagogic politics. In its early days, many Scottish Labour leaders came from Catholic backgrounds. John Wheatley (who set up the Catholic Socialist Society) and James Maxton from Labour, and Willie Gallacher, Communist MP for West Fife from 1935–50, are three influential examples. In more recent times this tradition has still given to the left some of its more powerful figures: Jimmy Reid, George Galloway (who wasn't brought up as a Catholic but has subsequently embraced the church), and Tommy Sheridan.

The Presbyterian radical impulse had a collectivist ethos and egalitarianism, or what Neal Ascherson called a 'levelling' in relation to authority and leadership (Reid, 2010: 357). It had a democratic spirit and intellect but was also deeply authoritarian, judgemental and conscious of status inside the church. In this it matched the contradictions of Scottish culture. It is beyond the parameters of this study to determine the role of Calvinism in contributing or holding back society – suffice to say it has always had its detractors – in modern times following on from Edwin Muir (1929), and those who look to make a more positive case (Macleod, 2001; Gay, 2013). The other powerful tradition, the Catholic Church in Scotland, felt the imprint of Irish immigration, experience of widespread poverty and discrimination, and the prevalence of anti-Irish prejudice across society.

The origins of the left and its relationship to religion are not difficult to identify in the seismic inequalities and injustices in late 19th and early 20th century capitalism, combined with the pull of organised religion over the masses in Scotland and the rest of the UK. Thus, the language of Scottish socialism drew heavily on religious values, beliefs and imagery even amongst non-believers. It was in the culture, people's backgrounds, and was a means of connecting with a constituency.

This could be found across the political spectrum of the left. Willie Stewart, Scottish ILP Secretary from 1912–36 said that socialism is 'in the highest and most lasting sense, the New Religion' (McCabe, 1994: 32). From Ramsay MacDonald and Edwin Scrymgeour in the 1920s to Jimmy Reid at UCS in the 1970s, a similar language would infuse socialist rhetoric: part Bible, part Robert Burns egalitarianism, mixed with morality and a belief in the collective power of the working-classes (Smout, 1986).

This visionary socialism was well suited for lifting either the congregation in the church or crowd at the rally, but it translated less effectively into a detailed programme of reform. There is a direct relationship between the idealism of some of the early socialists such as Ramsay MacDonald preaching an ethical, idealist socialism which was an abstract and invoked 'the Second Coming' and the grinding conservatism of the first Labour Governments of the 1920s. A link could even be made between this, Gordon Brown's potent oratory as a missionary man, and his complex record in office as Chancellor and Prime Minister. That might seem unfair about Brown but at the end of his tenure in office he was reduced to returning to the old comfort zones, for example lifting an audience at a London Citizens rally in the 2010 election with an evangelical call for a better world which bore little relation to his record.

Some of the left's usage of over the top rhetoric has in many places been the equivalent of demagoguery, seen in the examples of Galloway and Sheridan, who create cartoonesque worlds of simplicity, reducing nearly everything to a battle between good and evil. While these may appear like outlier examples, a new generation of left-wingers brought up in the context of a shrunken left and dismay at Cameron government cuts, often articulate a one-dimensional left posture of oppositionalism.

There is a deep left propensity born of religious influence and earlier injustices which sees the world in terms of 'us' and 'them': those who are principled and those who either have false consciousness or worse are 'class traitors'. This is summed up in the question, 'Whose side are you on?' It is less a question and often more a pointed accusation, demanding of people that they choose between two sides and in this it is profoundly influenced by religion, being saved or damned. It has been used down the decades, from the miners' strikes of 1926 to 1984–85, and its usage by parts of the left displays an unattractive anger, insularity and erecting boundaries. These are seldom comprehended by those making them – to whom are these heartfelt calls directed, what kind of response are they ideally looking for, and why do those making such statements seldom reflect on how they translate in the world of the non-left (which is the vast majority of people)?

More prevalent than the Galloway and Sheridan examples was the widespread practice by Scottish Labour politicians and the left to use sweeping rhetoric and rich metaphors to disguise thinking or doing things. There were several generations of Labour politicians who went to Westminster promising change, and while they made some fine speeches, did very little to change Scotland and their constituencies for the better.

In the era of the new left after the 1960s, one way to project your radicalism was to support various international causes such as Palestine or South Africa, which gave the freedom to not to have to think about things you had direct influence over, such as your local Labour council. That was the lesson of Galloway in Dundee in the late 1970s and 1980s, twinning the city with the Palestinian town of Nablus, being noted by the left and national media, but not ever bothering about mundane matters such as Dundee housing provision.

## Reasons to be Cheerful: Revolution and Laughter

Contemporary Scotland can be seen to be embarking on what has been called by Open Democracy's Anthony Barnett 'a revolution of the normal'. This entails the prospect of Scotland aspiring to become a mainstream, progressive European democracy (unlike the present day United Kingdom). This would be a gigantic, normalising shift, but would leave many of the shortcomings and dynamics of Scottish society unaddressed and isn't exactly a quantum leap compared to our lack of democracy, pluralism and voice.

The word 'revolution' has become associated with negative connotations aided by the forces of entrenched power and privilege, and it has also become synonymous with violent seizures of power and rule, coup d'états and ultimately the Leninist model of politics. Yet, 'revolution' has numerous interpretations and implementations. We have for example lived through an age of revolutions these last 30 years: the neo-liberal revolution of the West, the collapse of the Soviet bloc, and the defeat of the South African apartheid regime.

'Revolution' has been championed in a very different way by liberation groups, such as the Mexican Zapatista Army of National Liberation, who have embraced, as well as successful guerilla tactics, an understanding of the importance of play, fun and the power of love. In very different circumstances, groups such as 'The Yes Men' with their satirising of the World Trade Organisation (WTO) and corporate abuse by the likes of Exxon-Mobil, BP and others, have attempted to ridicule some of the assumptions of globalisation. Similarly, Billionaires for Bush have set out to showcase the financial elite's control of US politics, by showcasing the arrogance, ignorance and naked self-interest of the super rich and powerful.

All of these examples, in different circumstances, are motivated by trying to be subversive in a wider canvas than the usual left menu of politics. They start from a recognition that protest and dissent should utilise humour, imagination, poking fun at those with power and pretensions, and taking chances in the varieties and styles of opposition. For those who believe that the left has to be humourless and that the demands of the age are for a completely serious politics, two observations can counter this: first, the role of humour at points in the past amongst radicals and progressives, and second, the ways that reactionary ideas have been employed to undermine the left.

In the past, some of the finest progressive writers and thinkers have used humour and irony. A powerful example is Jonathan Swift's writings and his 1729 essay 'A Modest Proposal' whereby he proposed to solve the problem of poverty in Ireland by advocating the eating of poor people. Such a piece was intended to satirise the dehumanising of poor people which characterised supposedly respectable circles of the day. His most famous work, *Gulliver's Travels*, is a fable and journey into another world which plays with concepts of power, authority and what influences character, set in a society with no recognisable form of government, and where Gulliver, for all his size and strength, is not that intelligent, and is outmanoeuvred by the smaller Lilliputians.

## How to Challenge Our Inner Dave Sparts

More recent examples come from the way that the right has consistently portrayed the left as lacking humour, being over-earnest, and dogmatic, and in so doing contributed to undermining it. A hugely influential case is the *Private Eye* creation in the 1970s of the character Dave Spart, named after the German Spartacus League, and sometime resident of the London borough of Neasden. He offered a simplistic revolutionary message seeing in every issue the potential for overthrowing the system and freeing the masses.

Dave Spart still resonates 40 years on, for all the convulsions of politics and retreats of the left, as he conveys some inner truths about what it is to be left. Most left-wingers have a bit of Dave Spart in them, some more than others: an element of humourlessness and earnestness, feeling you have the right to lecture and tell people off, an over-concentration on everything being about politics, and viewing the world in a simplistic, binary way. Anyone watching Owen Jones feel so much anger at Tory cuts that he loses his temper, or Mehdi Hasan railing against the *Daily Mail* then it being revealed that he solicited getting a job with the same paper, will know that the spirit of Dave Spart lives on.

The left has not learned the two obvious lessons from this: one curbing their Dave Spart tendencies, but also recognising the power of humour and satire in defining your opponents. We have had 30 years of neo-liberal onslaught, market vandalism and dogma, selling us a worldview of crony capitalism and consultancy jargon as if it was the Ten Commandments and some kind of Second Enlightenment. It has battered and distorted societies, individuals, cultures and politics, and led to an Alice 'Through the Looking Glass' world where the right has stolen the banners of liberation and freedom, leaving the left looking like a defeated, retreating army hanging on to the notion of a 'better yesterday'.

The revolution of the right has been 'the god that failed' after Communism, but still its remorseless logic goes in the UK, US and across the West, seeking to devoir and destroy all before it: public goods (which seem not to be recognised by conservative opinion in the UK and US), strategic national interests being sold off to the City and foreign capital, and a war waged on the most basic social provision in some of the most unequal places in the developed world.

There is a rich terrain for caricaturing the array of characters who have acted as apologists for the neo-liberal era. There are the 'one-dimensional men' and women, to use Herbert Marcuse's descriptive phrase, who believe as capitalist buccaneers and self-starters that they have great insight into what makes success and failure in every walk of life. There are the new vultures of our age: the asset strippers, offshore tax dodgers and outsourcers who have tarnished every area of life from core public services to Grangemouth and football clubs. And there are the forces of finance capital from the City and banking and its related services of accountancy and contract law who so distort the British economy, politics and media reporting of both.

Then there are the army of consultants and advisers in think tanks and academia who are prepared to demean the English language to give greater legitimacy to the new 'masters of the universe'. Sadly there is even a culture of people who have grown up with all this and believe that in 'the century of the self' that everything is for sale from clean water to air, blood and body organs.

This is a wonderful cast from villains to willing accomplices for an imaginative opposition to have fun with. What is needed is the simple act of naming and giving shape to the kind of amoral individuals who inhabit this world. To tell stories about them, create bylines about their schemes and moneymaking dreams, and to identify the equivalent Dave Sparts of the right.

Satire, comedy, wit, theatre and creative imagination are a crucial weapon in any politics and the politics of orthodoxy and dogma seen by the right is openly inviting being portrayed in this way. Mainstream politicians will say that the above is too marginal and tangential to have any great impact, but over the decades such interventions can contribute to shaping and framing political debate by defining your opponents. They will say that the examples above are too left-wing, too irresponsible and too revolutionary. In this they are missing the argument of how to shift the political debate and aid change in a progressive direction.

## A Scottish Sense of Play and Subversion

No one would seriously propose setting up a Scottish equivalent of the Zapatistas, but other kinds of imaginations are possible which could even include virtual urban and rural guerilla forces (with the appeal of guerilla gardening for example already showing how the term can be reused). There have been some noteworthy cultural initiatives in recent years in Scotland which have shown some of these qualities. There was Bill

Margaret Curran in Space by Greg Moodie

Duncan's *A Wee Book of Calvin* (2004), which played with the 'self-help' book (it being a self-hate book), the Californisation of emotional currency across the West, and the stereotyping of Scots culture as all about an omnipotent, repressive Calvinism.

The singer/songwriter turned cultural imagineer Momus produced his staggering work, *The Book of Scotlands*, five years ago. In it he creates 150 plus parallel Scotlands of past, present and future, some nearly imaginable, some distorting realities, some phantasmagorical in their surreal madness and genius. These include tales of Hamish Henderson and Alfred Kinsey touring Scotland in the 1950s studying the sex habits of people, a magical story of a huge Black Swan which Scotland makes its raison d'être, and another where Scotland becomes the world's first 'post-industrial matriarchy'. This is an extract from one of his parallel Scotlands in a world without 'schools, offices, mortgages and cars':

> It takes us a while to adjust to the nervous energy of the Scots. Their society is constantly bombarded with information – not from above, but rather from below, from the grassroots… The Scots are post-money. They live for experience, for collaboration, for networking, for the intense sociability of the art opening, for the pleasures of the moment. (2009: 47–8)

This is a Scotland where people have 'the knowledge that life rewards those who love – but really love – to live'. This is the utopian imagination mixing the styles of William Morris, Gabriel García Márquez and Italo Calvino, while at the same time being profoundly Scottish. Two years after this, Momus penned *The Book of Japans* (2011), a novel exploring a series of Shetland-Japanese exchanges. The pro-independence site, National Collective, has also displayed humour and fun in numerous articles, and in particular the graphic cartoon strips of Greg Moodie and Rose Garnett (see for example the Moodie strip above). Another example, BBC Scotlandshire with its strapline, 'Och Aye the News', spoofs with what it sees as the parochial, partisan nature of the BBC's coverage. There are other examples, but they are much rarer than they should be considering the richness of Scots culture.

A central point concerns the type of interventions in political discussion. The last 30 years have shown that the conventional Fabian response to market vandalism has been totally inadequate. Fabian social democrats believe in gradualism, reasonableness and the power of evidence. They have been met by an ideological opposition informed by a set of theories of how the world works and human nature. They are dogmatic, economic determinists and not motivated by facts; therefore it is impossible to defeat them with the cold logic of empirical logic, showing as Richard Wilkinson and Kate Pickett attempted to in *The Spirit Level* (2009) that inequality hurts society and equality works better for everyone. In Wilkinson and Pickett there is no understanding of the importance of ideology; they believe facts can convince people and ultimately governments.

That worldview and the degree to which it is not interested in evidence came to the fore in remarks from the second Bush administration, when its spokesman speaking to the *New York Times* chastised their opponents notion of a 'reality based community', whereas they were motivated by something grandeur. They declared that, 'We're an Empire now and when we act, we create reality' (*New York Times*, 17 October 2004). This was met with incredulity and dismay from liberals and left-wingers, declaring that it showed the stupidity of George W. Bush and his supporters. But it did nothing of the kind. It illustrated that they had a political and ideological project about changing the US and world, that their opponents did not fully grasp.

The conventional centre-left approach in the UK and US in recent decades in response to the right has been to move right. This after all was the logic of the Bill Clinton-Dick Norris triangulation strategy and Tony Blair and New Labour; and while it won elections, its creation of what became known as 'the near-left' took them onto unpalatable territory and did not stop, but instead aided, the right. There was a pessimism in New Labour and the Clinton New Democrats; in the former Blair and key advisers really believed Britain was a permanently 'conservative country' and they only had a short-term lease in office.

The Blair-Clinton years critically misunderstood the battle for ideas and their opponents. They were not interested in building up an ecology of progressive ideas, and certainly not in any coming from the fringes or the margins; in the way that the conservative movements in the UK and US has done for several decades.

Thinking and acting differently about politics and social change has to entail dealing in the long term, and nurturing alternative centres and spaces which challenge the all-prevailing orthodoxies. One project I was involved in, called *Glasgow 2020*, looked at the future of Scotland's biggest city and involved thousands of people thinking and creating new ideas and futures. In this, participants came up with the idea of 'assemblies of hope' – spaces and places which were not controlled by the system, sat engaging with it on their own terms, which were not beholden to corporate or marketising logics, and which people felt they had created themselves (Hassan, Mean and Tims, 2007).

Some people really liked the term, 'assemblies of hope' and some saw it as too affected and middle class. Others appreciated the Scottish associations, and the word 'assembly', with its connotations of fluidity, soft power and not focusing on traditional institutions. Whatever view people take, this territory is trying to address big questions about agency and power, and how people can collectively come together and lever influence. But this cannot just be some vague expression of 'network power', it has to embrace and articulate the role and importance of values and ideas which will be explored later.

The realities of the modern world in Scotland, the UK and West demand understanding the destructive phase of capitalism, the unprecedented concentration of economic power in fewer hands, and the emergence of a near monopoly capitalism which most mainstream politicians do not want to acknowledge (including the Westminster classes and significant parts of Scotland).

This has to be recognised alongside the weakness of the left to think, act and be strategic. Instead the mainstream left is weak, in retreat and filled with doubts. The age of anxiety and austerity post-crash has produced a crisis of legitimacy and trust in contemporary capitalism across the West, but has also exasperated the crisis of the left, grounded as it is in assumptions of Western modernity and progress. In many of its assumptions historically the left has been as problematic as the right: economically determinist, routed in modernity, turning a blind eye to ecological concerns (which deviate it from its economic growth fetish to pay for social plans), and with a pliable view of human nature from Stalinism to Fabianism.

That requires a different kind of radicalism from that of the 19th and 20th centuries. Some of the answers, but not all, can be found in the left's diverse past before the state socialists took over. Scotland has many inspirational radicals and campaigners to draw from, ranging from the early Tom Johnston of *Our Scots Noble Families* to the Crofters and Highland radicals, and the ILP voices who were confident enough to be socialist and nationalist and not view them as incompatible. These can provide inspiration and road maps towards a different politics, but we will not find all our answers in the past, as the voices harking back to the 1970s were aspiring to. We will need to develop new ideas of social change, new philosophies and new practices which deal with the unprecedented scale of challenges of 21st century Scotland and globally. This new culture of curiosity, daring and imagination, demands a very different attitude and approach – learning and borrowing from the past, but consciously embracing and creating the future.

# CHAPTER TEN

# Now That's What I Call the Eighties: Scotland and Thatcherism

We have to ease the transition from declining traditional industries to thriving new ones. But tomorrow's Scotland cannot live on yesterday's jobs. Labour's strategy confines itself to resisting change. Our strategy is to encourage it. Far from increasing unemployment, this strategy offers the only hope of making real in-roads in Scotland's dole queues.

MARGARET THATCHER, *The Herald*, 1 May 1979

SCOTLAND HAS UNDERGONE dramatic change in recent years, but one of the most far-reaching aspects has been how a large part of Scotland sees and interprets itself. In the last few decades, Scotland began to reappraise itself as a political community, its radical credentials, what it meant to be a nation, and its commonalities and differences with the rest of the UK. Pivotal to all of this is the experience and perceptions of the tenure of Margaret Thatcher.

## How Scots saw the World of Thatcherism

The seismic economic and social changes which Scotland witnessed in the late 1970s and 1980s have become shortened to one word – 'Thatcherism'. This has become a metaphor for the scale and imposition of change, and with it the sense of loss of control, authority and status. Traditional Scots ways of doing things, whether it was in council estates, working-class culture, mining villages in Ayrshire or East Lothian, or shipbuilding on the Clyde, were ripped up and thrown away by what were perceived as external forces, synonymous with Thatcherism.

An examination of Scottish politics, media and public life over the period of the Thatcher government of 1979–90 shows a dramatic change in how it was portrayed. The early years of the Thatcher Government from 1979–81 saw huge economic and social dislocation, rising unemployment and factory closures, and widespread opposition to the administration.

This was told north of the border (as indeed it was south of the border) as a very British story. This was hugely aided by the ideological mood of the times, which was of right versus left, of the post-war consensus not just breaking down but being actively challenged by the radicals in the

Thatcher Government and the Bennite wing of the Labour Party. To some on the left all this was a simple re-run of the Heath years, who had begun with a radical right programme and anti-trade union legislation before being brought down by trade union opposition and the miners. As well as the post-devolution debacle hangover, politics in Scotland felt very British as Labour surged in popularity against the unpopular Tories, and the SNP disappeared into obscurity and bitter divisions post-1979.

The period 1983–87 saw the slow re-emergence of the Scottish dimension; the words 'no mandate' started to be used about the Thatcher government, 'the Doomsday Scenario' emerged – based on Scotland not voting Tory but getting a Tory government based on English votes – and the idea of 'the democratic deficit' entered public discussion as a description of Scotland's political situation.

By the 1987 election and the third Thatcher UK victory, a dramatic change had occurred. This was now interpreted not through a British or left versus right frame, but of the national dimension. Scotland had become a political community which increasingly did not have faith in Westminster and the British constitution, and instead wished to embrace greater self-government. Thatcherism was seen as 'alien', anti-Scottish and as an 'other': as something which Scots were not and had decisively rejected. This was an anti-Tory, social democratic, civic nationalist country – one thinking of itself in very different terms from how it saw the same government and more importantly, itself in 1979 (see Mitchell, 2014).

A useful way to understand this is offered by 19th century French philosopher Ernest Renan in his essay exploring 'What is a nation?' Renan, writing in 1882 just after the emergence of an ascendant Germany in central Europe, answered his own question by dismissing notions of language, race or geography. Instead, he posed that becoming and being a nation entailed what to 'remember' and what to 'forget' and in doing so what is just as important is the active act of what we choose and select to either 'remember' or 'forget' (Renan, 1882). This set of observations help understand how part of Scotland constructed a political community which has chosen to develop a partial version of the recent past, and in particular the Thatcher years, with continuing consequences.

Significant parts of Scotland changed fundamentally what they choose to 'remember and 'forget' between 1979–90. In the first period, there was an emphasis on shared values and experiences across the UK, references to left versus right, and the importance of the economy and class. All this was reinforced by what was seen as the devolution decade of the 1970s, which after the inclusive referendum of 1979 had seemingly not achieved anything.

In the second period, by the late 1980s, the cumulative effect of Tory rule from job losses to public spending cuts in the context of an increasingly anti-Tory Scotland meant that this was interpreted in a language of difference, and the politics of civic nationalism. The solution was seen as a self-government which moved on considerably from previous proposals of devolution. This shift involved a profound move in what Scots choose to 'remember' and 'forget', with consequences up to the present which need to be explored and understood.

This is played out in the party partisan interpretations of how 1979 is seen and who is responsible for Thatcher's victory and therefore, the decade of Thatcherism. Johann Lamont, Scottish Labour leader, said in First Minister's Questions in October 2013, 'It wasn't my party which walked through the lobbies to create a Tory Government under Margaret Thatcher'. She then warmed to her theme, stating to SNP benches, 'I know, they don't like to remember their own history. This is what the SNP did to Scotland, and Scotland will never forgive them' (BBC *Holyrood*, 10 October 2013).

A SNP counter-version of this gained ground in the 1980s as Thatcherism was seen to run roughshod over Scottish majority sentiment and opinion. This led to Labour's 50 Scottish MPs being labelled 'the feeble fifty'. Pete Wishart, SNP MP for Perth and North Perthshire, over 25 years later showed his still simmering anger, commenting, 'Never was so little achieved by so many in defence of so few' – the motto of the fabled 'Feeble Fifty', and drew the following lessons for today, 'The parable of the Feeble Fifty is one that has to be clearly understood… Scotland will never trust Labour to defend Scotland from the Tories ever again' (petewishart.wordpress.com, 13 April 2013).

Take these remarks in turn. Lamont's conveniently ignores the role Labour anti-devolutionists played in bringing down their own government – that people such as Brian Wilson, Tam Dalyell and Johann Lamont, who voted no to their own government's devolution plans, and triggered the no confidence motion which brought about the 1979 election. The SNP presents Labour as a party which perfidiously promised and then failed to deliver devolution after the people voted for it, and then stood idly by as Thatcherism ransacked the nation.

There is in both of these examples victimhood, anger and evasion of responsibility, along with the Scots characteristic of wanting to constantly revisit and rewrite the past. But there is also as will be explored later in this chapter, insularity, and seeing the epic changes which Scotland was going through as reducible to the villain of 'Thatcherism'. Both the year 1979 and the decade which preceded it were ones of epic global change which affected both Scotland and the UK, and the assumptions of the post-war era.

## Collective Memories and the Flashbulb Memories of Thatcherism

The different dimensions of this shift, how it has come about and its consequences needs careful study. One factor concerns how the past and memories are constructed – about the power of collective memories, and how the story of Thatcherism has become myth and folklore.

The experience of the post-1979 period has a spectrum of tones and moods and has become situated in a set of iconic images and causes: some of the early industrial closures, the miners' strike, the poll tax, the 'Sermon on the Mound' and Ravenscraig (even though this was shut by the Major Government).

The development of 'collective memories' are by necessity socially constructed, partial and the combination of deeply personal reflections. One leading writer on this, Eviatar Zerubaval, has observed that 'collective memories' with their aggregation of individual recollections narrow and eliminate numerous perspectives such as inter-generational memory as they continually remake and reimagine the past (1996).

Two other academics, Roger Brown and James Kulik, in the 1970s, invented the concept of 'flashbulb memories' to understand how we recall and reinvent key moments, events and incidents, and give more weight to certain pivotal, defining images (1977). In this they studied a range of high profile moments – the assassination of significant public figures in post-war US history – Malcolm X, Martin Luther King, Robert Kennedy. They made the case that we construct 'flashbulb memories' from a very specific part of our mind and memory. This creates a set of powerful images, filled with intricate detail and background, related to the circumstances when we first heard news of such an event. They pose that this is the notion of the 'Now print!' way people remember, with each recollection unique, captured and a creation of the social and individual setting.

The notion of 'collective memories' and 'flashbulb memories' provide a useful set of tools for analysing and understanding how Scottish society interpreted Thatcherism, the decade of the 1980s, and how it has continued to see it in the 20 plus years since the fall of the Thatcher Government. The period of 1979–90 has become crystallised into a set of iconic themes: the closing of traditional manufacturing industries, the poll tax, the Sermon on the Mound, and Ravenscraig. From these wider themes are evoked: of the loss of whole ways of life which had been built up over generations, the damage and destruction which many communities felt, the challenge to a certain kind of Scottish man and masculinity defined by the endeavour of his work, and the imposition of Thatcher's Government and Thatcherism on an unwilling 'restless nation' which never voted for her, or her ism.

If one phrase sums up the distinct Scots experience: it is that of the poll tax and the perception that Scots were 'guinea pigs', a phrase which carries with it all the redolent imagery of Scotland as a laboratory of social engineering of the New Right. This is beyond the revisionism of David Torrance in his thoughtful counter-history of Thatcherism north of the border when he tries to dismantle the 'guinea pig' and other theses (Torrance, 2009). It is beyond a mere examination of facts or looking at the poll tax in isolation; it touches a deep almost psychic nerve in Scots society about this decade and how it is remembered.

## How Scotland interprets the 1980s and why it matters today

There are key voices and witnesses in the Scotland of the 1980s. One would be novelist and writer William McIlvanney and in particular his September 1987 'Stands Scotland Where It Did' lecture and December 1992 speech to the post-election 'Democracy Demonstration' march. The 1987 lecture delivered to the SNP conference saw him state: 'We live under a government which has wiped out whole areas of Scotland and then cynically carved on the headstones: 'Regeneration'. Aye. Maybe in the next world' (1992: 241).

This was to McIlvanney not just a government that people like he opposed, but about taking Scotland into uncharted waters:

> ... we have never, in my lifetime, until now had a government whose basic principles were so utterly against the most essential traditions and aspirations of Scottish life. We have never until now had a government so determined to unpick the very fabric of Scottish life and make it over into something quite different... Under this government, it is not the quality of our individual lives that is threatened. It is our communal sense of our own identity. (1992: 245–6)

This was about fundamentals in terms of ideology, philosophy and politics. And it was felt at a deep personal level:

> For Margaret Thatcher is not just a perpetrator of bad policies. She is a cultural vandal. She takes the axe of her own simplicity to the complex-

ities of Scottish life. She has no understanding of the hard-earned traditions she is destroying. And if we allow her to continue, she will remove
from the word 'Scottish' any meaning other than geographical. (1992: 246)

The timing of this speech is critical to understanding its sentiments. It was
articulated in the shadow of Thatcher's third election victory of 1987 and
when a significant part of Scotland felt it and its values were under threat,
and under attack from her and her government. In this political environment, many Scots agreed with McIlvanney's thesis that Scotland's existence
as a nation, political community and its difference were in peril and could
be lost. He observed, 'At such a time we should at least consider what it
is we are danger of losing?' (1992: 246).

Five years later in 1992 in the wake of another Tory election victory,
their fourth consecutive triumph, its unexpected nature in the immediate
aftermath threw up grassroots activism in the cross-party 'Scotland
United' which culminated in the 'Democracy Demonstration' march and
rally in Edinburgh to mark the European Summit held in the city, and
Scotland's lack of democracy. This was a significant moment in Scotland's
public consciousness: a major international summit with the attention of
the world's media, the largest ever pro-home rule match with between
25,000 and 40,000 protestors filling Edinburgh's streets, as John Major
tried to slow down European Union integration.

McIlvanney caught much of the collective sentiment that day, and the
post-1992 election sentiments of a large part of Scotland for Labour and
SNP to put away their differences and unite for democracy and against
Tory rule. He also invoked a Scottish sense of pluralism and hybrid identities as a 'mongrel nation' which he felt was threatened by the dogma of
the British government.

McIlvanney was one of many powerful and eloquent public figures
giving voice to a Scotland dissatisfied with the status quo and Tory minority
rule, and demanding a democratic set of arrangements in how Scotland
was governed. Owen Dudley Edwards, in the conclusion to a collection
of essays inspired by *A Claim of Right for Scotland*, wrote at the end of
the 1980s:

Thatcherism has done everything it can to bribe, bully and blackmail
Scotland into bowing down before its gods of materialism and British
chauvinism, self-enrichment and self-regard, community destruction and
beggar-your-neighbour... (1989: 187)

Dudley Edwards went on to write that, 'Thatcherism is in an extreme
stage of alcoholism', and making a comparison between the experience

of Scotland and Ireland, took the view that, 'The SNP abhors violence; Thatcherism worships it' (1989: 188, 191).

Arguably the single most resonant soundbite of the Thatcher decade and Scotland was supplied by the unlikely figure of Canon Kenyon Wright, co-chair of the Scottish Constitutional Convention, an umbrella group bringing together Labour, Lib Dems, trade unions, local government. At its inaugural meeting in March 1989 highlighting Scottish desire for democracy and the opposition of Thatcher, he said:

> What happens if that other voice we all know so well responds by saying, 'We say No and we are the State?' Well, we say Yes and We are the People and in the last analysis, Scotland believes not in the 'Royal We' but in 'We the People'. (*Glasgow Herald*, 31 March 1989)

Kenyon Wright later reflected on the potency of the above quote, 'It was effective because it succeeded in encapsulating the central challenge that the Convention was making to the authority of the British state' (1997: 52).

The above comments and in particular the opinions of McIlvanney and Kenyon Wright form what can be seen as 'the official story' of Scotland and 'Thatcherism in a cold climate', to use David McCrone's phrase from the 1980s (*Radical Scotland*, June/July 1989). McIlvanney actually claimed in his 1987 lecture, in words he has never qualified or withdrawn, that Scotland as a community and set of values was under threat from Thatcherism and could potentially be reduced to a postal address. These were widely shared sentiments in the late 1980s in anti-Tory Scotland, but that does not mean that they cannot be critiqued to explore what kind of Scotland they were evoking.

This is a moral call to arms, of indignation, being affronted and evoking an older Scots sensibility of rejecting an asocial individualism and posing a socially informed communitarianism. Like many, I was hugely influenced and affected by the language of McIlvanney and others in the 1980s. They were giving a legitimacy and respectability to a politics which was rejecting Thatcherism and in so doing embracing a politics and culture of Scots self-government.

There were positives in this account but omissions and blindness to some of the shortcomings in our society – from huge health inequalities to the permanent exclusion of a host of people and communities from the life of our nation, economically, socially and culturally. One contradiction in the McIlvanney thesis was that Thatcherism was out to destroy Scotland with her 'cultural vandalism' attempting to lay waste to north of the border, but at the same time, he chose to ignore the multi-dimensional, complex nature of poverty and exclusion in Scotland which was not all down to Thatcher's 'evil' intent.

Some Scots writers such as Joyce McMillan propose that Scotland pre-1979 was practically bereft of poverty, hardship and suffering, recently writing that the 1970s saw 'the ending of homelessness and beggary' (*The Scotsman*, 13 September 2013). This over-states the degree to which Thatcher changed Scotland, and distorts and caricatures the society that existed pre-1979. While being less unequal than what came after, there is no doubt that it had not abolished hardship or inequality, and contained all sorts of bureaucratic insensitivities and intrusions into peoples' lives.

An examination of Scotland, pre-Thatcher, suggests that this was not exactly the social democratic paradise as it was defined after the event. In books such as *The Red Paper on Scotland* published in 1975 chapters analysing poverty and need by Ian Levitt, examining Glasgow by Vince Cable and by Donald Cameron addressing public health detailed the inadequacies of that period after three decades of the 'post-war consensus' (Brown, 1975). Levitt addressing poverty wrote:

> Today in Scotland there are over a million poor – even though we are generally better housed, clothed and fed than ever before. What this means is that one person in four has not shared the new prosperity that has come in the last decade. (1975: 317)

Levitt argued that the focus on growth, along with the belief in planning, modernity and the power of experts in the 1950s and 1960s, led authorities to ignore inconvenient facts which did not fit with their bright, optimistic picture of Scotland. One of these was the emergence of what he called 'the new poor' who challenged the assumptions of this outlook. Simultaneously, the evolving industrial structure of the economy, decline in traditional manufacturing and changes in employment, along with systemic low pay, all contributed to increasing poverty and hardship which by the late 1960s and 1970s had become significant in scale. He concluded his assessment with the warning that, 'The future can only be viewed with apprehension' (1975: 317).

The first response to 'official Scotland' in post-war times to the re-emergence of new problems and refusal of old ones to disappear was to ignore and deny them, and when that failed, the next step was to do what all bureaucracies do when faced with inconvenient facts, namely, to blame the people.

Take Glasgow in the 1950s and 1960s. This was the site of a formidable experiment in social engineering, in the remaking of the city, improving living conditions, and rebuilding the public and civic culture of the city. Massive slum clearance occurred razing parts of the city such as the Gorbals to the ground, new council house estates such as Drumchapel and Easterhouse emerged (originally called 'townships' in council plans before it gained a South African apartheid association), and motorways built through the centre of the city. Huge numbers of people were relocated from Glasgow to New Towns such as East Kilbride and Cumbernauld, while many others moved from the old central core to the new estates, many on the outskirts of the city.

There was immense hope, energy and positivity in all this. Authorities thought in the immediate post-war era that they could tackle Beveridge's famous 'Five Evils' of 'squalor, ignorance, want, idleness and disease' and create a brave new world where poverty and lack of opportunity would be a thing of the past.

Vince Cable, a Glasgow Labour councillor from 1971–74, reflected on the end of this expansive period saying that, 'Labour councilors saw new motorways, like blocks of multi-storey council houses, as emblems of a modernist, dynamic city' (Cable, 2009: 125). When the first problems emerged with people complaining about shortcomings in their homes or lack of amenities in the areas, the official response was not impressive, 'Initially, many councillors and housing officers refused to accept that there was a problem and developed a language for describing 'choosy' and 'difficult' people who lacked 'gratitude' for what the council had done' (Cable: 123).

None of this is in any way an apology for Thatcherism, but a call to begin to put the scale of its changes into historical perspective, and to not think that all the wrongs in our society emanated from her ism. And from this there flows the need to recognise the nature of society pre-1979, and the managed, ordered world of supposedly enlightened authority which characterised so much of public life.

If people think it is an exaggeration to argue that McIlvanney, in his understandable motivation to mobilise Scottish opinion to Thatcherism, invoked a selective, partial account which glossed over some of the uncomfortable aspects of Scottish life, consider the following. In the same lecture, McIlvanney wrote, 'I know nowhere less defined by materialism than Scotland'. He then went on to quote speaking to a French friend in Paris and their exchange:

> 'I like to meet you, Willie', he said. Then he shook his head. 'But you are so Scottish. Always the moral issue. The demand for justice. The world is not like that.' Many Scots have always felt that it should be. (1992: 247)

McIlvanney's response was to say, 'There is a deeply ingrained tradition in Scotland that we will not judge one another by material standards', the need to question the orthodoxies of 'measurement' and 'performance', and the belief in 'the deep humanity of the Scottish people' (1992: 248). This latter sentiment is 'not a hard system to apply. Its principles are simple enough. You want a measurement of people? Then, if you wish to remain Scottish, here it is. You will measure them by the extent of their understanding, by the width of their compassion, by the depth of their concern and by the size of their humanity' (1992: 248–9).

This is lyrically and poetically a potent and beautifully written stirring call to Scotland as a moral and political community; an active defiance to the politics of Thatcherism and a cry for compassion. What is not to admire in this you may say? On many levels this is correct, but the words of McIlvanney's French friend shouldn't be so easily dismissed. He says 'you are so Scottish. Always the moral issue. The demand for justice', and with these words McIlvanney is portraying a morality where good and bad, black and white are unambiguous, and then unproblematically acted upon by government, public agencies and others in Scotland. If only it were that simple.

## The Limits of Scotland's Moral Community

Instead, Scotland is marred by a profound disjuncture between rhetoric and action, between believing we are an inclusive, egalitarian society and the actual picture of seismic, inter-generational exclusion and poverty. What McIlvanney is giving articulation to is a Scottish sense of 'the good society', one informed by ideas of communitarianism and progressivism which have deep roots in our society, but which have become mistaken for the ideas of social democracy.

These traditions, which have produced a lineage of influential Scots thinkers such as Alasdair MacIntyre and John Macmurray (the latter of whom in very different ways was hugely influential on both Tony Blair's and Gordon Brown's political thought) are in McIlvanney's account reduced to a few homespun homilies and self-evident truths, expressed with all the power and gifts he has as a writer.

This defining period of Thatcher's Scotland has become one of the foundation stories of modern society, aided by the likes of McIlvanney who so eloquently captured the understandable rage against Thatcherism people felt and wanted to see expressed. Yet it has come to embody a sort of collective false memory syndrome about Scotland and Thatcherism which most of us have fallen prey to. It goes along the lines of, to take a couple of examples: 'Mrs Thatcher demolished Scotland's steel, engineering and mining industries' (Ascherson, 2002: 238) and 'Moribund dinosaurs like shipbuilding, coalmining and steel, living on state finance, starved to death in no time' (Oliver, 2009: 364).

BBC Scotland's *Thatcher and the Scots* programme saw presenter Allan Little observe, 'She remains unforgiven here', commenting that 'we have built her into our national mythology' (BBC Scotland, 1 January 2009). Thatcherism has become the convenient scapegoat for what we believe is wrong in Scottish society. It has become shorthand to define who we are by who we are not, what our values are by what we oppose, and crucially, who we have chosen our enemies to be.

The choice politically of who you identify as not part of your community or tribe is important. Majority Scottish opinion, and certainly most media and commentary views in the 1980s, increasingly painted the Thatcher Government as 'alien' and 'foreign', not just in its lack of a democratic mandate, but also in terms of its values, intent and ideology. This was an 'ism' at war with society, the very notion of which was meant to galvanise most Scots.

Nearly all Scots accounts of Thatcherism since, with the exception of solitary centre-right voices, have bought into this account. There are numerous other dimensions which should be acknowledged in terms of how most Scots interpreted Thatcherism. One is the politics of gender. The 1980s saw hundreds of thousands of men lose their jobs and their livelihoods, along with much of how they defined themselves as men and breadwinners. A whole generation of men working in traditional industries went from being 'big men' who were looked up to in the towns and places they lived to what can only be called 'walking wounded' – left behind, traumatised and without a sense of purpose.

The early years of Thatcherism in Scotland and the UK saw a widespread misogyny on parts of the left who thought it permissible to throw anything at her to show their rage and fury. There were 'Ditch the Bitch' placards in the early 1980s and in Scotland, an infamous SNP poster from 1980 which presented Thatcher as a blood-sucking vampire getting her hands on Scotland's oil.

While we like to think we have moved on, when Thatcher died in April 2013 there was an explosion of anger in certain parts of the left and communities which felt disposed and hurt by the consequences of her policies. There was the UK-wide campaign to get 'Ding Dong the Witch is

Dead' to number one in the singles chart. In Scotland there was a reaction in parts of society similar to places such as South Yorkshire and Wales that had been hit by huge job losses, plus the above sensibility that Thatcher and her ism were out to destroy Scotland.

The gendered aspect of all of this is pertinent. Thatcher as a woman, her impact on working-class male jobs, and on a society which was very masculinised and gender divided when she came to power in 1979, has to be recognised. In 1979 to take just one example of public life, Scotland elected out of 71 Westminster MPs a single woman MP (Dame Judith Hart); and middle-class public life was dominated by grey faced, grey haired men who ran local authorities, public bodies and businesses.

This matters to Scotland to this day: about how and why the vast social changes which have occurred in the decades since 1979 came about, what they mean and how they are interpreted. The Scotland of 1979 was very different from that of today, with a majority of people living in council houses and well over half of those in work belonging to a trade union. This along with Labour's dominance of local government gave the three pillars of what I have called 'Labour Scotland'. This was distinct from the direct expression of the party and enabled it having never won a majority of the popular vote to speak for, represent and have an element of control over a majority of the population.

The 'official story' of modern Scotland says that Thatcherism destroyed the British social democratic settlement to which most Scots along with many elsewhere in the UK bought into, thus paving the way for devolution, the Scottish Parliament and bringing us to the present debate on independence. But of course things were more nuanced than that.

The British post-war settlement and citizenship, which Thatcherism is so widely credited with dismantling, was actually in deep crisis prior to the election of 1979. Thatcher and Thatcherism were a symptom of this crisis, not the cause. For example, in the 1970s a series of global and domestic shocks weakened and then overturned the managed post-war economic order, ranging from the 1971 floating of the dollar, the 1973 OPEC oil price spike in the aftermath of the Arab-Israeli war, and the 1979 oil price rise which followed the fall of the Shah of Iran.

There was the 1976 IMF crisis in which Labour had to implement drastic public spending cuts while Prime Minister Jim Callaghan embraced monetarism and told the Labour Conference that 'we used to think that you could spend your way out of a recession… that option no longer exists' (Sandbrook, 2012: 478). The year before, Tony Crosland, once Labour's leading revisionist social democratic thinker, told local government that 'the party is over', preparing the way for Thatcher's centralist war of attrition (*The Times*, 10 May 1975).

This was a decade of instability, economic shocks and anxiety not just in the UK but across the world. The year 1979 saw dramatic change in Iran with the fall of the Shah and coming to power of Ayatollah Khomeini, the beginning of the end of the Soviet empire with the visit to Poland of Pope John Paul II, the introduction of Deng Xiaoping's market reforms in China, and Ronald Reagan embark on his campaign for the Republican Presidential nominate which would prove successful the following year and result in him defeating Democrat Jimmy Carter in the election (Caryl, 2013). Nevertheless, neither globally nor in relation to the UK or Scotland is 1979 a 'Year Zero', but the crystallisation of longer trends.

In a sense Thatcherism, as we have come to know and define it, predates Thatcher and even her version of the ism. This matters for Scotland now. Because if the changes and ideological agenda of Thatcherism was located in wider global and domestic shifts, then the yearning in part of the Scottish debate to go back to the certainty, order and compassion of society in 1945–75, to make a moral Scots version of the post-war British settlement, is not possible.

Part of the Scottish desire for greater autonomy and self-government is a 'Back to the Future' nostalgia which is not possible given this wider context. Global capitalism has dramatically changed from that of Keynesian planned management, which is sometimes characterised as 'organised capitalism', to one which is more disorganised, destructive and creative; and from a world which was flatter and more equal to one which has become a brazen apology for massive privilege and inequality.

A crucial element of Scotland understanding this is the meanings and memories we choose to invest in the word Thatcherism, and how we understand some of the epic economic and social changes we have lived through. The high, modernist Scotland of post-war times cannot be summoned back into life by collective will. Nor can a Scottish version of the British post-war dream be resurrected, which so many people understandably feel aggrieved at having lost. This means our future is going to be more potentially unpredictable, untidy and messy, and with that comes risks and uncertainty, but also opportunities.

CHAPTER ELEVEN

# The Sounds of Silence: Thatcher, Blair and Understanding the Past

Go into any place where history is stored and listen. Hold your breath. Hear how still it is. Librarians and archivists will keep their visitors quiet, but this particular silence has nothing to do with them. It runs through buzzing computer rooms and waits in busy record offices, it is always there. It is always there. It is the sound of nothingness. It is the huge, invisible, silent roar of all the people who are too small to record. They disappear and leave the past inhabited only, as murderers and prodigies and saints.

A. L. Kennedy, 'The Role of Notable Silences in Scottish History',
in *Night Geometry and the Garscadden Trains*, Polygon 1990

HOW SCOTLAND interprets and understands itself, who is speaking and has influence in public life, and what stories come to the fore, have huge implications. As we have seen this affected how Thatcherism has been seen, but also following on from it the experience of New Labour, the establishment of the Scottish Parliament and the dynamics of the independence debate.

The extended decade of New Labour's ascendancy was widely portrayed by many as problematic in Scotland. Even pre-1997, Tony Blair's identification of 'middle England' as a key constituency, the abolition of Clause Four from the party constitution, and the decision to have a devolution referendum, shored up Scottish tensions. Labour Party focus groups leaked to the press found huge Scottish misgivings about 'Tony's easy smile' and 'New Labour's promises with regard to Scotland'.

These sentiments found expression while New Labour went on to win three UK elections and poll impressively in Scotland. Yet, this occurred while much of the discussion on Tony Blair and New Labour, with some echoes of how Thatcherism was interpreted, saw it as a Southern English phenomenon, and not relevant to politics north of the border.

Similarly, the Scottish Parliament as an institution was for in its first few years either savaged or severely criticised in the media. These ranged from attacking MSP expenses and awarding themselves medals, to the high profile campaign on Clause 28, and the long running saga of the escalating costs of the Holyrood building project (which went through the roof from £40m to £414.4m).

Some of this dissatisfaction was the media tapping into the general anti-political and cynical mood of the public, but what was also evident was a disappointment and lack of connection with the way Labour in coalition with the Lib Dems governed Scotland. Under successive First Ministers – Donald Dewar, Henry McLeish, Jack McConnell – there seemed to be little clear idea of Labour's vision of Scotland and the purpose of devolution.

## The 'Community of Communicators' and the Importance of Silence

Critical in how Thatcherism, New Labour and the Scottish Parliament were represented was what William MacKenzie has called 'the community of communicators' (1978: 165). This is a term which describes those in public life who have voice, status and influence, and who contribute to the making and manufacturing of public opinion, determining the boundaries of what it is seen as permissible to debate and discuss in mainstream society.

A fundamental kernel of 'the community of communicators' are its characteristics, who is in it and why, and who is not in it and the reasons. Thus the entrances and exits to this community matter, as do, what Karl Deutsch in his seminal study of nationalism, called 'marked gaps', the importance of breaks and barriers, and in particular communicative barriers (1966: 100). This understanding of the 'marked gaps' aids awareness of just not what is discussed and who is discussing it, but the seismic silences and omissions which characterise too much of Scots public life, and which tend to go unacknowledged in many of the accounts of how Scotland sees itself: as this land of inclusion, compassion and egalitarian values.

MacKenzie's perspective, supplemented by Deutsch, (whose studies were enormously influential on Benedict Anderson's much cited *Imagined Communities* (1983)) allows us to see Scotland not just as a nation and society, but a social place, and a site of competing actors and voices, in public places, conversations, politics and culture.

A fundamental dynamic is Scotland's inter-relationship within the UK, and the evolving power dynamics and in particular, the power nexus of the 'world city' of London. In this Scotland has given expression to its own distinctive 'community of communicators' which has inhabited and animated its public life, politics and media, and defined many of the debates, sense of difference and values in wider society. There is a wider context here: of how politics, public conversation, and the place of main-stream media has evolved, including the long term crisis and decline of print journalism which can only be touched upon, but which I have written on elsewhere in relation to studying Scottish public life and its public realm (Hassan, 2014).

However, this Scottish community whose influence and status has been pivotal to the last three or more decades of public life north of the border, has an ambiguous relationship with the London 'community of the communicators'. Increasingly this latter group has grown insular, self-obsessed and lacking in any detailed understanding of the rest of the UK (let alone Scotland). And while no doubt some of those very charac-teristics could be levied at the Scots, and later in this chapter I will further explore some of their limitations, there is something problematic about the London group's take on the UK.

This represents increasingly a London-centric view of the world, uncri-tically aligned to London as the great 'world city' of the rich, powerful and privileged. Post-crash, Boris Johnson openly lauded London's achieve-ments at what increasingly looks like the rest of the UK's expense, stating that the city accounts for 12.5 per cent of the UK population and creates 25 per cent of UK GDP (on other estimates it is slightly less). There seems, even when talking to UK-wide audiences little sensitivity to the conseque-nces of the above – of a divided, unequal UK, which would reduce numerous regions' sole economic and social viability to servicing the needs of London and the South East.

Also relevant is that the Scottish community in areas such as politics and media is compromised and limited by the power of this London group. This is of course a discussion about the influence and views of two contrasting elites, but from the point of view of Scottish debates it is one of asymmetry and an element of condescension. London is the imperial capital of the UK and the economic powerhouse of the increasingly divided UK, and its elites believe that their interests and that of the Westminster, City and business insider groups comprise a worldview which 'UK plc' should embrace and to which opposition is unenlightened and reactionary.

Scotland's 'community of communicators' is found in and at the inter-section of a number of areas of public life: media, politics, culture. It is an elite, and in part is anchored in a number of familiar groups such as 'the chattering class' (which is sometimes referred to as the McChattering classes), the commentariat of opinion makers and commentators in public life, and in the arena and attitude of 'civic Scotland' which was explored earlier.

This community is by its nature a narrow, incestuous world, but is larger than those groups above, also including senior figures in business, public sector, and the voluntary sector. It is an insider group, one that points simultaneously in two directions at the same time: towards the centres of power of government and institutional opinion, and outwards to the public via the media, social platforms and communicative spaces.

The place and influence of this group can only be fully understood by locating it in Scotland's compromised public realm, and the degree of autonomy and distinctiveness it has in relation to the wider and more powerful London group of elites. Then there is how it is situated in the culture and terrain of Scotland's limited democracy and wider participation, what I have previously called undemocracy and unspace, with the latter aiding the prioritisation and status of institutional voices, narrow bandwidth of debate, and exclusion of those who are seen as too challenging or radical.

It is only be placing these groups in a longer historical story: of the managed society of the union and Scotland's elite-led incorporations, the evolution of territorial government from late Victorian times, the emergence of the quasi-corporate state in the 1920s and 1930s, and the 'high Scotland' of 1945–75, that it is possible to begin to understand Scotland's experience in recent decades.

It is this historical backdrop, of the limited nature of Scottish democracy, and the evolution of the closed order of much of society that allowed the 'community of the communicators' stance on Scotland to become so influential in the last three decades on Thatcherism, New Labour and the Scottish Parliament.

## Scotland's 'Children of the Echo'

A key question to explore here is: did the above groups contribute significantly to changing how Scotland saw itself in the 1980s onwards, or were they following pre-existing public opinion? Was Scotland's emphasis on seeing itself as predominantly left-wing, anti-Tory and anti-Thatcherite, part of something new, or just a modern version of an older story? And crucially, what was the mixture between the role of elites and opinion formers, and the general public?

Jarvis Cocker, of 1990s band Pulp, when talking about the continued obsession and cultural stranglehold of the 1960s, wrote, 'We are children of the echo. Born just after some kind of explosion, and doomed to spend our lives working backwards to try and get as close as we can to the moment of that Big Bang' (*The Guardian*, 10 October 2012).

Cocker meant that the 1960s represented a 'Big Bang' of art, creativity and activity which, as we travelled further and further from its epicentre, saw its original impulse grow weaker and weaker. Thus in the 1970s there were still significant elements of originality and imagination in Bowie, Roxy Music and punk; but by the 1990s 'Britpop' had become more derivative and conservative, and the cultural flowerings had become part of a wider heritage, self-reverential industry. Cocker argued that this never ending mining and referencing of the '60s and of a narrow interpretation based on the Beatles, Lennon and McCartney, was a law of diminishing returns which ultimately ended in 'Britpop' and the increasing dominance of retro culture.

The notion of 'children of the echo' can be used to see how Scotland's 'community of the communicators' have been first shaped and defined in their opposition to Thatcherism, but to an extent, captured and limited by the politics of the 1980s. Scotland and the onslaught of the alien, imposed Thatcherism has become a code for all that is wrong in society. The complexity of economic and social changes have become constricted into the view that Thatcher waged war on Scotland, shut our industries and took hundreds of thousands of jobs and livelihoods.

There is a generational account of Scotland in this which is synonymous with Baby Boomer Scotland, the cohort who grew up in the immediate post-war era, believed in its aspirations and values, and mostly associated with the ideals of the Labour Party. This group regarded the onset of Thatcherism as an onslaught on many of the ideas and values which they thought had become irreversible: full employment, the welfare state, redistribution, and a society which was becoming more socially mobile, filled with greater opportunities, and more economically and socially equal.

This explanation of Scotland has come to be 'the official story' of modern times: of seeing large parts of our politics and public life through the experience of Thatcherism. In the mindset of 'children of the echo', as the 1980s have retreated into history, a simplified, caricatured version of that decade and ism have increasingly come to define what we think and how we see the world.

This is not a defence or apology for Thatcherism; it is an argument against all-persuasive received wisdom and the notion of 'the official story'. Post-1980s and post-Thatcherism, Scotland increasingly saw itself as a social democratic, centre-left, inclusive political community, a place where Thatcher and Tories were unpopular and used as bellwethers, but from which wider consequences flowed. Scottish political debate had clear boundaries around what could be openly debated, set by invoking the ghost of Thatcher and in many accounts, Tony Blair. This ran seamlessly from the political projects of Thatcherism to New Labour, both portrayed as a negation of all Scotland stood for and believed.

Many high profile examples illustrate this including Johann Lamont's 'something for nothing' speech of September 2012. In this Lamont asked:

> What is progressive about judges and lawyers earning more than £100,000 a year, not paying tuition fees for their child to follow in their footsteps at university, while one in four unemployed young people in Scotland can't get a job or a place at college?

She then went on to pose that taxes would have to rise or services be cut in order to maintain existing policies and SNP pledges such as free care for the elderly and the council tax freeze. To think otherwise she claimed was to maintain the notion of a 'something for nothing society' with policies funded 'all on the never-never' (BBC *News Scotland*, 25 September 2012).

This is not about defending Lamont's intervention. The speech supposedly aimed to open a debate on what Lamont regarded as a closed area but by utilising the tabloidesque words 'something for nothing' and talking of 'never-never', it colluded with the language of reactionary ideas and the new right. This was the logic of Paul Sinclair, Lamont's main media adviser and previously Political Editor of the *Daily Record*. In this it follows the tramlines of media strategy so religiously followed by New Labour and how Alastair Campbell and Peter Mandelson corroded the party's social democratic DNA for newspaper acquiescence and headlines.

That was a dangerous, ultimately self-defeating approach for New Labour which offers a clear warning for Scottish Labour. Yet at the same time the response of the Scottish media and commentariat to Lamont was nearly uniformly dismissive, portraying it in a manner which closed down debate and avoided substance.

For example, Kevin McKenna in *The Observer* commented that 'Mrs Thatcher would have been proud' and that the views expressed by Lamont 'would have tickled the Iron Lady' (*The Observer*, 30 September 2012). Iain Macwhirter called it 'Nick Clegg without the apology' and 'the second longest suicide note in history', the longest in conventional political logic being Labour's 1983 election manifesto (*The Herald*, 27 September 2012). Ian Bell declared it 'the triumph of Blairism in a party that no longer seems sure what it means by a welfare state' (*Sunday Herald*, 30 September 2012).

Joyce McMillan stated that Lamont's 'fatal slip' left Salmond as 'one of the few Western leaders of our time with the courage and gaiety to buck the trend and to dare to offer a politics of hope' (*The Scotsman*, 28 September 2012).

This episode reveals a variety of factors about what passes for Scottish political debate, its boundaries and beliefs. First, it illustrates that Thatcher, Blair and their related isms, have become keywords which show what is permissible to debate in contemporary Scotland. To evoke them allows the likelihood of closing off serious discussion on politics, policy and ideas, and something placed beyond the bounds of consideration. Thatcher, Blair and related terms have become framing terms which allow any issue to be seen through a constricted and blinkered vision which prevents any challenge to the existing situation.

Second, what Macwhirter, Bell and McMillan, all fine writers and talents, are representing in the above is the inherent conservatism of large parts of modern Scotland. Their account on this and other issues seems to embody a land which defines itself by not voting Tory, but at the same time supports the existing status quo, and 'the settled will' of institutional Scotland. This account of Scotland is by its nature, conservative, elitist and limiting in its idea of democracy, yet seems to think it is radical and progressive doing the above. Equally revealingly large sections of the Scottish electorate seem to agree and collude in this, buying into a self-sustaining set of myths.

Numerous other examples indicate where Scots debate and opinion is closed down or is profoundly narrow and threadbare, preferring prevailing comforting stories rather than a wider debate. One recent case in 2013 is the subject of the bedroom tax, with numerous Labour and SNP politicians seeming to have nothing of any substance to say on the subject of social justice. To most Scottish politicians apart from Tories and Westminster Lib Dem ministers, 'welfare reform' seems to be something to be blanketly opposed, rather than remade and recreated.

This is the world of Scotland's 'community of communicators' and the reach and grip of 'the children of the echo', the framing and closing down of debates, thinking and choices, by constant reference to Thatcher, Tories and Blair. It represents the rise and stranglehold of a specific generational story, one which was shaped pre-1979, and which has never been able to come to terms with the rise of Thatcherism, the new right and the defeat of the post-war consensus.

As argued previously, the association of the complex ideological and big political and economic changes which began to take hold in the 1979s

with the catchphrase 'Thatcherism' is actually a one-dimensional caricature of the huge changes which were unleashed from that period onward.
There is a yearning for the quiet, simple, agreeable life in some of the
Scottish debate – a belief that we can just lock out the market vandals
who inhabit the corridors of Westminster, and continue as we previously
have done.

Part of this also falls within a search for who we are, and who are the
enemies and villains of the piece. This encompasses a collective desire for
the Tories to be the ones we chase out of the village, but given the lack of
powerful Tories north of the border we have to instead label others as
'tartan Tories'. This of course used to be what Labour people called the
SNP, but is now applied to anyone who deviates from the conformity of
public life. An added dimension is the seeming reluctance to identify real
villains, such as privatisers and outsourcers (the latter well-entrenched in
the Scottish state in the form of Serco, G4S and others), so we create
phantom ones aided by the weakness of the Tory Party.

Silences and omissions in the public life of Scotland tell us much about
where we are and what we stand for. Another revealing recent example
has been the implosion of Rangers FC, previously Scotland's biggest and
most successful club. The freewheeling, free-spending years of David
Murray's ownership went unchallenged and unexamined in the media,
and even to this day, two years since the club went into first administration and then liquidation, massive questions remain about Murray, Craig
Whyte and Charles Green.

The Rangers saga spawned a sub-industry of blogs, websites and
campaigns, but the mainstream press, football journalists and football
authorities, showed themselves pre-administration unable and unwilling
to question power, its uses and abuses, the lessons of which are more fully
explored later. It was given a name pre-Rangers crash, 'succulent lamb
journalism', indicating a world of access, favours and over-familiarity
which prevented proper journalism. In today's world of powerful elites in
business, corporates and politics, these characteristics distort and demean
public life and democracy in areas more important than football.

In significant sections of Scottish society there is a problem with power
and a groupthink mentality which reinforces conformity. This has increasingly become incongruous and problematic as our society has become less
deferential and institutions like the Church of Scotland and Catholic Church
slowly retreat, but a legacy and tradition of the 'high Scotland' and previous
closed order remains.

The first step in challenging the above and its constraints and complacencies is to recognise the limits of permissible public debate. The second is to understand that if we want to be the radical, egalitarian, centre-left nation which many Scots seem to, 'the progressive beacon' of Alex Salmond's language, then we will not achieve this by reinforcing conservatism, caution and the pseudo-people's language of institutional Scotland.

The independence debate gives an opportunity to actively choose which road we want for Scotland's future. One is the route of populism, superficial soundbites and catchphrases which stay clear of any detail, and instead engage in a shadow war about caricature and a war of position between political opponents. That is seen in the examples of Johann Lamont's 'something for nothing' speech and the crude calculations of Labour and SNP on the bedroom tax.

The other is to open up a more honest, radical and reflective set of conversations about our nation's future, which touches on such subjects as who has power and voice. This would contain bold ambition and idealism, but would also negotiate the uncomfortable terrain of political choices and trade-offs, and the distributional consequences of our decisions.

Aiding this latter approach requires greater awareness to the limitations of Scotland's public debates and spaces, about who has voice and who does not, and the composition and values of 'the community of communicators'. The historic debate on independence, the slow, weakening of power of institutional Scotland, and the emergence of new platforms and social media, allows for the potential of a new opening, if it can be galvinised to not repeating and reproducing groupthink and existing orthodoxies. This prospect will be explored in concluding chapters of the book.

A socially just, egalitarian Scotland does not come about by being imprisoned in our past, and a mythical, imagined past at that. At some point we have to stop using the constructs of Thatcherism and New Labour as shibboleths which make us feel good and tell us what we are not, and put them back in the box of history. This is not an argument or apology for their philosophies, but against faux radicalism and the conservative grip and use of the past. As Jarvis Cocker wrote,

> We, the children of the echo, should get a life. We, the children of the echo, should know better. Time to move on.

CHAPTER TWELVE

# What went wrong with Professional Scotland?

'Why politics?'

'Power, Michael. Power. And don't let any politician fool you that they're in the business for any other reason. They may want power to do great and wonderful things for, mankind, but at the end of the day, the only reason to get into politics is because you want the power the other guy's got.'

HELEN LIDDELL, *Elite*, Century 1990

THE DYNAMICS OF Scottish public life, society and the networks of civil society, combined with the limited nature of Scottish democracy, have resulted historically in a disproportionate emphasis being placed in institutional Scotland. This has often been where Scots have defined their autonomy and part of their identities, aided by the expansion of Scottish administration and government from late Victorian times onwards.

The complex dynamics of institutional Scotland have made a huge contribution in the evolution of society to the present day: the maintenance of the 'holy trinity' of the Kirk, law and education post-union, the creation of territorial mechanisms of government with the Scottish Office (the first such territorial department within the UK), the expansion of the semi-corporate state in the 1920s and 1930s drawing business and trade unions together with government, and the huge social experiment of the post-war welfare state.

There is much to be positive about in this contribution historically, but we also have to concede its shortcomings: its lack of democracy, its paternalism, its collusion with elites and its perpetuation of a closed Scotland and a land where much of the public good was defined and run by 'committees of the great and good'.

Today institutional Scotland faces multiple challenges: the squeeze on public spending, popular expectations which assume incremental improvements, the decline in deference and trust, and increasing demographic pressures from an aging population to the relative decline of young people as a portion of the whole population.

An additional problem is how in institutional Scotland the political and policy classes undertake their work. This can be seen in the multiple and related crises of the policy classes, academia and government, which has a deleterious effect on how Scotland does its politics and policy.

## Who and What are the Policy Class?

In the post-war era the challenge to government, public bodies and the civil service in how it responded to some of the great issues of the day saw the rise of a professional class of experts, technocrats, administrators and managers. In Britain, this group came to be seen as a 'Fabian class' so named after the late 19th and early 20th century Fabian socialists, George Bernard Shaw, H.G. Wells and Sidney and Beatrice Webb, who believed in the power of rationalism and gradualism (as opposed to revolutionary socialism). They had an abiding faith in what they called 'permeation', by which they meant the slow changing of what had been reactionary elites into progressive ones by a kind of select entryism and persuasion.

A significant element of this professional class engaged in deliberating and making policy, for which there was an increased demand in post-war Britain and Scotland. There was an expansive welfare state that needed policy, processes and administrative structures: there was the NHS, nation-alised industries, a huge housing programme of slum clearance and house building, town planning and more. This was an era of grand design, ambi-tion and hope, and a whole new stratum of society saw themselves at the vanguard of a programme of ambitious social engineering which believed in limitless change: of human nature and indeed in places of creating a new kind of mankind free from want, need and ignorance.

This era has been tarnished and trashed repeatedly by reactionary right-wing opinion so it is important to recognise what they got right. The post-war era of Britain and Scotland from 1945 to 1959, from Clement Attlee's landslide Labour victory to Harold Macmillan's Tory third term and 'you've never had it so good' saw huge social advances. This was a time of rising living standards for most, full employment (for men), and a national home building programme which saw Labour and Tory outbid each other on how much they could build each year, with Macmillan winning promising 300,000 new homes a year (rising to a postwar high of 413,700 in 1968 comparing to 135,117 in 2012, the latter the lowest since the 1920s (Hicks and Allen, 1999; *Channel Four News*, 3 October 2013).

The same was true in Scotland. Scotland's cityscape, and in particular Glasgow and the West of the country, changed fundamentally. New Towns rose (East Kilbride 1947, Glenrothes 1948, Cumbernauld 1955), while in the wake of wartime Secretary of State for Scotland Tom Johnston's formation of the North of Scotland Hydro-Electric Board in 1943, a huge post-war expansion of hydro-electric stations followed, inspired by the achievements of the American New Deal (Miller, 2003).

David Gibson, Convener of Housing at Glasgow Corporation in the 1960s conveyed this spirit of can-do optimism when talking about a 'thrilling' prospect for 'the many thousands who are still yearning for a home'. He acknowledged that his style might be brusque at times but it was all for social gain and the betterment of the greater number, 'It may appear on occasion that I would offend against all good planning princi- ples, against open space and Green Belt principles – if I offend against against these it is only in seeking to avoid the continuing and unpardon- able offence that bad housing commits against human dignity' (Devine, 1999: 561). This was the language of social engineering and the high point of modernity, of believing that not only new living conditions, but a new society and new mankind, could be cast from their efforts.

Many of us had direct experience of this 'Brave New World' and its inherent positives. My parents moved to Ardler on the north-west corner of Dundee in 1968 to a council estate dominated by six tower blocks but also characterised by green spaces having been bought on the grounds of the former Downfield Golf Course which the council had purchased.

My parents' experience of Ardler was liberating and uplifting which matched that of many other working-class families. We moved from a small and antiquated flat in Dundonald Street behind Dens Road Market to a clean house with large rooms, central heating and built-in fixtures and fittings. In the period of my childhood, covering the 1970s, there was little crime and vandalism or unemployment, while the area was a mix of people from different backgrounds including teachers, shop owners and bank managers.

This was the positive of 'Labour Scotland'. My parents felt secure in employment and in their lives, and were optimistic about the future for themselves, their son and the country. Of course the country they felt an identification with was the UK, as 'Labour Scotland' very much saw itself as part of Britain.

There were shortcomings in this benign, caring world. All our houses had piped television provided through a special socket in the wall and sometimes the local rental company would switch the signal off late in the evening losing all channels. Part of the logic was the council's disapproval of anyone erecting an outside aerial and disrupting their neat, planned aesthetic. Eventually this began to breakdown in the mid to late 1970s, but at the same time the first large-scale public spending cuts occurred.

Slowly the atmosphere began to change, and the security and optimism of my parents and their friends and neighbours began to weaken.

There were significant limitations in the above vision of Britain and Scotland. For a start some of the issues which post-war planners faced were so long term and ingrained it proved difficult to tackle their origins: the historic underinvestment of British industry, the amateurish clubland nature of management (equally sent up with obstinate trade unions in the *I'm All Right Jack* 1959 film with Peter Sellers), while the British upper classes showed their disdain for the idea of making things, manufacturing and displayed a deep seated anti-industry prejudice.

Today's policy class is not shaped by a grand mission of making the better world, eradicating poverty and blight. Instead, it is mostly concerned with its own self-preservation, making sure in a more unpredictable world that it secures its place, status and funding, and engaging in empire building, turf wars and policing the boundaries of organisations and influence. Much of this is typical bureaucratic activity, but it takes away from wider social benefit and progress.

Increasingly, the policy class is dislocated from everyday lived life in how they see and understand the world. A good example of this is the way health and education policy is talked about and analysed. In numerous specialist studies in Scotland and the UK, these address what can be called the system level of policy, government and institutions and the official ecology of government papers, policies, announcements, aims and objectives, measurements and targets.

What this ignores is the interaction between this very specialised, rarified 'official' world and how people live, and the crucial importance of this exchange, i.e. the real impact of policy. This is in policyspeak, the ethnographic dimension of policy. Sadly it is much easier, less time consuming and challenging to look at interpreting the world through the narrow gaze of how systems and institutions understand things, but profoundly wrong.

An illustrative example of this insular, disconnected intelligence is provided by a report by NESTA (National Endowment for Science Technology and the Arts), a creation of the New Labour 'creative class' years, inappropriately titled *Radical Scotland* which addressed the issues of 'public sector reform' and 'innovation'. However, it did so from a remarkably narrow and distant place, commenting on and critiquing Scotland at the macro-level of outputs and measurements without having any engagement with the real Scotland.

The report ignored any connection with the everyday lived experience of Scots, whether public service users or workers, and instead, offered a snapshot of a far distant world from a policy class who literally could be describing another civilisation (Bunt et al, 2010). This accountancy style logic where change is about public sector productivity (itself a problematic term) and template consultancy speak is the kind of thinking which can practically be bought off the shelf (or think tank/research agency) and adapted to suit circumstances. It is part of the problem of how public policy is done, contributing to a circular reproduction and legitimisation of orthodoxy, and abdicating the role of government and others from leading, questioning and developing new policy and ideas. It is of course, on another level, costing government and public bodies, many millions of pounds, yet does not have a sterling record of achieving better policy and results, instead often used to validate a certain elite way of seeing the world.

## The Crisis of the Academic Class

The expansion of the higher education class, universities and colleges across the post-war era has come with similar pressures. The 1960s increase of higher education came in a period of economic growth and a belief in government as a force for public good, and knowledge and understanding as progressive, enlightening and noble, making the world a better place. At the same, the coming era of universities and colleges being reduced to a more instrumental role was heralded in the connection of higher education and economic growth, which was first pronounced by government in the Robbins Report on Higher Education in 1963.

The 1990s expansion of higher education was a very different one from the 1960s, initiated after a decade of high unemployment (and youth unemployment), and where a culture of managerial orthodoxies, knowledge as a commodity and something to be measured, and a business model of thinking about education, became the norm. Added to all this, the Labour Government of Tony Blair in 2004 introduced student tuition fees for England, Wales and Northern Ireland of £3,000 per year, which were raised by the Conservative-Lib Dem Government of David Cameron in 2010 to £9,000 per year, and which will inevitably rise in future years.

The state of modern academia in Scotland and the UK has become an increasingly diverse one with divergent and conflicting interests. Scotland's 19 universities and higher education institutions come together in the lobbying body Universities Scotland which sees the future as more market orientated, involving greater competition and fees. At a UK level, the self-appointed Russell Group of 'top universities' (24 institutions including two from Scotland: Edinburgh and Glasgow) push for greater freedom,

independence and the right to be able to charge above the current level of
£9k tuition fees. In 2010 two thirds of all UK university research monies
were awarded to Russell Group institutions.

Allowing for the above differences it is possible to identify some common
characteristics about Scottish academia in relation to policy and how it
engages with government and wider social concerns. There is a seismic
disconnection between academia and the outside world, seen in the removal
of most academics from public policy deliberations and debates which
have a relevance to the Scotland outside academia and practical policy.

Scotland's small academic community even in devolved areas such as
health and education are mostly not fully engaged in policy debates relevant to the life of the nation. Instead, they are being influenced not by the
external drivers of how better health and education can be identified and
become policy solutions, but by the internal drivers of management speak,
measurement and career protection and advancement. There are exceptions in this, which will be acknowledged below, but for the best part
academics have become overt specialists, defenders of a very narrow range
of intelligence and work, and part of a Weberian style iron cage bureaucracy. Some respected academics such as Patrick Dunleavy of the LSE and
Iain McLean of Oxford University have felt they had enough security and
seniority to be able to criticise the Research Exercise Framework (REF).
Dunleavy sees this as contributing to the commodification of knowledge
and related to the widely discredited New Public Management (NPM), which
arose in the 1980s in relation to a marketised model of public services
(LSE Blog, 10 June 2011).

Contemporary academia is filled with the jargon talk of 'knowledge
exchange' and 'knowledge transfer', the former now used more regularly
than the latter, and the catch-all term of 'impact'. Everything in how these
UK wide systems operate in 'the knowledge union' that is the United
Kingdom mitigates against any real, lasting sense of 'impact'. Then there is
the emergence and over-concentration on what is called STEM intelligence
– meaning science, technology, engineering and mathematics – which has
research and status funding priority over other disciplines, and promoted
by such august bodies as the Royal Society of Edinburgh.

There are exceptions both individually and as institutional clusters.
These include bodies such as the Fraser of Allander Institute at Strathclyde
University, the Centre for Cultural Policy Research at Glasgow University,
and the Glasgow Centre for Population Health, which has pioneered work
on health inequalities and 'the Glasgow effect', more of which later. However,
these organisations work in an institutional culture which mitigates against

the development of successful policy, research and work, whereas it is near-nigh impossible for one body to develop a different means of policy innovation and engagement.

## What has happened to Government?

Government itself has played a central role in this situation coming to pass. It has been a leading player in the rise of technocratic, managerialist specialisms, first in the immediate post-war era, then again in the 1960s, and subsequently in the 1980s and onward. It has presided over several different waves of expert knows best redesigning policy phases: the Brave New World of 1945, the white heat of technology of the 1960s, and the economic determinism of the 1980s onwards.

The role of government today has changed because of this, how it sees itself and the external world. First, there is the language that government uses in its pronouncements and engagements with other public and professional groups. There has been over the post-war era an incremental rise in jargon-laden and obscurantist terminology, often imported from the latest buzzwords from the US government, think tanks or policy entrepreneurs. Thus, we have the invoking of words and concepts such as 'co-production' (a big favourite with New Labour in its early days in office but having a second life currently in Scotland), 'nudge' (big with the Cameron Conservatives who admire the idea of behaviour management), 'asset based approaches' (a particular in-term of the former Chief Medical Officer Harry Burns), and ubiquitous terms which can be utilised in every occasion such as 'world-class' and 'stepchange'.

Many of these are advocated by public bodies that want to give the impression they are at the cutting edge of the latest fads. The reality is more prosaic. There is an increasing tendency of the policy class towards conformity and groupthink, and because of this in terms of funding and status, the need to give the impression to other influencer groups that you are on the inside and part of the in-class. This is part of the phenomenon of an insider language (with a concomitant insider thinking) of the new class, many of whom are on the public payroll and work in public bodies, which has given succour to an outlook which is about corporate interests and a mantra about Scotland and the world economy, which is deeply unattractive and unsustainable.

This leads to the situation of people using words of which they have no real idea of their meaning, talking sentences filled with jargon, and demeaning and distorting the English language. More seriously, as explored more fully in the next chapter is that numerous government departments and public bodies, end up articulating a worldview and set of values which are profoundly troubling: are reactionary, about winners and the global elite and not about tackling some of the issues about power and voice.

One lesson of the Creative Scotland controversy and its aftermath at the end of 2012 was the insight it offered into the expectations and language used in the artistic community. Despite the campaign of leading cultural figures which saw the removal of the Chief Executive, there is in a small community a desire to be part of an insider group. This manifests itself in a near-complete closed loop set of deliberations, whereby Creative Scotland set out a mission statement, people looking for funding tell funders what they want to hear, and then Creative Scotland think they are being informed by artistic and cultural practice.

This produces a cycle of conformity and dependency and cultural organisations in this case adopting the official, prescribed language, often without understanding or believing in it. This is a problem for everyone involved in that such bodies fail to understand the need to articulate the values they represent in their work and want to see embodied in their external relationships. It is a problem for bodies such as Creative Scotland, for how are they to understand and to develop appropriately if they are fed back what people think they want to hear?

This closed loop begs the question about where the original ideas, dissent and innovation come from in such a set of exchanges. Despite the Creative Scotland stramash, the fundamentals of this set of relationships have not been addressed. This touches on a wider truth about public sector development and reform, not aided by some of the silo based, inward looking influences which act as a restraint on how public services are more change orientated, properly focused and outwardly directed. Such characteristics should not be equated with some kind of Thatcherisation of the public service, for without this sort of intelligence and reflection too often public services become guardians of those who work for them, and fail those who need them most.

There is a longer perspective to this tale. The Scottish Arts Council was founded in 1967, emerging from the Scottish Committee of the Arts Council of Great Britain. In the first 30 years of its existence from 1967 to 1997, there was not one parliamentary question, debate or inquiry: so much for parliamentary accountability and scrutiny of the Scottish Office pre-devolution.

This began to change post-1997, with preparations for setting up the Scottish Parliament and the institutional furniture and assumptions shifting.

Thus, in 1998, a Scottish Arts Council decision to withdraw funding from Wildcat Theatre Company produces a Scottish Affairs Select Committee inquiry with its then director, Shona Reid, and chair, Magnus Linklater, finding themselves in uncharted waters of having to answer in public for a decision they have taken with public monies. Both left shortly after. This example underlines the absence of democratic accountability pre-Parliament, and that we are now in an age of transition, where these old methods no longer work, but we are still finding our way, hence some of the tensions in the Creative Scotland controversy.

## The Place of the Professional Classes

The professional classes in Scotland and the UK were once filled with a sense of near limitless possibility about the positive changes which they could be at the helm of. There was a belief for much of the 20th century that the limitations on human life and opportunity could be lifted, and a more equal, fairer version of society brought into existence.

This would have been of course a society made in the shape and name of the professional classes from health and education experts, to town planners, architects and designers and local government senior staff. It would have been profoundly rational, tidy and well-ordered, with each individual knowing their place and working to the greater good. One of the many fascinating Scottish public information films made after the Second World War extolling this vision talked of the positives of 'planned freedom', which was the mantra of the age, but also a very Scottish concept: freedom, but for a greater, specified purpose.

That benign, structured world never fully came into existence, and instead a sense of retreat emerged in this class from the ideals of enlightened wisdom and authority. In its place, there has emerged a sense of defeatism, disappointment and pessimism in such professional groups. This has been driven by what are perceived as the failure of their social experiments from New Towns to social work, but also by the related Conservative and right-wing attack on the progressive credentials of such professions being a mask for protecting their self-interests. At the same time many members of the public have become less unquestioning and more challenging of various elites and professions who people believe have a direct day to day impact on their lives, and find the once insufferable paternalism and know-all attitudes something they no longer have to resign themselves to putting up with.

However, this professional class sense of disappointment should be understood. Many professionals now feel they have a reduced status in the eyes of many, but perhaps even more importantly, they feel let down by the actions and role of many of the people. By this, some professionals are of the view that the public have failed in what was previously a social contract between the two, professionals and public. In this the professionals were committed to a social project of making society better, fairer, more ordered, cleaner and healthier, and the people would respond by being grateful and moderating their behaviour in recognition of new public services and public policy.

The post-war era did not work out in this prescribed way with most of the social problems proving more endemic and deeply rooted. Very few professionals will articulate this in public, but with their role and status under more scrutiny, the great social experiments of post-1945 having run their course, and people inclined to be less benign and malleable, something has shifted. In private discussions, senior professionals will admit their disappointment and even anger at what some of them see as the lack of gratitude of the public.

Several years ago I ran a discussion with senior council officials of one of Scotland's local authorities. When exploring a particularly challenging key policy issue which was controversial and lacked public support, I asked the officials what they would do to overcome this, and more than one of them responded in near-uniform chorus and said 'Fuck the public then'. Basically, they revealed that public reticence had pushed them close to the end of their tether, and articulated an anger and resentment which, it appeared, they regularly expressed to each other in private.

The veneer of respectability about much of what passes for public discussion in Scottish institutional life often masks much more deep seated, even primordial feelings of rage, emotion and hurt. It overlaps with what has been called by others not in print as 'a zone of politeness' by which there is a cover and ethos of being well mannered, never losing your cool or talking in a manner which reveals if you are personally annoyed. While understandable to an extent, these parameters prevent a greater awareness of what professional groups think and what motivates them, and the arc from the great post-war hopes to where we sit today.

## After Disillusion: A New Social Contract for Professionals

The longer-term consequences of this professional pessimism remains to be seen. It is now commonplace and fashionable to knock the kind of enlightened optimism that previously built the welfare state and NHS, and say that this now means the current disdain of any radical social change will forever be the dominant outlook. This is neither attractive nor necessarily true.

There is in the current disposition in professional opinions a bewilderment, lack of confidence in people and their capacity to make informed choices, and perhaps most strongly, an inability to let go. Where this goes throws up numerous different scenarios. One option is the continuation of reactionary social engineering as we witness in the UK and US, which in the former has seen the championing by the Conservative-led Government of doctrinaire welfare proposals such as the bedroom tax. These are proposals championed on the grounds of 'fairness', given a ridiculous Orwellian name, 'the spare room subsidy' and which are disproportionately hitting disabled people. Six months into the bedroom tax, Scottish local authorities made up eight of the top twenty areas in the UK with the most people affected and put into arrears by this measure. The most hit areas in Scotland with the percentage of people in arrears as a portion of those affected was: Clackmannanshire 67 per cent, Dundee 47 per cent, North Lanarkshire 46 per cent, South Lanarkshire 45 per cent and Edinburgh 45 per cent (TUC, 19 September 2013).

Such policies are the consequence of professional dislocation and the environment created by the nurturing of new right thinking and policies. It is a frightening insight into what kind of society would be created if this set of circumstances are allowed to continue. In short, the end point would be a UK with a nightwatchman state meaning minimal government, little publically owned and controlled public services, punitive welfare and a Dickensian society.

British progressive opinion has failed to mount an adequate defence against such a challenge and instead has appeased and colluded with it. This is after all one of the lessons of the New Labour era, which is a more complex period than often simplistic interpretations of the left present, but which undoubtedly at its Blair-Brown dual monarchy centre saw Britain as a 'conservative country' and thus one where those forces needed to be accommodated and fed.

An alternative path has to start from recognising the shortcomings and pitfalls of the present and that it is unsustainable in the future. Yet it has to understand the important role that professional groups play in a developed society and the potential they have for aiding and supporting social change. Are we really going to buy into the conventional wisdom of cynicism which says because there were huge problems in the immediate post-1945 and 1960s periods, which we should give up? That we should stop asking that professionals contribute to making a better, fairer world, challenging inequality and privilege and engaging in continuous self-criticism and self-improvement?

A new social contract for professional groups, which invites them to be part of a bigger, bolder national project, tackling some of the huge issues of Scottish society is required. This needs a different model of professionalism from the Fabian era of paternalism or new right inspired era of retreat, and draws from this experience, recognises the harm caused by the 'missing Scotland', and sets out to draw together society.

Once upon a time social workers, teachers and even some lawyers had radical aspirations and an intent to contribute to challenging injustice and inequality. No more can that be said of any significant sections of most professional bodies. The state of Scottish society requires that such forces shift from their current pessimism and detachment to one of active engagement and optimism. This necessitates considering the formation of initiatives such as Social Workers for a New Scotland and Teachers for Self-Determination, which put their professional responsibilities centre-stage in how we overcome the huge challenges that Scotland faces.

These groups would address how we can transcend the limited democracy of modern Scotland which aids cynicism and defeatism, and contribute to a radical public culture and professionalism. One of the central features of this would be how we bring up and nurture Scotland's children, so many of whom live in poverty and blighted lives, and how we support and care for disadvantaged children and their families. If the Scotland many of us aspire to is about anything it is reaching out to our children who the current status quo so conspicuously fails, and acting from the premise that this is the responsibility of all of us. Starting from this, a particular onus falls on the professions, to lead, inspire and contribute to mending a society which has left so many behind and seemed to give up on them.

This entails a change in institutional Scotland, in the public, private and voluntary sectors, and the rest of us. It has to have a new leadership culture and an esprit de corps which makes it one of its central aims to overcome the divisions of the 'missing Scotland', inequality and the generations of learned helplessness which have been built up, and which does this in a partnership between professionals and the people.

This would involve an ethos of leadership very different from traditional professional Scotland, the consultant class, or the new right radicals. It would challenge the non-leadership evident in too many public bodies which hide behind status and process, as well as the defeatism evident in parts of the professional classes. Instead, it would draw on ideas of adaptive, dispersed leadership, the importance of supporting emotional intelligence and organisational justice, and champion the intermediate class of leaders who already show by example how to embody values, character and change.

What this would even begin to look like is one of the great questions of Scotland which requires thinking and answering, and which I will attempt to offer some thoughts on in the concluding chapters. One fundamental in this is that such an approach has to deal with the terrain of Scotland's limited democracy and unspace and the terrain of values, voice and vessels. Scotland's professional classes cannot adopt new thinking and practices in isolation; they have to be part of a great reforming movement of Scottish society.

# CHAPTER THIRTEEN

# The Emergence of 'the Third Scotland': Values, Voice and Vessels

What are a policy's empathetic consequences – how does it affect all that we are connected to? How does it affect the natural world? Does it sustain life, or does it harm life? How am I personally connected to its consequences, as a human being? What, if anything, makes it beautiful, healthful, enjoyable, fulfilling? What causal system does it fit into? How will it affect future generations? Is it fair and does it make us more free? Will it lift spirits, and will we find awe in it?

GEORGE LAKOFF, *The Political Brain: A Cognitive Scientist's Guide to your Brain and its Politics*, Penguin 2009

In short, Mr Parlabane, there is no place for you here in the future. This is the new Scotland, a new country, with new standards and a new morality. I must not allow it or its institutions – nascent and ancient alike – to be disparaged and prejudiced by the diseased mind of a wee shite like you. For this reason, I order that you be taken from this court, henceforth to a place of confinement, there to dwell in perpetual fear of being chibbed and humped by rabid schemies.

CHRISTOPHER BROOKMYRE, *Boiling a Frog*, Little, Brown and Company 2000

One of the critical dimensions in the public life of Scotland (along with most of the West) is the challenging question of what is called agency, by which is meant collective agents or bodies that people see themselves in, feel they own, and have a sense that they can bring about wider change through.

## *The Retreat of Traditional Politics and Institutions*

This process has increasingly come to the fore because of the hollowing out and decline of previous bodies and institutions which acted as agents of social and political change. Scotland has witnessed these last 30 years the retreat of trade unions who have declined from well over half the workforce at the end of the '70s to under a third today (which is still significantly ahead of the UK figure of one-fifth). The character of Scottish trade union membership (as with UK) is of an aging, public sector work-force, with little presence in the growing parts of the economy.

Then there is the long withering of the Church of Scotland and Catholic Church memberships. The Kirk's high point in members was 1955, the same year of the Scottish Tories' Indian Summer when the party won over half the Scots vote. This was a deferential, ordered, patrician society, one of compassion, but punitive authority, of the welfare state, but built on the legacy and gains of Empire and the British imperial project.

There is a direct link between the decline of the Catholic Church in numbers and religious observance, and the emergence of megaphone diplomacy by leading Catholics such as Cardinal Winning and Keith O'Brien on matters of sexuality, the family and ethics. The two leading religious bodies acted as a kind of societal 'Old Firm' where at their peak they morally policed their own respective closed communities. This after all was how the historian Bob Crampsey interpreted the practice of the football equivalent from its outset in the early 20th century. Fortunately, the church version of this has steadily weakened, which is more than can be said for the football rivalry.

Finally, we come to the state of the political parties. The Scottish Labour Party is in a shrunken, atrophied state, devoid of energy and purpose; its version of 'Labour Scotland' long moribund and with the party barely understanding that this requires a break with the past and a completely different politics.

The Scottish National Party's membership has risen in the last decade under the second period of Salmond leadership (more than trebling but from a very low base historically), but is still small compared to the days of mass parties. An SNP membership of over 25,000 make it by far the biggest party in Scotland, but does not compare with the post-Hamilton honeymoon the SNP enjoyed when Winnie Ewing caused an electoral earthquake with her 1967 by-election victory, and within a year the SNP had 120,000 members (most of whom disappeared within a year or two of the by-election).

However, all Scotland's political party memberships would not be that sizeable a spectrum of Scottish society, as it represents less than one per cent of the whole population. Put this in proper perspective. Adding all of the mainstream parties in the Scottish Parliament, along with the SSP/Solidarity and UKIP and the BNP, would not equate to the full houses regularly achieved at Ibrox as Rangers FC stormed away with the Division Three title in 2012–13. And just to underline the point: this comparison is overly favourable to the political parties as it maximises their appeal (counting many inactive and lapsed members), while understating the global reach and appeal of Rangers.

Britain's governing party, the Conservatives, as recently as 1992, only a political generation ago, had by far the biggest membership in Scotland at 35,000, then nearly twice their nearest challengers, Labour. Now the party that says its whole *raison d'être* is the union, as well as having only one Westminster MP has a membership which is the equivalent of an average Motherwell FC home gate. The Scots Tories in the spate of 20 years have begun to disappear from the face of Scotland, from our streets, towns and communities, with the exception of a few isolated pockets of local government bravely holding out against all the odds.

The UK Tories are facing a similar evaporation, with towards the end of 2013, on favourable estimates, a mere 134,000 members, which has more than halved since David Cameron became leader (*The Independent*, 18 September 2013). So maybe the Scots Tories fate is a harbinger to come for the UK party – one of no members, few foot soldiers and funded by the City and offshore Hedge Funds. Such a politics of elites, privilege and power could produce an even more right-wing, free market determinist politics which will distort British politics, and prove even more unpalatable to most of Scotland.

There is an assumption across large sectors of Scotland, despite the above, that collectively as a society we know how to do political and social change. This viewpoint fails to account for the collapse of the above three pillars: trade unions, churches, and political parties. It is barely aware that it is living off the dwindling legacy of past generations and their efforts; citing and referencing each of the three without recognising their diminished existence. This is given validation and continued legitimacy by the modern mantras which make many Scots (at least the politically engaged) feel good about themselves. That is we don't vote for the Tories, didn't like Thatcher, and rejected the values and ideas of Thatcherism; we are a land opposed to permissive individualism and greed and hold true to our centre-left, progressive values.

Unfortunately this assertion does not stand up to any great scrutiny. Change does not come solely from institutional Scotland and enlightened authority. Nor does it come from the myths and ideology of 'civic Scotland'. Nor does it come from ideas being floated on their own, isolated from wider social forces. Instead, change comes from a crucial combination of three factors, values, vessels and voices.

## The Importance of Values

Each of the three will be examined in turn starting with values. Values matter and inform what characterises public life, what we do, how we interpret it, our actions, behaviours and the wider outcomes of society.

There is a prevailing assumption in much of Scotland that the values of our society and institutions are good values; that we have progressive, inclusive values which inform policy, practice and politics, and that we have collectively taken a positive decision to turn our back on the free market vandals gathered at the border.

This perspective is an anchor for many Scottish attitudes in policy, ideas and politics. It aids us being self-congratulatory and to avoid self-reflection on some of the less comfortable truths about Scottish society. And importantly, it externalises most of our challenges and problems: they are massed over the border in the British state and political parties and the dominance of market determinism in them. This doesn't do us any good in Scotland for it is another variant of believing our own myths and folklore that have arisen these last few decades: that we are so progressive, inclusive and egalitarian, and have rejected the pseudo-free market dogma of down south.

In this conjecture, significant parts of public life and agencies find it comfortable to have a near complete absence of self-examination, self-criticism and reflection on the limits of current practices. Numerous groups of professionals I have worked with over the years, when pushed in the intimacy of exchange and challenge, find it difficult to leave their 'official story'. They may even know in part some of their shortcomings, or that they have to embrace a corporate language and set of values they feel no affinity with, but their identities are so wound up in it that they cannot let it fully go or openly criticise it. Sometimes pointing this out leads to interesting observations. At one recent discussion when I brought up the subject of values, one specialist consultant in the area dismissed it with the claim, 'There you go. Always the purist', while a senior manager said, 'Why do we need to talk about this?' This tells us something about public life and the cultures of some of our leading organisations.

An example can be found in the ripples which emerged from the Creative Scotland controversy of 2012 which saw two of its leading figures go and the arts and cultural community up in arms about the practices of the public body. At the time Chief Executive Andrew Dixon left, two papers were presented to the Board on how the body understood its public mission and remit. Speaking to people about this crisis as it evolved, some did not feel that Creative Scotland's impasse was about ideology and values, but about personnel and practice. Thus some of the central figures involved saw the crisis over with the two senior staff removed. One told me that the Board papers represented, 'the end of Creative Scotland and its values as we have known them' and 'the reassertion of a different set of values'. Normal service would be resumed with the 'good guys' victorious and the villains vanquished.

This revealing observation glosses over the reality that the battle over Creative Scotland was animated by ideology and values. This was about the Scottish version of 'creative Britain', and the idea of creativity, innovation and the arts as the embodiments of the class of global winners, instrumentality, economic policy which has no political economy, and the branding, bland monoculture worldview which reached its apex in the New Labour era.

Philip Schlesinger, Director of the Centre for Cultural Policy Research at Glasgow University in charting the above odyssey observed that, 'The Blairites were the first major populisers of the creative industries thinking that has now circled the globe' (2013: 276). Within this is an ideological interpretation of the world centred on a belief in the boom times of a different kind of capitalist economy, 'the knowledge economy', requiring skills, multi-tasking and talent. This draws from American academic Richard Florida and his much cited book, *The Rise of the Creative Class* (2003) which emphasises the characteristics of urban clusters to aid innovation, and which was embraced by New Labour, and its assorted cheerleaders, the British Council, NESTA and Design Council, and north of the border, Scottish Enterprise and Creative Scotland. A set of ideas, this was a validation of the good economic times, and while it has circled the world and become embraced by UNESCO, this deeply Anglo-American hyperbole has offered no convincing explanation of how it fits into the world post-bubble, post-crash. And yet it still survives.

Returning to our example, it served the interests of both sides to not portray the Creative Scotland episode as about ideology and values. The staff of the body knew as anyone in public life does that the corporatisation of language and its 'creative class' mindset does not win hearts and minds and is the adopted outlook of a narrow insider class in the UK and globally who employ an ideological Esperanto – a vocabulary with its own key jargon words which makes it clear they are part of the new elect.

The artists and writers who choose to mount a campaign of resistance had a variety of views, with some no doubt seeing ideology as part of this (and any alliance running from writer James Kelman to composer James

MacMillan has many shades). But for the most part, publically and privately, they choose the ground of how Creative Scotland operated in practice, and its notion of business models and art as investment, writing in their open letter to the body that, 'This is not about money' and instead was 'about management' (BBC *News Scotland*, 9 October 2012). This was an evasion of the deeper dynamics, namely, the ideology and worldview which lay behind all of these organisational actions.

The wider lessons from the above is that the ideas which have so distorted and weakened public service and the idea of the public good in England are not completely alien to us or external. They are already rooted in Scotland, deep in the public sector, in outsourcing, consultancy speak and practice, and the long-term decline of the traditional way of delivering public services.

Our collective failure to understand that this is a fundamental battle of values hinders us in the extreme. Public services all across Scotland are being remade by this, overtly outsourced and fragmented and given over to groups such as Serco and G4S, while even more perniciously and widely, existing parts of our public services give over their internal mandate to this unappealing view of the world. The defence against this cannot be to retreat to the old public services model of service and duty which was paternalist and patronising. Nor is it possible to ignore the terrain of values and just fight over practice and process; instead the contest and articulation of ideas has to be brought into the light and become explicit.

A penetrating study by Tom Crompton for Oxfam UK addressed some of these fundamentals – namely how do we nurture and implement the appropriate values to aid social change. He identified two sets of values – intrinsic or self-transcendent values and extrinsic or self-enhancing values: 'Intrinsic values are associated with concern about bigger-than-self problems' while 'Extrinsic values... are associated with lower levels of concern about bigger-than-self problems...' (2010: 10). Crompton believes that the majority of people in the UK hold intrinsic values and think them more important than extrinsic values. He also states that, 'There is no such thing as value-neutral policy' (2010: 13), an obvious truism and a challenge to parts of the mainstream policy world. Addressing values though is one only part of how social change become real.

## The Power of Voice(s)

The notion of voice is critical to understanding the dynamics of public life. This is about a number of dimensions: addressing the language and underlying philosophies of how people speak and interact, and challenging the increasing disembodied language of the consultant class, experts and the professional classes.

Voice though is about something much more far-reaching and important which is explored on Albert O. Hirschman's book, *Exit, Voice and Loyalty* (1970) on the idea of collective voice and power which was referenced in the introductory chapter. Hirschman posits that traditionally the left have focused on the idea of loyalty based on class and solidarity, whereas the right has talked of exit focused on consumer behaviour and individualism. Both have tended to downplay the potential of voice, because it is so powerful and unpredictable, and potentially does not necessarily correspond to their didactic views of human nature and behaviour: in one we are all co-operative, in the other selfish.

Hirschman's concept of voice sits with MacKenzie's 'community of communicators' and Deutsch's 'marked gaps' in public life. It can add insight and understanding into who has and does not have voice, status and influence in any situation or conversation, and who is included and who is excluded.

The Scots have a propensity in public and professional contexts and discussions to be oblivious to who is included and even more so who is excluded. There is a mirage or mood music of inclusiveness, and a token reference at best to those who are disadvantaged or living in challenging circumstances, but it rarely moves further forward. Thus numerous MPs and MSPs cite that they are speaking up for that dread term 'hardworking families' and occasionally will mention 'those who are struggling or poor', particularly in relation to welfare reform and such issues as the bedroom tax.

This Scots myth of connectedness and inclusion is what I have called the complete absence of any interest in 'relational space'. By this I mean an awareness and acknowledgement of who is involved in an exchange, conversation or relationship, the dynamics of power, and who has status and why, and who is missing and why.

Andrew Marr, the broadcaster and quasi-pillar of the British establishment, talking about the flowering of ideas in Edinburgh during the Scottish Enlightenment said in an exchange with Andrew O'Hagan on radio, 'all Edinburgh was involved in the discussions of the Scottish Enlightenment' which brought forth no challenge or counter-argument (BBC *Start the Week*, 2 May 2001). It is a comment which reveals a complete historical ignorance of the age he was invoking, of class, gender and profession. What Marr of course meant was that 'all Edinburgh' that mattered – a minute slice of the population – that had status, respect and money had a say which is a very different matter.

This failure to grasp the importance of 'relational space' is a manifestation of Scotland's sense of itself as this deeply egalitarian society with few barriers, hierarchy or class distinctions. This attitude can be seen as widely prevalent in many comments on the independence referendum, where people's own views become wish-fulfillment and are then translated into statements about the state of the nation. One amongst many examples was from the writer and musician Pat Kane who reflected that with one year to the referendum, 'This nation is in conversation' (*The Guardian*, 15 September 2013). It is only five words but they are five troubling words, written with hope and spirit and belief that we can change Scotland. Yet given this was in a newspaper piece where Pat had the space to explore, qualify and situate his remarks in understanding who is in conversation and who isn't, were illuminating.

Telling ourselves comforting stories about our society and democracy, and not talking openly about our truncated state of limited democracy or the weak nature of society for those most vulnerable, does not aid change. It only aids unrealistic expectations, disappointment, and the continuation of the status quo.

Therefore the idea and practice of voice matters as does posing it as a direct counterpoint to the conventional left and right ways of doing politics and society, emphasising class and solidarity or consumerism and individualism. Human beings are more than these caricatures, and Hirschman writing at the end of the 1960s was an acute enough observer to note that the main future challenge would come not from the Berkeley new left, but the emerging new right who would take the notions of 'exit' and hyper-individualism to destruction.

This is part of the context of searching for and nurturing Scottish voice and voices today: the retreat and diminishing of the left, and the rise of the market determinist view of the world. Just because Scotland is far less down the road to the latter than the UK, while offering us an opportunity, does not mean we can be completely sanguine, or see the solution in reflating and buying into old leftist rhetoric and hopes whether around Labour or independence. The idea of voice means noticing the narrow bandwidth of public life and conversations, reflecting on the 'missing Scotland', and changing how we think about public services, society and how politics and social change happens. But to even begin to do this requires a third ingredient along with values and voice.

## The Third Dimension: The Need for Vessels

Finally, we come to the terrain of vessels. This is about a sense of collective agency which people feel they have created, in which they have a sense of confidence and ownership, and can see themselves and their views represented and articulated in the DNA, ethos and day to day practices. It is about places, spaces and bodies where people can find their genuine voice, rather than have to speak through the codes and rituals of the system, and where they can sense that their values are being nurtured and nourished, not tokenistically presented by an organisation talking one way to people, and another way to the powers that be, whether politicians or businesses.

Once people felt confidence in political parties, trade unions and churches, but for the vast majority of people, this is no longer the case. Trade unions and churches still have community footprints in places and on specific occasions or issues a wider voice which will be heard in public, but they are increasingly living off their past reputations and mandates. In relation to trade unions and the increasingly fragile, fragmented and anxious world of work this is not a positive development, and it can be observed that the retreat from political and civic activism encourages cynicism and the belief that politics is a closed set of elite conversations, and this become a vicious cycle. Taking Hirschman's ideas of 'Exit, Voice and Loyalty', there has been across two generations, a mass exit from the traditional institutions of how to do social change which has left large acres of public life in the hands of professional interest groups.

How do people create and own vessels in which they recognise themselves and their interests? First, such bodies cannot be part of the system. They cannot be offshoots of government, the corporate sector of the professionalised voluntary sector. Second, they cannot depend on their existence and funding from such bodies, and cannot be at the beck and call of the state or business. It isn't possible to set up a Community Empowerment Network and have it funded by BT Scotland; that changes everything about ethos, values and ownership. Third, it has to develop a careful balancing act: not part of the state, or beholden to it, but engaging with it as an independent entity. Fourth, in practice, incorporation or oppositionalism has to be equally avoided; society, the nature of the state and civil society are more complex than such one-dimensional approaches.

There are already examples of initiatives which have successful found a sense of the three Vs: values, voice and vessels, and negotiated the above. One would be London Citizens which began life as the East London

Citizens Organisation (TELCO) and then spread city-wide at a community activist level, beginning in trade union and church groups. It has developed into an entity with a genuine, powerful voice listened to and respected by politicians from Gordon Brown when Prime Minister to Boris Johnson as Mayor of London.

An attempt was made a few years ago to set up a Scottish Citizens equivalent drawing from and with the support of London Citizens, but it failed for reasons unclear. One possible contributory factor was that London Citizens didn't fully understand that Scotland was different, and another may have been that the Scottish initiative was not sufficiently grass roots led, instead developed at the leadership level of the churches, STUC and SCVO. Whatever the reasons, that failure was unfortunate and the terrain of the idea, of a Scottish Citizens or something similar, is one worth revisiting.

Bringing these three dimensions together: values, voice and vessels, entails thinking and acting differently, looking at what passes for public life, dialogue and conversation, and the issues of who has a mandate and mission to speak or act on a subject. It is not about a dry exercise in evaluating what happens already and finding it inadequate, or posing what occurs versus some utopian idealised participatory democracy. Instead, it is about noting the truncated democracy we live in and the compromised nature of much of the public realm. From this we need to have an understanding of ideology (either having one, its absence, or that of others), the power of voice and the damage of the silences and omissions of so much of life, and the need for all of this to be about more than talking but about doing: a practice of social change.

## Beginning to Do Social Change Differently

What is missing in Scottish debates is an awareness of how to advance and nurture social change, and connected to this, build alliances and movements, and create new forms of voice. These would amount to developing an embryonic ecology of self-government, which shows people self-organising, mobilising and resourcing their own lives and priorities, leading to a culture and practice of self-determination. Such an approach would be very different from the paternalism, statism and control managerialism which has been the predicable diet on offer from our mainstream politics and most of institutional Scotland.

Fortunately there are increasing signs that the character of this benign authority, managed and cossetted society will not remain unchallenged into the near-future. Scotland is not immune from wider trends seen across the entire West and is as influenced by the crisis of authority and institutions, the decline in deference, and loss of trust in professional expertise. Now this may take longer to find form and shape in Scotland, but is already evident, and could potentially emerge with a very different voice compared to the embrace of hyper-individualism and corporate capture which have so shaped the last three decades of Anglo-American capitalism.

Another future dynamic will be 'the lost decade' of the UK economically with its resultant austerity and pressures on public spending and choices. This is going to open up a debate about expectations, demands and what is sustainable, and in particular, the distributional consequences of public policy. Scotland did in the first decade of devolution conspicuously avoid having such a debate, but more difficult financial times which will come post-independence vote, irrespective of the result, may prove to be the catalyst for this long overdue reflection.

There has been a range of welcome interventions, creations and happenings aided by the spur of the long route to the 2014 independence vote. These include fuzzy, messy, disputatious spaces which have increasingly challenged the sanctioned version of 'civic Scotland' and 'the official story' of mainstream authority. This can be seen in such activities as the Radical Independence Campaign (RIC), the Jimmy Reid Foundation, the Poverty Alliance's Poverty Assemblies, and groups such as National Collective.

Each of the above have created spaces and places which have sat outside institutional Scotland, not being about access to power and insider status, and have brought people together in a genuine and mostly uncontrolled or unorchestrated way. There is also something interesting in the use of the word 'assembly' in the work of the Poverty Alliance; it seeming to be that the system does top down expert initiatives such as endless Commissions (Christie Commission, COSLA Commission on Local Democracy etc., to the point we could imagine a Scottish Government Commission on Commissions). 'Assembly' which was also invoked by a recent independently planned, bottom up Citizen's Assembly conveys cultivating, gathering and soft power. It offers the intention of a very different approach.

## *The Importance of 'the Third Scotland'*

These approaches are part of what I call 'third Scotland': the activities and contributions of a range of people who don't easily fit into the boxes of institutional life. One characteristic of them being a 'third Scotland' is that one restricting version of the independence debate between Yes and

No is between two competing elites and two establishments. There is the old 'Labour Scotland' version, slightly feeling sorry for itself, put out of power and place, and tarnished and not quite sure how to get its act back on the road. Then there is the new SNP Scotland, which is all filled with ambition, drive and motivation, bright, shiny and sensing possibilities, but still at its heart an establishment, albeit a new one. That seems a very constricted choice: between two camps and two elites, and independence apart, not that different visions of society.

'Third Scotland' is not establishment based or focused, and while it is not perfect or with all the answers, aided by the independence referendum it has seen a welcome unleashing of activity and energy. It is not based in institutional settings or anchored in a relationship of funding or dependency on the state or corporates. People have made it happen because they wanted to: there is an element of DIY Scotland to some of this, and of a practical culture of self-determination evolving and becoming something interesting and different.

There are all sorts of limitations however. The actual numbers involved are small, resources are scarce, and most of these activities involve self-selecting people. Groups such as the Radical Independence Campaign (RIC) also contain an unreflective, unrealistic leftist nostalgia which is not conducive to the politics of 21st century Scotland (or anywhere in the West for that matter). I have in previous chapters explored the terrain of this left revivalism, but there are many positives in what is happening which may have a long-term significance.

The narrow bandwidth of large parts of 'official Scotland', its complacencies and orthodoxies are being scrutinised and found wanting. A new generation of twentysomething activists who have seen their parents and their own education shaped by marketeer and consultant language where everything is reduced to brands, products and a spurious, contrived 'choice', have said in small but growing numbers, that they want more. Not more of the same; but a very different kind of life, politics and society.

Then there are the emergence of new voices and opinions in public life which is a challenge to the generational gridlock and society of elders which Scotland seems to have been permanently stuck in these last few decades. There is a gender dimension to this, with some of the male only exclusion zones of public life (*Newsnight Scotland* being a good example) being criticised or more often than not bypassed, and a whole plethora of social media sites and platforms opening up a less organised, disputatious set of discussions.

The 'third Scotland' has both on and off social media, a horizontal, more egalitarian, fluid and less demarcated way of working; many of the groups which have formed will be short-lived, temporary and not become permanent fixtures. This is characteristic of the networked communities which the likes of Catalan sociologist Manuel Castells has talked about and identified in his *The Rise of the Network Society* (2000–2004) which is related to Zygmunt Bauman's notion of the crisis of modernity and the fluid, impermanent lives of 'liquid modernity' (2000).

All of this is the opposite of the hierarchical, narrowly specialist, accredited, status defined and closed conversations of government and business. They also have a certainty in their near-permanence and importance institutionally, often in many cases when bodies have passed their sell-by-date (one example being the plethora of business membership organisations, CBI, IOD, SCDI, Scottish Chambers, all pursuing the same subscriptions).

The boundaries of this 'third Scotland' are porous enough allowing for entry and exit, not well-defined or policed by gatekeepers, marking a fundamental difference with 'official Scotland'. Some parts of the voluntary sector would sit in or part within the 'third Scotland', but many of the bigger NGOs and aggregators such as SCVO with their propretial ownership of the term 'the third sector' and their contractual relationship of near-dependency on government, would not. All of this represents some kind of shift in organisation, activism, influence, and how power manifests itself and is expressed.

What seems to lie behind a lot of this is a rejection and loss of patience with the closed society with its sense of control and permission. People have been saying more and more, 'I have authority' and 'I have a right to do this', and not waiting for permission and licence from some institution. This is only happening in small numbers, but it seems to have the potential of being the beginning of a watershed change: of a generational shift towards self-organisation, self-help and a sort of embryonic mutualism.

This is a culture of self-determination beginning to take form, and irrespective of the independence referendum, it reflects wider changes in society: the decline in deference, the decade of austerity inflicted on the UK and Scotland, and a growing belief by some that they can take power and voice into their own hands. That is the beginning of a very different Scotland.

CHAPTER FOURTEEN

# A Scotland Beyond Labels and 'the Official Story'

If freedom has won, how does it come about that human ability to imagine a better world and to do something to make it better was not among the trophies of victory and what sort of freedom is it that discourages imagination and tolerates the impotence of free people in matters that concern them?

ZYGMUNT BAUMAN, *In Defence of Politics*, Polity Press 1999

... when we reject the single story, when we realise that there is never a single story about any place, we regain a kind of paradise.

CHIMAMANDA NGOZI ADICHIE, 'The Danger of a Single Story', TED Talk, 7 October 2009

THIS CHAPTER EXPLORES where Scotland is in relation to its modern defining stories, the problems and inadequacies with the mindset of 'official Scotland', and what can be done to challenge this, before its closing sections will explore the terrain, content and viability of different ways of advancing social and political change.

## The Limits of Tribalism in 21st Century Scotland

This book has advanced the notion that the conventional ways in which the mainstream political community see Scotland are barely adequate to describe and face the issues of a modern society and the future. The paradigms and labels of unionist versus nationalist, and left versus right, have together defined most of 20th-century Scotland, and still hold sway and attraction for some. It is also true that the independence referendum with its Yes/No question and debate, has given some added impetus to this outlook.

It is not enough in early 21st-century Scotland. The reasons for this are manifold. The challenge of market determinism and vandalism which we have to live with and endure these last three decades does not automatically mean that the left is vindicated or the main vehicle for opposition. In fact, the left historically share many of the same characteristics as neo-liberalism: economic determinism, a blinkered belief in modernity and progress, an absence of understanding the limits of growth and ecological crisis, as well as a sense that human behaviour is infinitely malleable. Both are projects of social engineering believing they can remake the human soul.

But it is much more than that. The terms, left and right, and unionist and nationalist, speak to past certainties and the human condition of needing to label and box things to understand them. It is understandable to want to name things, but by this focusing on boundaries and who is within and without certain communities, discussions are limited and closed down. There has always for example been a central paradox running through the idea of being left. This is that at its best and boldest, this was a lodestar for a universalist project of liberating humanity, freeing us of blight, prejudice and the limiting of people through their background or vested interests. But of course this was not a universal project in how it enacted its politics and vision. Instead, it was a partial mindset which constantly talked an exclusionary language; when it talked about 'we' and 'us' that community excluded conservatives, reactionaries and liberals. Those groups historically have been much more open and pluralist in how they have at least described their politics.

An underlying strand underneath all of these terms is that of the power of tribalism, of identifying and proclaiming who you are and who you are not. This is part of what it is to be in human: tribes, gangs, associations. But in this area it has been taken too far, of thinking in binary terms which distort complex, nuanced debates. Most of Scotland does not see themselves reflected in the certainties of the Yes/No vote, rightly judging the debate as one more of ambiguity and shades of self-government.

Then there are the realities that for all the certainties of those within these labels, they are now less powerful, all-encompassing and defining political projects. They are in essence political terms and definitions which come out of the Enlightenment and the harsh experiences of 19th-century industrial capitalism. These terms have defined and shaped in positive and negative many of the ways we think of the modern world, but they have become increasingly diminished and not relevant for many of the world's problems. For example, it isn't just possible to add together a 'Red-Green' politics to answer the ecological crisis, because the left is beholden to economic growth. Or that the politics and science of medical ethics which will throw up all sorts of challenges on technology and what it means to be human and even at some stage, post-human. The world of left versus right offers us no guide on these and many other areas.

## Inbetweener Scotland

Writing the above I feel a slight sense of guilt and anxiety. Part is an awareness about how some of this will be read in the world of certainty, labelling and tribalism: that I will be condemned as being not 'one of us' or not grasping the historic necessities of the age we live in. But it is much more than that. It is about the mix of the personal and political, and namely, that I, like many others come from a tribe, the left.

There is a host of factors at work in this: personal background, the influence of parents, families and friends, and the dynamics of culture, identities and politics. The inter-play between this recognition of a wider social environmental influence and the deeply personal should at least be brought into the open. I grew up in a working-class community in what turned out to be an age of managed, ordered capitalism which not coincidentally was also the period of 'high Scotland' speaking and acting with a progressive voice. My experience was that of hundreds of thousands of other Scots, of my parents having secure jobs, experiencing rising living standards, and perceiving my future and that of my peers as being one of greater opportunities in that increasingly more fair and open world.

These characteristics hugely shaped a part of this generation, and those of us whose formative childhood years spanned the end of one era, the transition years of the 1970s, and the beginning of another, have been affected by this. In a sense, we are 'inbetweeners' in two meanings: one in terms of social class, coming from the working-class and ending up in middle-class professions, but never being wholly of the traditional middle-class. The second is this critical age of dramatic change which was the 1970s which saw not just Scotland, but the UK and global capitalism, undergo enormous disruption.

The first group in relation to class makes up a significant section of Scottish society, in some estimates of Scotland post-1979, up to one-third of people, and the key group who have driven many of the debates on politics, the constitutional question, and centre-left values since, and many of whom have continued to identify as working-class as a statement about roots, status and how they see class. Many Scots brought up working-class have viewed the term 'middle-class' as being synonymous with 'sell-out', not having a social conscience, voting Tory, or living in a Scots suburban equivalent of *Terry and June*.

The second experience of being an 'in-betweener' is perhaps less clearly understood. It situates people between the security and positivity of the baby boomer generation, and the economic and social doubts of those who only experienced Thatcher's Scotland and after. There is in this an awareness that the fabric of society, peoples' lives and whole communities sit in a set of dynamics, some of which can dramatically change, parts of which people can shape and affect, and elements of which happen without people being able to influence. There are two dimensions to seeing this: one emphasising powerlessness and apolitical attitudes, as in, 'what is the point of politics, community involvement, activism?'; another, stressing the fluidity and impermanence of any social period or gains.

On the basis of evidence alone Scotland is not that different from the rest of the UK on class. In the last Scots figures 66.1 per cent saw themselves as working-class, while in the UK the latest figure was 61 per cent; but this does not of course mean that such terms have the same meanings in different places and over time (Paterson, Bechhofer and McCrone, 2004; Heath, Savage and Senior, 2013).

Both of these 'inbetweener Scotlands' have been enormously influential, finding voice in politics and culture, and in the arts, theatre, TV and literature. They are explored in the novels of William McIlvanney, James Kelman and Janice Galloway, where the rising expectations of the first group are often framed against the harsh realities and disappointment of dashed hopes in part of the second group as the 1980s developed.

Both these strands profoundly influenced and shaped my experience and how I interpret the world and live my life. For a variety of reasons, rooted in my parents politics and outward looking engagement with people, I choose to through the difficult rapids of the 1980s remaining hopeful, centred on believing in the capacity of people to affect positive change. And despite the neo-liberal onslaught of the last few decades, I even more firmly remain of an optimistic disposition.

However, our world is a complex, contradictory one, and this has to be recognised in any assessment of the interplay between the societal and the personal. Having grown up in a supportive, loving working-class family and community, I feel a personal responsibility to act and understand in my life in a way which attempts to aid existing working-class communities and people. Sometimes this means directly being involved in a host of community projects, on other occasions, challenging the middle-class comfort zones of much of polite society.

In this I think the terminologies of left versus right and unionist versus nationalist just don't really do justice to the change we have lived through, contemporary Scotland, and our different possible futures. There is little research on this but most people do not see themselves reflected and represented in these terms to any great extent.

Such terms offer a politics of certainty, understandably motivated by the narrative of difference, and an attempt to erect signposts for a collective future. They state what we are not: emphatically not Thatcherite, Tory or market determinist, and some of what many of us are: a more centre-left, autonomous politics based on self-government. But they also limit how we see ourselves, and Scotland as a political community. For if most people do not see themselves in these terms, this reduces those political conversations to a minority pastime, to one of the elect and a selectorate. And just as crucially, the articulation of these labels gives a false sense to the political world that puts its hopes in these terms, that this is enough to guide the complex trade-offs and decisions governments and public bodies have to take, when this is not the case.

We do however need to explore, define and be aware of the values and philosophies which inform government and the public realm. Technocratic talk, managerialism, or the cult of consultancy jargon, are not only not adequate, they are variants of the 'masters of the universe' zeitgeist which has so distorted politics. The language of the tribe actually insulates people into thinking it is enough to defeat this worldview, whereas a comprehensive re-assessment and re-statement of what our values are and how they shape our practices is needed to even begin to do this. It is to this end that the rest of this book is focused.

## What are the Defining Stories of Modern Scotland?

In present day Scotland there are a number of defining stories which increasingly have come to say who we are, how we see ourselves, and how we differentiate ourselves from others. Underneath the six myths of modern Scotland identified in Chapter Two, three pivotal accounts are identifiable which, while they can take many forms and names, can be called the Scotland of the egalitarian impulse, the democratic intellect, and the nation and culture of popular sovereignty.

First, Scotland is shaped by an egalitarian impulse, Jock Tamson's bairns and all that, and the belief that as a society we have rejected the worst excesses of Anglo-American capitalism. This argues that we are more virtuous, moral and filled with a mission of compassion, honour and duty: a Scottish ideal of 'I am my brother's keeper' as evidenced in William McIlvanney's pronouncements during the Tory years of Thatcher and Major.

Unfortunately Scotland is one of the most unequal places in the developed world. We are only marginally less unequal than England, itself distorted by the presence of London, the most unequal city in the rich world.

The UK is on some estimates the fourth most unequal country in the developed world, only surpassed by the USA, Portugal and Singapore, and an independent Scotland on current trends would be only slightly less unequal (Dorling, 2012: 349).

Second, is the evoking of the democratic intellect and pride in Scotland's curiosity and imagination of the mind, its inquisitiveness in relation to ideas, and our generalist educational traditions which many belief are more open and less class bound than England. Yet, the Scottish education system with its lad o'pairts was never this hallowed world of liberation, never particularly child-orientated or friendly, and has in recent decades remained a virtually closed system particularly in school education: inward-looking, lacking dynamism and over-influenced by interest groups.

Finally, there is what I believe is the most persuasive account of Scotland in recent times: that of the sovereignty of the people and of popular sovereignty. This argument as we have seen in Chapter Six believes that Scotland as a distinct political and historical space has been defined by a distinct notion of authority, power and legitimacy, with a direct lineage from the Declaration of Arbroath of 1320 to the present day.

Scotland is not in any legal or literal political way a nation of popular sovereignty. If it were, our society and democracy would look radically different from today. The experience of Thatcher, 'the democratic deficit' and the poll tax, would have been substantially mitigated and resisted. The talking shop that was the Scottish Constitutional Convention of the late 1980s and early 1990s would have been more than a gathering of alternative elite Scotland.

More crucially, our democratic practices would be more varied and vibrant, and concerned with the 'missing Scotland' and forgotten voices who are excluded from democratic politics. There would be in a culture shaped by popular sovereignty a whole raft of processes and practices by which the people gave voice and expression to their collective views. There would be a plethora of democratic forums and forms: referenda, deliberative and participative forums, and a diffusing and dispensing of power beyond the political classes and institutional Scotland. That 'deep democracy' is far removed from the Scotland of today.

Therefore there is a seismic chasm between how a significant part of Scotland sees our characteristics as a nation and society, and the more complex and less complimentary reality. What is self-evident from this is that Scottish society – whether reinforcing and believing in this or more detached and distant – seems to be comfortable and unquestioning of this disjuncture.

This seems, without trying to be too dramatic, a rather damning account of progressive and centre-left Scotland, and of the dominant accounts of it – SNP, Labour, 'civic Scotland' and a wider social democratic sentiment beyond party allegiances (see for another take on this: Gallagher, 2009). This is a social democracy by and for professional groups, insiders and elites, but one certain radicals and left-wingers have chosen to buy into the myths believing the mirage of Scotland as fact.

What do we do to change this state of affairs? One option would be to go down the free marketeer and deregulation road, embracing the orthodoxies which have dominated British politics. There is fortunately little public, institutional or professional support for such an approach. Another more influential approach would be to embed the technocratic managerialism of the consultant class, and use the crisis to instigate a public sector transformation of being more selective and charging: this is the approach of the Crawford Beveridge review (Beveridge et al, 2010).

A radical Scottish project would take these mythologies and ask the question: does Scotland want to be true to how many people see it and imagine it? It would work with the grain and characteristics of Scottish society and use them to build popular coalitions and public support to act upon and champion the values people believe most embody contemporary Scotland. In this, such an approach could learn something from those recent British political projects, Thatcherism and New Labour, which went with the grain of power, privilege and the new global classes, and in so doing claimed they were the future and that all opposition was outdated and stuck in the past.

## The Gap Between Words and Actions

A Scotland that was shaped and acted upon these three accounts would be a place which sat in the proud tradition of the inventors, imagineers, agitators and radicals of our past at its best. A more egalitarian society would act upon the seismic inequalities which disfigure our nation, and face up to the powerful elites in business, wealth and land who control and dominate many of the decisions of our society.

A Scotland of the democratic intellect would begin rethinking learning and education, challenge our narrow notions of knowledge and intelligence, and look at how to bring innovation and dynamism into state education. A key concern would be, rather than just being complacent about education, to begin to address issues of Scotland's underachievers in class, place and gender, and prioritise literacy and emotional intelligence.

Finally, in the area of popular sovereignty we would attempt to overthrow the over-prescriptive, tightly controlled bandwidth of what it is possible to imagine politically and as the popular will. We would endlessly experiment with different formats, and encourage spaces and resources which sit outwith the system or beyond the system's ethos. We would do something about the 'missing Scotland' and begin to establish some basic rules about how and who should conduct a modern democracy: how we can agree and disagree constructively, challenge disrespect and the non-listening and non-engaging which so often passes for dialogue and conversation in our politics and public life.

A Scotland that did these things would be in the spirit of how we think and see of ourselves today, but crucially, it would feel and be a very different place. Two central questions concern whether we are firstly, really serious about these values as a set of statements and foundation stories which tell us who we are, and second, if we are, then how do we go about advancing and enacting them?

To address this honestly involves looking at the gap between our myths and stories and reality, and between how we talk and our actions. This is an arena which disables left and progressive politics the world over. Barack Obama in his book, *Dreams from my Father*, reflected on this in the US and black nationalism:

> It was the distance between our talk and our actions, the effect it was having on us as individuals and as a people. The gap corrupted both language and thought: it made us forgetful and encouraged fabrication; it eventually eroded our ability to hold ourselves or each other accountable. (Obama, 2008: 203)

While all of this was going on, the mainstream was moving in a very different direction as Reagan was changing in America with what Obama called 'his brand of verbal legerdemain' (2008: 203) which won over large parts of white America. Obama concluded from this experience the limits of the politics of identity and race, and then from this the need to build a wider coalition:

> The continuing struggle to align word and action our heartfelt desires with a workable plan – didn't self-esteem finally depend on just this? It was that belief which had led me into organising, and it was that belief which would lead me to conclude, perhaps for me the final time, that notions of purity – of race or of culture – could no more serve as the basis for the typical black American's self-esteem than it could for me. Our sense of wholeness would have to arise from something more fine than

the bloodlines we inherited. It would have to find root in… all the messy contradictory details of our experience. (2008: 204)

The first Obama quote has obvious resonances with the comforting stories of Scotland's social democracy which many seem happy to live within, ignoring the gap between words and actions. This distorts and demeans who 'we' are and it erodes, as Obama understood, our abilities to hold ourselves and others to account. The second is about the particularities of black America in the 1980s, identity politics and race, but it can also be seen as addressing the faultlines in community politics and any kind of politics which is inward and not addressing the messy, contradictory patterns of modern life. This has obvious relevance to Scottish politics with its tribes, labels, name-calling and love of boundaries.

Yet it was revealing that one of Scottish Labour's most thoughtful voices, Douglas Alexander, in a speech in September 2013 choose to evoke parts of the Obama quotes above to explore the limits of Scottish nationalism. Introducing Obama's quotes, Alexander wrote that, 'Despite the evident differences between the ethnic nationalism of '80s Chicago, and the civic nationalism of Scotland today, his insight remains both powerful and relevant'.

After citing Obama's observation about the gap between words and actions, he reflected that, 'As soon as I read these words, their relevance to the nationalists' claims here in Scotland seemed obvious to me', and continued, 'the centrality of the nationalist question to Scottish politics and their continued determination to avoid responsibility for every ill (while claiming credit for every success) has hollowed out and constrained too many of Scotland's debates.' He then goes further to link Obama's emerging awareness in the 1980s of the limits of community and black politics, as being relevant to Scotland and the SNP today, citing that the 'messy contradictory details of our experience… rings true to me as a constituency Member of Parliament' (Alexander, 2013).

Alexander has been a rare example post-2011 of a Scottish Labour politician bravely and openly prepared to ask difficult questions of his party and tradition. He has on occasions done so in a language and tone which has been beyond the partisan name-calling, but here he falls back into the bunker. The narrow analysis he puts forward citing what is wrong in Scotland is itself a major part of our collective predicament and Labour denial and evasions which demeans all of our public life.

Think about Alexander's comments on Obama's words and action points. Has Scottish Labour ever adequately reflected upon, or offered an analysis of the inadequacies and any kind of apology for the mistakes of

50 years of 'Labour Scotland'? None of any substance or conviction; and such a move like Labour in opposition under Kinnock and Blair, or the Tories post-1997, would be a first move in renewal. It is also self-evident that Scotland's shortcomings in debate and dynamism are much deeper and more historic than blaming it on the supposed obsession with the constitutional debate of these last 40 years plus (one Labour politicians along with Lib Dems seem to forget that at points they were an integral part of).

But it is wider than this. There is a systemic evasion in Scottish public life between words and deeds. It covers all political traditions and perspectives, and parts of institutional and 'civic Scotland'. It has been one of the characteristics of our politics, whether it was the 19th-century Liberals, Scottish Labour when it was the dominant party, or contemporary SNP: all of them like to embrace radical and progressive credentials, but have been or in the latter case, are becoming, parties of the Scottish elites and establishment.

This has been allowed to happen because of the institutional groupthink of large parts of public life, in politics, the professions and media, which have defined those sectors. There is as Alexander says a 'false conceit of moral superiority' which infuses too much of Scottish life. In recent times, 'the fog of war' and exaggerated, distorted rhetoric between Labour and SNP has strengthened this propensity, but has to be seen in this longer historic context. Scottish Labour were the leading party of the nation for 50 years and in terms of 'place making' Scotland could be seen as a 'Labour place'.

Many Labour politicians cannot help themselves, blaming all of contemporary Scotland's shortcomings on the SNP and the limits of Scottish nationalism. Alexander is not the only Labour politician speaking like this, with Margaret Curran asking 'what has devolution ever done for Easterhouse?', forgetting that Labour built and then ran the Glasgow council estate that was Easterhouse for decades (*Daily Telegraph*, 24 September 2013). There is a cognitive dissonance going on here: of Labour politicians finding reality too difficult and then seeking sanctuary in a Scotland they have created in their own mind. But my point is that they are not alone in this, merely the most outspoken in what is the prevailing mindset of our public life.

## What do we do about 'Official Scotland'?

How does official Scotland see contemporary Scotland? Amongst its many shades and variants is a belief that government, institutional Scotland and professional groups are working towards a better, fairer society; that slowly and incrementally progress is being made in policy, ideas and outcomes. A contributory factor in this is Isaiah Berlin's notion of 'symmetrical fantasy', humanity's search for shape and meaning in what is often messy, fragmented times. Berlin expressed this when he stated of his hero Alexander Herzen that he:

> ... believed in reason, scientific methods, individual action, empirically discovered truths; but he tended to suspect that faith in general formulas, laws, prescription in human affairs was an attempt, sometimes catastrophic, always irrational, to escape from the uncertainty and unpredictable variety of life into the false security of our own symmetrical fantasies. (Berlin, 1981: 211)

These are the undoubted characteristics of the 'high Scotland' of progress, modernity and hope of the 1945–75: filled with noble intentions but implemented with limited democracy and based on the continuation of elite power. We are now coming up for 40 years since the end of that era, but still many of these values and attitudes remain embedded in the institutions of public life.

To some the maintenance and preservation of these is deemed essential to defeat the marketeering, right-wing agenda of the UK Government. Others go further, seeing the rejection of the ideological approach which has taken hold down south as being evidence that everything is alright here. Iain Macwhirter recently wrote that travelling the length and breadth of Scotland he saw that the 'country is in a good shape right now'; he did add the caveat 'at least on the surface', but then continued, 'Is there a cottage left in Scotland that hasn't had an extension built on to it? Is there a town that doesn't have an annual book festival?' (*Sunday Herald*, 13 October 2013). The answers will be that most cottages do not have extensions, or most towns do not have book festivals.

The Scotland which portrays itself as the country of free tuition fees, free care for the elderly, free prescription charges and the council tax freeze, and which defines this as the universal expression of Scotland's social democracy, is in reality an extension of this safety first, complacency Scotland. This is not an argument for or against such benefits, but more fundamentally noting that the absence of acknowledging that these are not redistributive or effective in terms of helping those in most need, and their regressive supporting of the most middle class and affluent in our society, is telling. Some of Scotland's supposedly most radical and left-wing voices are content that the ultimate expression of our progressive credentials is the distribution of resources from the poorest to the most affluent.

What the above account tells us for one thing is the exhaustion of numerous established alternative approaches to how they critique this state of affairs. To take one example – the incorporation of the 'asset based approach' in government and public agencies, and in particular of the former Chief Medical Officer Harry Burns, who has championed such an analysis. In his perspective and that of the Scottish Government, an 'asset based approach' has been stripped of its radical community grass roots approach, and has become the individual, 'deficit model' pathologising what are socio-economic and structural issues. Lynne Friedli has systematically analysed the language of government and public bodies and found that compared to its challenging origins, the 'asset based approach' is now used to legitimise the appropriation of a deeply reactionary agenda which talks about 'welfare dependency', an 'underclass' and other new right terms (Friedli, 2012).

At the announcement of his departure as Chief Medical Officer for a prestigious and newly created academic post at Strathclyde University, Burns went on to chastise those who talk Scotland down and underplay the changes in health outcomes which he believed he had presided over, commenting, 'We shouldn't be negative. We are looked upon as a country which has grasped the issues.' He then compared the challenges society faces and issue of social change with the example of Sir David Brailsford, cycling coach and Team GB's successful Olympics cycling team, stating, 'The principle behind it is the same as won the cycling team all those gold medals... Small changes in a lot of areas deliver a big change in overall performance' (*The Times*, 23 January 2014). This is how some of the leading figures of professional Scotland think of delivering change: not only top down and comparable to professional sport, but all about motivation, individual factors and the latest fads of behavioural science.

Another example is that of community education and the associated community development approach which mushroomed in the 1970s and then became embedded in the 'local socialism' of Labour councils such as Lothian and Tayside in the 1980s. Community education at the outset was influenced by a critique and understanding of the limits of professionalism, but quickly aspired to being one itself, shifting from empowerment to gatekeeping. This can be seen in the retreat of the Central Belt teaching universities to focus on the profession of community education. This led to the slow departure of any sense of radical development, relationship to broader practice across Scotland and critical self-appraisal. The same models are still cited as 30 and 40 years ago such as Edinburgh based Adult Learning Partnership (ALP) and the same intellectual reference points, namely, Antonio Gramsci and Paulo Freire. Alongside this profession has grown the Community Learning and Development (CLD) approach, which is much more open and focused upon partnership working, makes less grandiose claims for itself, and thus, has more potential.

In more recent times, another perspective has grown up which has emphasised the themes of wellbeing, confidence and the power of positive psychology. A key text is Carol Craig's *The Scots' Crisis of Confidence* (2003). This took aim at the over-concentration of structural issues as an explanation of Scotland's problems, most crucially, the relationship with England and the prevalence of poverty. Craig's account challenged this, attempting to open up a wider debate, but in so doing, choose to ignore or downplay these structural factors. It thus quickly became appropriated by government and public agencies, and the McConnell Labour-Lib Dem administration who saw it as a way to avoid talking about power and voice. It thus proved a case study of how an analysis, if it was deemed helpful or unthreatening by institutional forces, could quickly become part of 'official Scotland' and thus become incorporated and then marginalised as the political cycle moves on.

Finally, a part of the professional policy class sits part inside while critiquing the system – offering an analysis which mixes managerialism, consultancy and an element of new age spiritualism. This is the world of policy and ideas entrepreneurship, where influential areas such as public health cross several specialist boundaries. Despite the contribution of individuals like Phil Hanlon from Glasgow University and the work of Glasgow Centre for Population Health (GCPH), there is a problem in the endless quest of some policy professionals to find unconventional answers. Without an ideological framework or understanding of the world, this can end up in in a search which results in embracing millennialist thinking, fads and even worse, new right thinking ('welfare dependency', 'underclass') without knowing its political dimensions.

A vital dimension missing in the above is that of voice, which brings to the fore the issue of interpretation and translation. Across Scotland's truncated, limited democracy, hundreds of thousands of people are silenced, marginalised or ignored; worse this is compounded by the way mainstream society – whether it is politics, media or public bodies – assumes it can speak for such groups in the media or corridors of power. There is a cumulative depowering and delegitimising of 'the missing Scotland' in this process, which disfigures and curtails democratic decision. The above groups, some with the best intentions and some not, seem more than content to maintain this culture of exclusion, as their status and privilege has emerged in such a divided, fragmented society where those with authority and access guard it. At the minimum, we could at least begin to note the self-appointed interpreters and translators and question their intentions.

The mainstream view of Scotland does not have a complete absence of opposition just because of the marginalisation of established alternative views. There is the critique from the populist and new right and the mindset of the London Scots, two worlds which overlap in for example, Andrew Neil, Fraser Nelson, editor of *The Spectator*, and Iain Martin, a former *Scotsman* editor. Neil has been a leading advocate of the new right critique of Scotland labeling independence as offering 'a permanent socialist nirvana' (BBC *Sunday Politics*, 20 October 2013). Nelson and Martin have regularly taken aim at Scotland, characterising it as the land of the burgeoning state and endless public spending; the problem is that this cartoonesque vision of Scotland has influence because of their access to London media platforms and the political classes.

This is crucially recycled and represented back to Scotland where it meets two very different responses. The first is that it plays into the Scots' crisis of confidence of our professional classes and their mixture of intellectual miserablism and complacency; and the second is that it reinforces the left-wing belief that Scotland is this land of socialist practice and intent. In the latter, the politics of hard right and the left find a common ground and purpose that they barely understand.

Not all London Scots have views such as Andrew Neil et al, and many have much more mainstream and moderate views at home with much of Scottish society: the likes of Andrew Marr, Jim Naughtie and Helena Kennedy being cases in point. Instead, they have a subtler and perhaps even more problematic view of Scotland because it is less offensive and overt.

Marr, Naughtie and Kennedy contribute to an outdated, out of step concept of Scotland, resolutely stuck in the past, focused on Labour, and dismissive to condescending of the SNP and independence. Marr, at a recent Edinburgh International Book Festival event, railed against 'anti-English prejudice' in Scotland, and when challenged by myself and others, took umbrage in *The Spectator* saying that the presence of the 'London Scots' was 'irritating for Scottish commentators' (*The Spectator*, 31 August 2013). Naughtie and Kennedy both have public Labour leanings (Kennedy being a Labour peer in the Lords), while the former has been close to former Prime Minister Gordon Brown (producing a book with him on John Smith).

This 'London Scot' version of Scotland is partly a generational one and shaped by their childhood and formative years. Naughtie left Scotland, for example, in 1977 to go south, so his understanding of Scotland is informed by memories and experiences of that past land. Marr left in the mid-1980s. Such prominent public figures have become part of a London liberal media establishment whose focus is on things other than Scotland: Westminster, the UK's global position, and international affairs. Small isn't beautiful in this world, it is something to be disparaged.

All of this contributes towards a series of disconnected, disjointed conversations and what are broken stories of Britain. The UK political, media and business elite world based in London and the South East have grown increasingly insular, self-obsessed and intolerant of other views, with the nature of power in the UK and the territorial dimensions within it, including Scotland, of little interest. This attitude then entrenches a problematic view of the UK which has little common ground or language with Scotland, thus strengthening the slow decoupling and detachment of the UK. This may not matter to some of a Scottish independence persuasion or some radical Tory English and Ukip voices, but if the UK remains it matters to all of us.

CHAPTER FIFTEEN

# The Change We Can Become and the Power of Dreams

... a map of the world that does not include utopia is not worth glancing at, for it leaves out the one country at which Humanity is always landing. And when Humanity lands there, it looks out, and seeing a better country, sets sail.

OSCAR WILDE, *The Soul of Man Under Socialism*, 1891

THE PLAYWRIGHT Peter Arnott has written that, 'Scotland is an argument'. It is a succinct, poignant phrase, laden with different meanings. It offers the prospect of pluralism and debate, but it also hints of the old cantankerous male (often drunken Scotland). If 'Scotland is an argument', it implies certain kinds of conversations and even voices are drowned out, and talked over without having the confidence to interject, and that as the views and opinions fly forth, some participants over-dominate, while others fail to even notice the silences and non-contributions of others.

There is a paradox at the heart of 'Scotland is an argument' which needs bringing into the open. Are we talking about creative or non-creative conversation, and with the emphasis on talking, what of the qualities of exchange, reflection and listening, qualities too often downplayed or ignored?

Then there is alongside this emphasis on difference and disagreement, underneath it an over-arching sense of a lack of real variety and contesting views, and in mainstream life, the validation of consensus. This exists in institutional Scotland, but it has also spawned left and nationalist variants. There is a democratic case that too much consensus is a bad thing: indeed the philosopher Chantal Mouffe argues that consensus is an impossibility, a fraud and a kind of democratic deceit (Mouffe, 2005). This makes the case for a theoretical hyper-pluralist, radical democracy which may be impossible, but which the current modern Scotland falls well short of.

How do we begin to imagine change from where we currently sit as a society? The idea of the utopian imagination post-Soviet Union has been in dramatic retreat, tarred with the association that the first step in the creation of an actual utopia is to work out who to exclude, from the Soviet gulag to Nazi Germany's concentration camps. Russell Jacoby in *The End of Utopia* observed that this closing of utopian possibilities has had egregious consequences: namely, the rise of a new political set of orthodoxies connected to managerialism and neo-liberalism (Jacoby, 2000).

Jacoby believes that the utopian imagination needs to be differentiated from the physical creation of real utopias, and celebrated as intrinsic to how we think of societies and radical change. Stephen Duncombe in his inspiring book, *Dream*, makes the similar point that utopia should always be a journey, never a destination; in so doing it acts to enable the gap between present location and ideal endpoint to be identified, the road and type of travel, and the resources required to undertake it (Duncombe, 2007). He connects this to the power of political dreams writing, 'The dream, if it is truly a dream, is never meant to be realised…' and goes on:

> Instead, they are meant to inspire and to guide to be a lodestone to orient a political compass. Unlike programs or plans or even the reasonable dreams of progressives past, the dream politics I am describing offers no comfortable quietude in claims of realisation, no disillusion or disengagement in a goal not met… They also provide something that progressives currently and desperately lack: inspiration and direction. (2007: 169)

Duncombe believes that in the last century the most radical and successful dreammakers were Nazi Germany, with the Soviet Union and Mao's China not far behind. Nazi Germany had an understanding of the power of spectacle, theatre and ritual in their quest for racial supremacy, genocide and world domination. Duncombe poses from this that we have to learn valuable lessons and imagine the idea of 'ethical spectacle' which invokes a different dramaturgical culture compared to the conventional left. He writes:

> Dreams are powerful. They are repositories of our desire. They animate the entertainment industry and drive consumption. They can blind people to reality and provide cover for political horror. But they also inspire us to imagine that things could be radically different than they are today and then believe we can progress towards the imaginary world. (2007: 182)

Duncombe with his colleague Steve Lambert runs the Centre for Artistic Activism, which looks practically at how to develop a different kind of politics and culture, centred around creative activism. In this they bring centrestage the idea of the utopian imagination and role of dreamscapes in a politics rooted in real social change, campaigning and an understanding of radical history. Their work is founded on a set of fascinating processes which asks people to explore the tantalising proposition: 'Imagine winning' on a key issue of social justice, and then invites them to visualise that world, telling them, 'you have won', now describe that world, what it looks, feels, sounds and even smells like.

It is a liberating experience. It invites people to park their imagination on the other side: in the world of the radical utopian impulse, in a place people shy away from and usually leave in their subconscious. Duncombe and Lambert then ask people sitting in their utopia to think of what comes next: if you have won, 'then what?' Their observation is that the ultimate destination of much left activism is often the end of politics itself, and even the end of having to be an activist.

The other observation is that left and progressive activists find it uncomfortable to imagine the prospect of 'winning' and fundamentally changing the world. It is an insight they have repeatedly found running workshops on creative activism across the world, from the US to continental Europe, Kenya and Scotland. This they argue is damaging, because it is only in visualising and imagining the prospect of 'winning' and the radically different society which would come about, that we can embark on the journey towards this.

## Insider and Outsider Scotland

The independence debate at the moment could not be further removed from this, for all the edifying efforts of 'the third Scotland' challenging the mainstream. For the last three years it has taken the form of two competing establishments standing off, both believing that they have the right to exclusively speak for Scotland, both with an entitlement culture, and both with over-passionate supporters who think they represent more people than they do, and that they have the right to shout down, hector and insult opponents.

This reflects the dynamics and contesting of power in Scotland and centrally, the insider/outsider divide which characterises society, politics and public debate. Insider Scotland represents those with a stake and/or voice in the system, and have something significant to lose by fundamental change. Outsider Scotland are those without institutional stakes and voices, and who have less to lose by far-reaching change; indeed given the narrow confines and boundaries of insider Scotland they have the prospect of being able through change and uncertainty to challenge and shake up the existing state of affairs.

Within the core of insider Scotland sits the Scottish Government, political parties, public bodies, business and voluntary sector. It is inhabited by organisations such as COSLA, the STUC, SCDI and SCVO: a kind of alphabet soup Scotland we are all meant to know the meaning of the various acronyms and their importance. The idea of 'civic Scotland' sat comfortably in all of this in the 1980s and 1990s, but has been in retreat and decline for years, and now looks it may never recover from the SCVO manoeuvres of 2011–12 to try to have a two question referendum on Scotland's constitutional future.

It is of course not an entirely harmonious or homogeneous world, seen in the contestment between pro-independence and pro-union opinion in this environment. Yet what unites them is important to stress: an attitude which can be called continuity, safety first Scotland, and whatever the constitutional status of the nation, the maintenance of their privilege, position and access to defining the terms of debate.

Insider Scotland maintains the truncated, atrophied democracy and perceives it as an aid in the continuation of this order. Therefore, the distorted politics this produces is one emphasising those who vote, have assets and an awareness of how to make their voice heard. There are generational, gender and professional aspects to this. The contours of insider Scotland are influenced by the realities that those who are more affluent and older vote more frequently and are more adept at articulating their self-interests.

Outsider Scotland contains groups excluded from the 'official Scotland', who have self-organised to form the 'third Scotland' that has arisen in the

Raft made from Clyde flotsam by Martin Campbell, as part of public art event
'Nothing about us without us is for us' led by Matt Baker and Tara Beall.
*Photo by Mark MacLachlan.*

vacuum left by the decline of 'civic Scotland'. That shift itself represents a small but significant move – from insider to outsider Scotland – in the current debate. The prevailing characteristic is of people with less influence and status, who do not operate in the insider trading of the corridors of power. Yet this group has access to resources, spaces and networks, making them very unlike most of the politically disengaged.

'Outsider Scotland's' clarion call would be 'Nothing about us without us is for us'. This demand for empowerment has become increasingly used across the globe – from Scotland to the USA to India – by disenfranchised groups, challenging what they perceive as closed, notionally democratic political systems which operate increasingly for the benefits of those with voice, and insider status.

That the independence referendum has so far been a contest mainly within the arena of insider Scotland limits its appeal and prospect of engagement and change. It places it in the context of Scottish politics and public life as an elite pastime which for most people is nothing more than a spectator sport. To shift this entails that our public discussions stop being defined by the interests of those with assets and voice who have something to lose from change, and that we start addressing the wider concerns of those without voice. And for this dramatic shift to occur, the three areas of values, voice and vessels explored earlier needs to be addressed and acted upon. An 'outsider Scotland' which became more organised, motivated and outspoken would be a significant historic development, and call time on the self-preservation society.

## The Psychologies of Self-Government and Self-Determination

To aid this entails a culture of change which is about more than political parties and politics, and instead embraces a wider landscape: one of culture and psychology.

Too much concentration has been put on our historic and contemporary debates on the idea of politics as the sole means and gateway to bringing about change. There has been a left variant of this, a Labour version and a Nationalist articulation, but it is wider than that. It is a response to the experience of the managed, negotiated Scotland which has limited any democratic voice and prioritised institutional opinion. This has led political and activist interpretations as viewing change as coming about in a very narrow terrain: that of formal politics and institutions, i.e. on the system's homeground, which somehow then miraculously transforms it, freeing and liberating all of us.

How wider societal change occurs is about a much richer canvas than just addressing the world of politics. This entails a staged approach. First, we have to stop seeing politics as primarily about institutions and institutional change. There is a default in numerous conversations even in informed circles to see change as about what this or that institution does. In the professional classes there is an inability to think about change in which they are not central or part of; this displays a lack of self-reflection and self-criticism, but also how 'insider Scotland' maintains its position.

Second, even independence has been framed in this way by the SNP: 'the full powers of a Parliament' rhetoric of many a Scottish Nationalist politician focuses all attention and expectation on a political institution and politicians. What it leaves unstated is the wider societal change and transformation which is central to any culture of self-government and self-determination.

Third, an approach which addresses cultural and social change more, and which invests less in politics would look and feel very different. It will draw from a wider set of references, inspirations and intelligences, and have a richer history and set of experiences which more connect to how people see themselves and see their lives. Everything about it would be different compared to the narrow confines of politics: its language, its understanding of difference and pluralism, and how we as a society see ourselves. Crucially, it would not look to politicians to initiate change, but see ourselves as the change: from the controlled order of permission and mandate to that of 'I do have authority' we have already seen partly emerge.

Finally, all of this has to embrace the psychologies of self-government and self-determination. What this involves is understanding that all life is not about politics and institutions, and even that the structural versus individual divide which has so characterised left versus right is a cul-de-sac. In any complex society and situation, both the structural and individual matter, and critically, the motivations, mindsets and attitudes of people – the psychologies they have – are of critical importance.

However, a meaningful psychology of self-determination goes well beyond this to champion change and a different idea of society. Self-determination theory poses that for individuals and societies to thrive there has to be three qualities: autonomy, competence and relatedness (Deci and Ryan, 2002). These offer an analysis grounded in an evidence base which allows for a less institutional way of understanding Scotland, and brings individual empowerment into the equation, while addressing the deep economic and social inequities which disfigure our society.

This also could encourage a vital shift in our debate – from self-government to self-determination. The first term, self-government, describes the current situation, of politics and political change as being seen as about institutions and a very prescribed set of processes not open to all. The second term, self-determination, is about 'us' as a society, and about change which includes politics, but also issues of who has power and voice, and importantly, the psychologies of this. The shift from the first to the second is a major one: from a limited, closed set of possibilities, to imagining and beginning to create a different Scotland. This second approach can be seen within the environment marked out earlier by Stephen Duncombe and Steve Lambert and their idea of creative activism.

There are already examples and lessons from some of our neighbours on the above. Ireland, post-crash, has had to embark on some difficult discussions and re-appraisals which have challenged some of their conventional foundation stories and more recent identities such as 'the Celtic Tiger'.

The Irish experience is salutary to compare to Scotland (and indeed the UK) leading up to and post-crash. Ireland with its 'Celtic Tiger' rhetoric and celebration of property, speculation and casino capitalism principles, played as fast and loose as the UK did, believing it could undertake a Faustian pact with the forces of globalisation and finance capital.

Post-crash, the Irish political and economic classes are fully focused on the project of 'restoration' and of rebuilding economic growth on the same ground as before: positioning of an open Irish economy, attracting inward investment with a competitive and low tax environment, and property growth. This is not that different from the UK under the Cameron and Osborne Tory-led administration, but there has been a widespread public and intellectual debate in Ireland about the meaning of the crash, and the consequences for the fragile state of Irish politics and democracy.

A central figure in this debate has been writer and journalist Fintan O'Toole, who has written two bestselling books on the Irish crisis and situation, *Ship of Fools* (2009) and *Enough is Enough* (2010). Such popular counterblasts to the groupthink and grip of economic illiteracy, fantasyland thinking and orthodoxies have so far not been produced in Scotland.

O'Toole's analyses combines an understanding of the economic bubble thinking which transfixed the Irish (and British) political, media and business elites, with an acute sense of the democratic and wider cultural terrain: namely how was this possible in a country which has as one of its foundations the overthrowing of British colonialism and a populist republicanism at the heart of its public life? O'Toole believes that Irish 'official republicanism' is nothing but a sham, and that the depth of the crisis requires fundamental action: namely the refounding of a 'new republic'.

What is refreshing and challenging in O'Toole's two books is that he takes the myths and folklores of the Irish Republic, and uses them to measure the mess the country is in, how their elites have fallen short, and use them as a clarion call for change. All of this has relevance to our debate in Scotland.

O'Toole made the comparison directly nearly two years ago, following the publication of *Ships of Fools* and *Enough is Enough*, and with Scotland's independence debate beginning to take shape. In a piece entitled, 'Independence is Having No One Else to Blame', O'Toole looked at both countries and explicitly addressed the importance of collective attitudes:

> You have to take responsibility for the choices you make. You end up feeling more disillusioned but also more grown-up. It's a bittersweet outcome. There are still follies and delusions but at least they're your own. This is the real choice. The options are not economic misery under the union or permanent boom-times under independence. They lie more in the realm of collective psychology. Do you want to have the safety net of an auld enemy to rage at when policies don't work and the world turns mean? Or do you prefer to look at yourself in the mirror, in all your glories and stupidities? (*The Times*, 5 June 2012)

Such a powerful statement has a resonance for the current Scottish debate, but as importantly, for the highly controlled, orchestrated nature of public life historically which has contributed to this state of affairs. O'Toole's observations point towards the need to kick against the narrow confines of what has been deemed political in Scotland to this day: that it is about formal politics, institutions and politicians, with even independence associated in the cause of the SNP's argument with the Parliament assuming full powers.

In this curtailed politics, much is beyond discussion and off the radar with the silences being as telling as the noises they counterpose. In this concentration on formal and official politics what is left therefore unexamined is the role of cultural and societal transformation in any ideas of change. A politics of institutions and politicians addresses the unequal world as a given, and not unconnectedly, plays to increasingly small audiences and box office appeal – whether it be in party memberships and identification, or voting.

A very different approach to self-government would evoke the politics implicit in Naomi Mitchison in April 1953 when she wrote to Roland Muirhead:

> It seems to me that you are bound to assume that a self-governing Scotland is going to be immediately morally better, and I don't see it unless there has also been a revolution. I can't see how the people who are likely to govern Scotland under any democratic system are going to be any different from the undoubted Scots who are in positions of local power. (quoted in Harvie, 1977, 283)

This entails talking about power, who has it and who doesn't, and critically, issues of ownership and control. The mistruths told by revisionist social democrats such as Tony Crosland in the 1950s and New Labour in the 2000s that ownership no longer mattered, and with proper regulation everything would be fine, has been proven to be a falsehold. The new right dogmatists show this when they say simultaneously that ownership does not matter and that it is only out of touch socialists who care about it, and then in the next breath, that only private ownership can deliver efficiency and innovation.

An approach which is about more than narrow politics has to go beyond power transferring from London to Edinburgh, and changing what flags are flown over government buildings. Many perspectives have criticised the Scottish nationalist account which concentrates on this transfer of power to the exclusion of economic and social change:

> In place of sleek lawyers, professional politicians, rich businessmen and their placemen running our lives from London, what do the SNP propose? Sleek lawyers, professional politicians, rich businessmen and their placemen will run our lives from Edinburgh. (Flynn, 1978: 1)

The above quote is not from 2014 or even 1999, but from that long distant world of pre-Thatcher: 1978. It summarises this outlook with an irony and disdain,

> Coca Cola is bloody awful for your teeth when its bottled in London. But once the bottling plant is located at the foot of Edinburgh's Calton Hill (the proposed site of the Assembly), Coca Cola is positively health giving (1978: 1).

There are still some independence supporters who subscribe to the above point of view. It has become a degree more subtle in the intervening period. But basically it says to those looking for a more radical politics and culture, that this is not what is required now. All that is needed, so it is argued, pre-independence vote is to win and then afterwards we can focus on the kind of society we desire. This thus puts the argument for independence in abstract, discombobulated terms: about sovereignty, freedom, the people, and places a naïve faith in any post-independence dynamics.

Former SNP MP Jim Sillars eloquently articulates this perspective when he writes that on the day of the independence referendum, 'absolute sovereign power will lie in the hands of the Scottish people' (2014: 1). Sillars is enough of an old-fashioned socialist (who refuses to define himself as a nationalist) to know that there is no such thing as 'absolute sovereignty'.

The analysis of 1978 above, while a little worn, like that of Naomi Mitchison in 1953, still carries weight. The shape of a future Scotland is being made in the here and now by the collective efforts of those for change, and those pursuing the continuity independence option of the SNP leadership (along with the content free analysis put forward by pro-union forces so far). A politics all about the principle of constitutional change will unsurprisingly produce a Scotland where power lies in a few hands and issues of economic and social change are far off the political agenda. Whereas a culture which has a ferment of debate and discussion challenging the status quo and offering alternative routes pre-independence vote, has more chances of bringing about wider change, opening up debates and scrutinising those with power and privilege.

This debate offers many layers of nuance: politics, culture, psychologies, and underneath all of these the opportunity to act upon and change the collective stories which define us and tell ourselves and others who we are and who we are not. Related to this is the impact of our collective memories of how we have seen and interpreted the recent and near-past; this current debate whatever the outcome offers a rare prospect of reshaping and reframing how we see our past.

In the last couple of decades our collective stories have been told increasingly through the prism and experience of Thatcherism, her ideology and the 'alien rule' of her government. As we have seen, the Scotlands of pre- and post-1979 are the equivalent of hinges in how many see the economic, social and political changes of modern Scotland, with 1979 reduced to the equivalent of a 'Year Zero'. This is an increasingly exclusive generational account, of the baby boomers and Thatcher's children, which has diminishing resonance on those younger, who have grown up under New Labour or who are even younger. So far, this version of Scotland has remained entrenched, aided by the dominant generational voices in public life and media who continue to see this as the reference point through which they understand politics and culture.

This was understandable in the Thatcher era and its immediate aftermath, but not when we are nearly quarter a century from the downfall of Thatcher as Prime Minister. It begins to become the equivalent of people years ago repeating tales of 'the winter of discontent' and 'the dead going unburied in the streets' as a way of portraying Labour Britain in the 1970s, or the memories of mass unemployment and hardship along with the Jarrow marches in the 1930s. One was used against Labour for nearly 20 years by Tories and the right-wing press. The second was used by Labour and left opinion well into the 1950s to stigmatise the Tories. Both eventually fell into folklore and stopped being potent political weapons; the same will eventually happen with Thatcherism, Scotland and the 1980s.

The independence debate allows the prospect of putting this near-history into the category marked 'history', to understand it more fully in the sweep of the great changes which have happened, and to reach a more nuanced position on the economic and social transformation that has happened in the course of one generation. Even more the current discussion allows Scotland the opportunity to make a new set of stories, moments and images which are equally historic. Whatever the result, the debate offers us the opening to throw off the negative stereotypes and inferiority complexes which we have too often told ourselves (encouraged by others): that we are too wee, poor, divided and just too Scottish to ever amount to anything and govern ourselves. A Scotland in which a significant part of our society embarks on such a journey would begin to feel and look like a very different place from now.

## Possible Scotlands: A Claim of Right for the Common Good

In the immediate there has to be encouragement of initiatives opening up space and dialogue on our future and change which aid all of the above. In this we can draw from examples and folklore in our own past, as well as imaginative examples from around the world.

One option drawing from Scotland's nationalist traditions and mythologies with a small 'n' is to utilise the resonance of the *Claim of Right* with its evoking of people power and standing up to injustice. It is also part of a nationalist ethos which in its last variant in *A Claim of Right for Scotland* drew on a number of strands, invoking popular sovereignty with Labour, Lib Dem and SNP politicians supporting it (although the latter did not officially sign the related declaration of March 1989 which led to the Constitutional Convention). It was also influenced by green, feminist, communist perspectives to name but a few.

'A Claim of Right for the Common Good' could utilise nationalist mythology owned by a broad swathe of the political spectrum to develop a road map to a different kind of Scottish society: one which rejects the market determinism of the Conservative-led UK Government, and the stasis and complacency of institutional Scotland. It would take the Scots idea of 'the common good' and mark out a modern, democratic idea of this, which informed public services and the public realm.

Even sympathetic commentators on Scottish nationalism have noticed that significant parts of it have often been quiet or lacking in detail on the societal vision which they claim is inherent in their politics as they talk and invoke centre-left, social democratic credentials. This is because the SNP is a 'catch-all' party, and that it is a nationalist party before a centre-left one, but the development of something like 'A Claim of Right for the Common Good' would take it more firmly into explicitly social democratic territory. This is the agenda a significant part of Scottish voters are looking for answers from, and are still not adequately getting them from SNP, Labour or 'civic Scotland'.

A very different example comes from Finland and an ambitious national programme, *Mission for Finland 2030* initiated by the Finnish Government. This began as a government project, but large parts of it were given over to outside agencies such as creative designers, artists and think tanks. For a country like Finland, which has a built-in respect for authority and even more powerful permission culture than Scotland, this was a major leap into the dark.

*Mission for Finland 2030* could be seen as a technological fix upskilled to the scale of a nation with all the negatives those words imply. However, it also came up with eight national aspirations for Finland in education, learning and innovation. In allowing it to sit outside the system, and then embracing it, Finnish authorities were playing at the limits of their rationalist based culture, and knowing that its findings would be taken seriously and implemented. It is relevant as well that the main findings and recommendations sat within the modern Finnish story that parts of its society likes to articulate about itself; i.e. using their myths to aid rather than hinder change and innovation.

There are numerous other examples from around the world that can be examined to understand how to best frame a national set of conversations which is wide, generous, participative, not captured by the system, and listened to and engaged with by those in authority. There was postcrash the example of the Icelandic constitutional process which saw a small country rebuild its democracy and renew and strength its progressive credentials. Then there was the Australian National Convention which drew together 1,000 citizens, who met and deliberated on ten national priorities, which the government gave a binding commitment to formally respond to.

All of these examples illustrate that it is possible if we wish to break out of the Groundhog Day Scotland of endless proposing yet another Constitutional Convention, or another Commission. The former body, which some such as Cannon Kenyon Wright like to declare set up the Scottish Parliament, did nothing of the kind, because it was a talking shop which did not have that power. Admittedly it did contribute to changing the prevailing mood music on what kind of Parliament was being conceived of in the late 1980s and early 1990s. More importantly for today, the Convention was about politicians, institutional figures and alternative elites: in a sense Scotland's 'committees of the great and good' excluded by Thatcher. This was already a politics fraying at the edges 25 years ago; now it is threadbare, discredited and unimaginative. Future ventures about the shape of our democracy or society cannot be left to such exclusionary, top-down ventures.

## Democratising Scotland

There is also the hollowed out nature of what passes for democracy in Scotland which is profoundly limited, excluding large parts of our country, and aids a culture where scrutinising power and privilege seem to be permanently off the radar. The comedian Russell Brand tapped into a widely held sentiment about the nature of the United Kingdom and British politics, with his mix of anger, dismay and faux-revolutionary zeal at the political and business elites, but Scotland is not completely immune from this outlook or a model democracy in any respect.

A number of very basic measures could begin widening the democratisation of Scotland. This would start with the most basic political democracy. One measure would be to initiate a 'Get the Vote Out' campaign before the big vote, headed up by a non-partisan body such as SCVO. This could draw on such successes as the work of the Vincentian Partnership for Social Justice in Ireland, bringing together four faith groups which has engaged in political and civic citizenship with the aim of driving up turnout at elections. Their work entails three stages: exploring with people the reasons to vote, how to register, and the process of how to actually vote; the different ways of finding out more on key issues; and how to assess and understand candidates. The results have been impressive over the course of 15 years – and working extensively in six areas of previous low turnout they have produced increases in participation between 12 per cent and 31 per cent (The Vincentian Partnership for Social Justice, 2012).

Another step would be a national voter registration drive to reverse the exclusion and self-withdrawal from the electoral register. There is now a long-term decline in the completeness of the electoral register across Britain from 1970 according to the Electoral Commission. Those aged over 55 years have registration levels above 90 per cent, whereas 17–24 year olds have 44 per cent registration levels. Scotland has a similar picture, with a significant issue in Glasgow with only a 74 per cent completion rate of the electoral register which has 'fallen sharply over the past decade' (Electoral Commission, 2010: 63).

How we interpret and see the act of voting needs to be rethought in an age where we are bombarded with populist requests to take part in this or that talent contest or TV vote. The art of voting – what it means, the power and potential of it – needs to be refreshed and made anew in these circumstances. The 2010 UK election saw a huge chasm between classes and ages in voting. According to Ipsos MORI the AB group had a 76 per cent turnout compared to DE's 57 per cent, while the over 65 year olds had a 76 per cent turnout and 18–24 year olds a 44 per cent rate. This is the distortive politics of the truncated electorate which leads to politicians concentrating their efforts on those who vote and are older and more middle class.

All sorts of civic and marketing drives can be employed to address this, but more fundamentally, voting needs to be seen as opening up the prospect of social change. When voting is seen as important and a harbinger of momentous things to come, then people turn out to vote. One case study was the 1998 Good Friday Agreement (GFA) referendum in Northern Ireland which produced a 81.1 per cent turnout. So far Scotland's experience of stand-alone referendums in 1979 and 1997 has not produced impressive turnouts, with 63.8 per cent and 60.4 per cent respectively.

Political democracy is only the first step in beginning a campaign to democratise every aspect of Scottish society – economic, social and cultural. This is where some uncomfortable truths need to be addressed about Scotland and the left both here and in the UK. For example, the dynamism and popular instincts of the new right have these last few decades seized and ran with this agenda. They have taken words such as 'freedom' and 'choice' and made them synonymous with their agenda. They have made, until the bankers crash at least, the vested interest groups which are unaccountable and out for themselves those of progressives: trade unions, the public sector, and professional groups who operate in the public realm.

Despite the cataclysmic events of the crash, the right are still using the financial crisis as a way to widen their attack on the welfare state and public spending. What many on the left fail to realise when they are critiquing the right is how they are even more using the democrat mantle to undermine progressive values. For example, under the Cameron Government we have seen across England the rolling out of foundation hospitals, free schools and elected police commissioners. The official Labour response to these is one of dislike but confusion: to argue about details and process and concede or evade the principle. Does anyone know if current Labour Shadow Education Secretary Tristram Hunt is for or against free schools? No, is the answer.

Whether people like foundation hospitals and free schools is not the point. The right have seized the agenda of freedom, choice, and wider participation. What is the left's response heard beyond its own boundaries? It seems to suggest that you cannot elect police commissioners as they are a waste of time, and that free schools will become the preserve of middle class, self-interested parents. However, in so doing the left positions itself on the side of anti-democracy and the old order, when it should be criticising the limited democracy of foundation hospitals and free schools, and outlining ways to envisage self-governing hospitals, schools and public services.

In Scotland, this debate has barely got out of our comfort zones. The SNP government had planned to implement elected health boards in part as a result of public opposition to the closing of A&E services; yet when it tried two pilot exercises it found little public appetite. The response of institutional Scotland including health authorities and professional groups was to breathe a sigh of relief and say how unworkable and cumbersome it would have proven. But that is what democracy does: it is uncomfortable, unpredictable and even involves some time and costs.

The wider Scottish sentiment is to emphasise our difference against innovations such as foundation hospitals and free schools. We have been at this for the first decade plus of devolution, since the Blair administration embarked upon its 'choice' agenda of public sector reform in its second term: academy schools, foundation hospitals and more. The political and policy response north of the border was to view these as unwelcome and unnecessary compared to the professional, integrated ethos of our health and education. These are benefits but behind them also lie professional interest groups and the words 'producer capture'. And while Scotland hasn't gone done the full marketisation route of down south we have not been immune to the reach of 'corporate capture' and the encroachment of Serco, G4S and A4e into public services. Indeed, our collective faith in the efficacy of public services allows much of the debate to remain blind to their shortcomings and inconvenient realities such as the presence of the new vested interests across Scotland with lucrative contracts: Serco for example provide Glasgow City Council's IT infrastructure in a ten year contract worth £265.5 million of public monies.

The dominant responses of the left and nationalists to the above involves often ignoring these realities. So, for example, the forward march of commercialisation in public services is met by externalising this to only happening south of the border. The market determinists, corporate vultures and ideologically driven think tanks, 'the enemy within', are all massed at the border and shaping Westminster village discussions. This ignores that for all Scotland's centre-left sentiments this is part of the business of modern life; equally in our invoking of all things Nordic we choose to ignore irrelevancies such as facts: namely that the Nordics have embraced privatisation, outsourcing and marketisation, and that large elements of the Swedish or Danish left feel exactly the same sort of loss and disorientation that parts of the Scottish and British left do.

Then there is the ultimate sanctuary – the invoking of abstract creations and the historic collective agency of 'the people'. This imagined and yet supposedly omnipotent construct is meant to be all-powerful, all wise and completely sovereign. Yet they are only those things in a surreal, otherworldly way. Are 'the people' sovereign running hospitals, schools or other public services? Are they sovereign in governing what passes for local democracy in Scotland, or Glasgow City Council's decision to outsource its IT to the vested interest group Serco (whose byline is the threatening 'bringing services to life')?

Sadly they are not because what the abstract invoking of 'the people' entails allows two contradictory assumptions to be held. One is the Scotland of popular control and 'we are the people' (the Canon Kenyon Wright declaration; not the Rangers FC version), and the other is that 'the people' are subsumed in professional group self-interests. In this latter case, the actions of the education unions such as the Educational Institute of Scotland (EIS) and health bodies such as British Medical Association (BMA) with their articulation of Scotland's social democratic for the middle classes, is somehow deemed to be by some proof of the power of 'the people'. This is a collective delusion that has been allowed to go on for too long, aided by Labour, Nationalist and Lib Dem politicians who have wanted to tell us comforting stories and have a quiet life.

The journey to this historic debate and what happens after September

2014 has to evoke a deeper radicalism than this. This has to entail going past abstract constructs of imagined 'peoples' and the closed shop of professional groups talking a pseudo-progressive language. Instead, we have to dare I suggest do something heretical and learn something from the successes and language of the right.

Thus we could, rather than defending the existing configurations of public services, begin to map out a different settlement. The idea of democratising public services could be taken back from the interests of the few, the middle classes, the pushy and the corporate classes and outsourcers. After all what is being proposed is a populist, limited, even fraudulent democracy, whereas a radical approach would envisage a deep seated, sweeping democratisation of public life. What have we exactly to be scared off in this? That people will occasionally make the 'wrong' choices and not be sufficiently progressive. That is what happens in democracy, and the present does not exactly work in favour of egalitarian outcomes.

Underneath this there is this fear in elements of the left that 'the people' cannot be trusted with the revolutionary role they have been entrusted with. This is what leads to the invoking of them as an imagined community, one step removed, rather than a reality; so that they can be constantly conjured up and invoked as a cause and claim, rather than seen as the contradictory force they really are.

A programme to begin democratising Scotland would be a bold, ambitious one which would change the face of politics, society and every aspect of public life. This would extent out from public services to areas such as the voluntary sector, business and corporates, and address such thorny issues as corporate governance, the ways in which Scottish businesses can be different from the failed model of Anglo-American capitalism, and the extent to which 'the third sector' is really that different now in its ethos and practices from the state and private sector. The possible detail of this is explored in an Afterword to the book.

There has to be a wider spectrum of debate about what politics is than what is currently on offer. Within politics many conversations turn by default to the state of public services and a predicable menu of possibilities. There is amongst part of the professional classes, the technocrat-consultancy approach of the Crawford Beveridge independent budget report commissioned for the Scottish government with its want of revisiting free, universal services (Beveridge et al, 2010). Then there is the managerial intelligence seen in the Christie Commission with its incremental caution and belief in re-ordering priorities towards preventive spend (Christie, 2011). And finally, there is the strange alliance between professional groups, parts of the left and SNP which presents existing public spending as some kind of enlightened social democratic state to be defended.

None of these three responses are adequate to meet the pressures and expectations people have for public spending. A debate about greater democratisation, choice and decentralisation is going to come. It would be wise to not leave these powerful ideas in the hands of the Taxpayers' Alliance and other right-wing groups. And it would be helpful if the Scottish debate could move off the mixture of defensiveness and complacency which characterises so much of this, and away from the confines of the conservatism on offer from the Beveridge and Christie reports.

This is a potential agenda which could invoke parts of an earlier Scottish and British left radical tradition, and an era when it was alert to who had power and who did not, was interested in decentralism and suspicious of state power. Yet it also belongs to more than the left and one tradition. It could challenge the conservatism of the left, but also the complacencies of Scottish nationalism, and the intricate web and mosaic that is the self-preservation society of large swathes of public life. This would be a philosophy, mindset and set of ambitions which could define much of our public debate, and be worthy of the historic debate Scotland now finds itself with.

CHAPTER SIXTEEN

# The Limits of Politics and the Potential of Scotland International

Scotland, admittedly, has some advantages that Ireland did not possess at independence. It has the same sectarian divide but at least it doesn't map easily on to political loyalties to create a toxic fusion of religion and politics. Its debates on independence do not risk teetering into civil wars. The emblems of an ethnic Scottishness (kilts and clan tartans) are so daft and bogus that nationalism has had to take a more rational, civic, shape. There's an admirable element of hard-headedness in the Scottish position: thanks a lot for the Empire and the industrial revolution but now that they're gone, we'll be off too. It may not be as heroically romantic as the Irish struggle, but cold pragmatism may be more useful to a new state.

FINTAN O'TOOLE, 'Independence is having no one else to blame', *The Times*, 5 June 2012

Leadership, some cynic has said with truth, consists in watching which way the crowd is going and then stepping in ahead. It means the creation of a group power rather than the expression of a personal power. It means either the utilisation and leadership of an existing group mind or the creation and leadership of a new one. Leadership cannot exist without the capacity to persuade, and to make explicit the dimly felt wills of the mass in a common endeavour.

JAMES A. BOWIE, *The Future of Scotland: A Survey of the Present Position with Some Proposals for Future Policy*, W. & R. Chambers 1939

THERE HAS ALWAYS been more to Scotland and public life than the world of politics: there have been other ways of representing and articulating collective identities and how people define themselves. At the same time, the power and reach of 'high Scotland' has never even at its peak been as far-reaching and omnipotent as both it and its opponents liked to think.

The reality of 'high Scotland', whether in the early 20th century – the 1920s and 1930s – or at the height of welfare state Britain in the 1950s and 1960s, was with its paternalism, progress and social control the only Scottish story evident to many. Counter-stories to this did exist, which can be called 'low Scotland', and were made up of working-class voices, cultures and organisations.

Identifying the idea of 'low Scotland' (as in 'high' and 'low' politics) does not necessitate validating the legends and myths of 'radical Scotland' which have been explored earlier. It does require though the need to recognise that the coalescing of immense forces which came together at the onset of the industrial revolution, with brutal industrialisation, population movement within Scotland, emigration and immigration, threw up huge concentrations of wealth, power and poverty.

These huge movements brought forth the rise of socialist and working-class politics as Chapter Eight explored as well as cultural and social consequences which remain to this day. Thus, one result of the changes in society in the 19th century, and a cultural expression of 'low Scotland' was the popularity of football, which from the outset was a 'people's game' with a large working-class involvement, whereas in England its origins were in the upper classes and public schools.

Scotland has a long pedigree in the world of football, the importance of the 'Scotch professors' and role of Queen's Park FC who invented the modern game and a host of Scots explorers who taught the world how to play. There were the working-class men who became heroes and inspirers of generations which to this day extends to the pedigree of Scottish football managers who have succeeded in the English Premiership (Alex Ferguson and Kenny Dalglish being the obvious examples) (see Goldblatt, 2009).

Football matters in Scottish society, and this concluding chapter explores tensions in the game between the authorities, the fans and the issue of the media and how power is held accountable. It then addresses how social change and a different politics and culture can be nurtured, before addressing the wider international dimension – of where Scotland chooses to sit geopolitically, the different choices we have and what these mean.

## The People's Game and Why It Matters So Much in Scotland

Football provides an illuminating case study of the changing dynamics of Scottish society. It can throw light on the scale of the closed order world that so defined Scotland in recent memory, and how it has been increasingly weakened, hollowed out and come under sustained scrutiny. All of this has relevance for a politics and culture of change which connects with everyday experiences, emotions, fears and dreams.

In January 1971 in the New Year Rangers versus Celtic fixture, the tragic Ibrox disaster occurred towards the end of the game, when part of the ground known as Stairway Thirteen collapsed, killing 66 people. It was an emblem for all that was wrong with the game and with inadequate safety standards at grounds. There had been four previous incidents at Ibrox. In 1902 (25 were killed at a Scotland v. England game), and three in the previous decade at Stairway Thirteen, all at 'Old Firm' matches – 1961 (two killed), 1967 (11 injured) and 1969 (29 injured). Rangers knew that a potential disaster was waiting to happen, as did police authorities and football commentators such as Archie Macpherson.

Two wider factors from this tell us about the Scotland of this era. Firstly, the BBC in London said that they did not trust BBC Scotland to properly cover the disaster. This played into the prevalent belief that sports journalists in Scotland were nearly exclusively pro-Rangers and would not sufficiently hold the club to account. The other was that in a subsequent civil action Rangers were told to pay damages to the family of one of 56 victims of the 66 (Charles Dougan) who died as a result of traumatic asphyxia. Despite this verdict, Rangers fans closed rank around the club, and no part of the Scottish media pushed to explore the implications of this verdict.

Fast forward 40 years and the slow implosion of Rangers FC saw the pernicious existence of 'succulent lamb journalism' whereby leading journalists such as the BBC's Chick Young and the *Daily Record*'s Jim Traynor would regurgitate Ibrox press releases in the age of David Murray (it proving no surprise that when Rangers were liquidated Traynor resurfaced as Rangers Head of Communications for a year).

When Rangers went into, first, administration in February 2012 and then, liquidation, in July of the same year, the barriers and conformist codes which held up this outlook began to break. Social media sites began to ask awkward questions of not just Rangers, but Scottish football authorities. At first these people were dismissed by the football establishment and the mainstream media as 'internet bampots', but this proved to underestimate their qualities. Social media authorities such as RangersTax-Case (winner of the 2012 Orwell Price) and Phil Mac Giolla Bhain mined away obsessionally at the detail of Rangers downfall. Some of this wasn't attractive: the former over-stated the nature of what became known as 'the Big Tax Case', while the latter in his own words was driven by his 'hatred of Rangers' and desire to do them harm. The point was that they filled a vacuum left by the mainstream media and began to challenge the existing order. In the wake of this traditional media followed: with the likes of Channel Four's Alex Thomson, BBC Scotland's Jim Spence, and co-presenter of BBC Scotland *Off the Ball*, Stuart Cosgrove, recognising the longer tail to this story.

The second potent strand of this was the explosion of fan power in the summer of 2012. The football authorities, faced with the implosion of the old Rangers, wanted to stitch a deal up keeping the 'new' Rangers in the top-flight league. This would traditionally have been how things were done. However, faced with this old-fashioned shoddy stitch-up, the football fans of the non-'Old Firm' top clubs rebelled. Organising in social media forums, the fans of Aberdeen, Dundee United, Hearts and others, stated that if their club chairman acquiesced to such a deal they would boycott their clubs in the next season. Faced with this unprecedented pressure, the clubs buckled and voted to not allow the 'new' Rangers to become part of the Scottish Premier League.

This then continued into the lower flight of the game. The football authorities after their first rebuttal tried again, insisting that the game could only survive Rangers out of the top flight for a brief sojourn, and that the best face-saving compromise was for Rangers to start their new life in what was then League One, the division below the top flight. Thus started the whole cycle of social media and fan power again, with supporters of the 30 lower league clubs finding expression and voice in their collective opposition to what was being proposed, and indicating that they would withhold their support from their own clubs if this came to pass. The end result of this was that the 'new' Rangers were voted into Scotland's lowest league, Division Three, a compromise which left many of their fans aggrieved and hurt, but which also fast-tracked the 'new' club back into league membership.

All of this was about much more than football and represents a huge moment not just for Rangers, fans of the game and the authorities, but for Scottish society. Something significant and long-term happened in the summer of 2012 which has deeper implications. This was one of the first occasions in modern Scotland when the institutional barriers and controls were broken and overturned by popular opinion.

This had not happened in any other walk of public life. Even the poll tax non-payment of 1989–90 did not stop the tax which was defeated by the voters of southern England (and in particular the Tory humiliation in the Eastbourne by-election in late 1990). From the other side of the political spectrum, Brian Soutar's 'Keep the Clause' unofficial referendum on Clause 28 in 2000 and the 'promotion' of homosexuality in schools, while it scared the new devolved administration, did not actually stop the legislation or get ministers to back down.

It is not an accident that the first major instance of institutional control being challenged and over-turned should happen in football. It is redolent of the importance of the game in society: in history, identities, numbers and the sheer resonance it has within communities the length and breadth of the land. Scotland is one of the most football-obsessed nations in the world; according to writer Simon Kuper, the third most fanatical nation per head in Europe, after Iceland and Cyprus (Kuper and Szymanski, 2009).

The football authorities in Scotland, the SFA and SPL, were similar to many other parts of society: treating their clientele with a historic disdain bordering on contempt, and in thinking via literal interpretations of their rulebooks that they could do what they liked. For years the SFA was seen as filled with old buffers and backwoodsmen, and then along came to it and the SPL, two technocratic, pragmatic bureaucrats with their MBA jargon filled speak: Stewart Regan at the SFA and Neil Doncaster at the SPL (now SPFL).

They attempted, in the summer of 2012, to combine the worst of the old and new: doing what they liked in the interests of the big clubs, while justifying it in the new language of the managerial class. Something snapped and they pushed the old stitch-ups too far. The continual humiliation of the English language in their consultancy talk infuriated people; and there was the issue of natural justice and a 'new' Rangers not being allowed to just continue as if nothing had happened.

Fan power defeated this and broke the levees which surrounded the machinations and justifications of how the Scottish game was run. The long-term consequences of this are many. Football fans showed that they are not passive but can organise, be coherent and have influence. The modern business models of the game based on TV rights and global branding were seen as not being the sole dynamics in deciding what is good for the game.

It was a painful episode for some. Many Rangers fans felt picked upon by the other clubs, and some of them singled out the likes of Channel Four's Alex Thomson and BBC Scotland's Jim Spence for their opprobrium. Many Celtic fans, while professing that this was the right course, in their hearts missed their old rival which gave them much of their meaning, and in particular, felt a void where once there was the circus of regular 'Old Firm' games.

Something profound had happened. Seismic, difficult change occurred. The old way of doing things dressed in the unappetising language of the corporate world was prevented. Institutional carve-ups and arrogance can only continue so long in a society where people have a say and are motivated and educated. It will be interesting to observe where the next 'revolt of the masses' will manifest itself, and where next authority will be challenged for taking the people for granted. But happen it will and with this Scotland will fundamentally change more.

There is also another dimension to all of this worth exploring. This is the role of working-class culture and of political activism in and around football in a way which is not seen in conventional politics. Sport of course has always been political. Barbara Ehrenreich's idea of 'collective joy' describes gatherings which have in their activity an element of spontaneity, unpredictability and even dangerousness (2007). The example of 'the Mexican wave' was one such phenomenon at football grounds, before it was corporatised and sanitised; this has a cycle by which spectators become participants and then spectators again.

The complex changing nature of football in Scotland saw football fans at many clubs kick back against the inexorable corporatisation and marketisation of the game. Passionate supporters of the big clubs such as the Green Brigade at Celtic and Blue Order at Rangers took a stand against the way their clubs were run and increasingly made public political stands. One of the main ways they did this was expressing themselves by huge banners they showcased at their home grounds.

The Green Brigade's response to plans to put the remembrance poppy on Celtic strips saw them unfurl a huge banner at Celtic Park declaring, 'No Blood Stained Poppy On Our Hoops' and stated 'Your deeds would shame all the devils in hell' and the words, 'Ireland Iraq Afghanistan'. This provoked a *Daily Mail* headline, 'Shame of Celtic after fans stage a "blood-stained" protest against wearing Remembrance Day poppies' (6 November 2010). Rangers fans, incensed by the myriad maneuverings of the Board and Directors post-liquidation, had finally started to protest: the Sons of Struth supporters group unveiling banners at games stating 'It's Our Club and We Want It Back' and 'Spivs Out! Let Your Voice Be Heard!'

There are many layers to these protests and banners, much of which has remained untold. This is not to argue that everything these fan groups do is attractive or edifying. The controversy at the end of 2013 surrounding the Green Brigade's actions prior to an important European match, where they unveiled portraits of William Wallace and Bobby Sands, and a banner stating, 'The terrorist or the dreamer? The savage or the brave? Depends whose vote you are trying to catch or whose face you're trying to save', created a minor cultural storm. To some of the Green Brigade, this was a natural expression of their Irish republican roots, to other Celtic fans and the club, the final straw and UEFA fined Celtic £42,000 for what they called an 'illicit banner' (*Daily Mail*, 13 December 2013). This combined with fan misbehavior at a Motherwell away game resulted in the club taking action against some of the Green Brigade (*The Scotsman*, 10 December 2013).

Yet, the bigger picture is of the self-organising, motivated groups who undertake these campaigns, create networks and make these banners. At clubs like Celtic, Rangers and Aberdeen, fans make their own banners and run what are in effect self-education classes on art, painting and creativity. This is a politics of working-class activism the length and breadth of Scotland, at odds with the corporatisation of football, and in a very different space from where 'official' politics have ended up.

This is people remembering and creating living histories of their clubs and communities, taking on the football authorities, and engaging in a wider politics beyond the game, seen in the campaigns against the Offensive Behaviour at Football and Threatening Communications (Scotland) Act 2012. Whether people agree or disagree with some of these activities and stands taken, or bemoan the over-dominance of football in public life, something important is going on in all of the above with lessons for society.

## How to Defeat Minority Report Scotland

For too many in Scotland what is viewed as politics is drawn narrowly and inflexibly. This is understandable in those who want to retain the status quo and their position in a system which works well for them. However, it is a prevalent view in large parts of the left and nationalist opinion. To begin to change Scotland this mindset has to be challenged and a wider sense of politics and human experience has to be articulated and allowed to flourish.

Two reflections illustrate the problems of the limited palate on offer. Pre-2007, when Scottish Labour still saw itself as 'the natural party of government' endlessly into the distant future, a Labour minister in the devolved administration said to me, after I had produced a book on the future of Scotland through the idea of stories, 'I liked it when you wrote your Fabian Society pamphlets and you didn't do this story stuff'. Move forward a few years, past the Scottish watershed of 2007 and the SNP coming to office, and an SNP minister proposed to me that independence was straightforward and simple and would only take 'the extension of the Scotland Act 1998' to cover all aspects of domestic policy and everything else.

What the above conversations exemplify is the narrow frame of reference of most of the Scottish political classes and two points emerge. First, most, if not all, of this class are only able to see the relevance of traditional policy thinking: whether this is the politics of 'modernisation' in Labour circles or just the plain institutional conservatism of large parts of the SNP, and are closed to anything that is more creative, bold and risk-taking.

Second, there is the limited notion of how some see independence. This is not in any sense about far-reaching, fundamental or transformational change. Instead, it is all focused on 'the full powers of the Parliament', and of change which is seamless, without any upheaval, and certainly no rupture, and does not address or investigate wider cultural or social change. In summary, it poses independence as the continuation of status quo Scotland but with a fresh broom in charge. That is a very limited form of change which will not excite and deliberately excludes the vast majority of the population.

Beginning to challenge this minority report Scotland involves a range of activities. It entails us stopping seeing politics as solely about politicians and independence. It involves political change as being about wider forces such as culture, identity and the personal; and this goes for the narrow framing of independence so far. It means the institutional closed shop of too much of our public life has to begin to be questioned. Why should we take as face value the so-called enlightened elites in education, health, law and the media, that they are the peoples' champions? And we have to begin to recognise that beyond the narrow bandwidth of a constrained 'official' politics, a more disputatious, diverse, self-organised politics and cultural activism is emerging which points to a very different and much more pluralist Scotland.

More profoundly, doing this involves two key components: addressing the issue of ideas and ideology, and understanding the importance of priorities and time. In the first, the concepts of self-determination in politics, culture, philosophy and psychology are kernel to moving beyond socialist nostalgia and managerial conservatism. When combined with the triptych of values, voice and vessels, this offers the potential of challenging the closed conversations of 'high Scotland'.

Aiding ambition, boldness and radicalism requires a nuanced strategy and addressing the issues of timescales. Thirty years ago, Bernard Crick wrote a Fabian Society pamphlet entitled *Socialist Values and Time* in which he explored how to nurture and advance progressive values (1984). He argued that much of the rhetoric and language of what passed for radical politics was unreflective and based on what could be called an 'instant gratification culture' of the left.

Previous generations used to talk about achieving socialism 'in the lifetime of the next Labour Government' or 'fundamental and irreversible shifts in power' as if they could be enacted by sheer human will power and wish fulfillment in an instant. Crick argued that such attitudes represented an immaturity and, even more made disappointment, retreat and defeat more likely, disillusioning people and activists, and leading to either apathy or even worse a swing to the right.

Taking a different tack, Crick argued that those on the left needed to adopt a much more bold and nuanced politics at the same time and 'campaign on three different levels'. These he identified: '(i) short-term tactical reforms within the system to build a basis of popular confidence for advance; (ii) middle-term strategies to change the system; and (iii) long-term persuasion to work a new system in a new spirit'. He concluded with the observation, 'These levels do not contradict, they complement each other so long as the distinctions about time are clear' (1984: 37).

The political intelligence of Crick's analysis of timescales is relevant for the politics of far-reaching progressive change and for the dynamics of the Scottish good. Thirty years after he wrote this we live in a world in which the word 'strategy' (like story) is ubiquitous: simultaneously everywhere and nowhere at the same time (Freedman, 2013). Yet, if we are serious about, for example, rebuilding the public realm, making sure that public goods such as education and health are not treated like commodities, and acting upon the desire to be a more egalitarian society, there needs to be a differentiated approach about how we move towards that.

Thus, the current debate either from SNP or Labour lacks such an awareness of the radical intention and destination of policies, and so is compromised in all sorts of trade-offs in the here and now. For example, the SNP's policy on corporation tax in an independent Scotland is to be 3p below the UK government, and thus linked to their policies; while New Labour in office engaged in a Dutch auction of steadily reducing the main rate of corporation tax in Gordon Brown's ten year period as Chancellor from 33 per cent to 28 per cent. A politics of timescales would begin to ask what is the legitimate contribution to ask businesses to make, and not make the mistake of falling for the argument that buying corporate orthodoxy is the same as being pro-business. In relation to public goods, this would involve asking what is desirable about being able to buy education and health, two key components of being a civilised society, and begin to take appropriate action in how these services are run and taxed.

This has to be located in a politics which recognises the wider contours of the Scottish debate and its UK implications. If we survey the possible and preferable Scottish futures, given the majority of Scots do not want to live in a conservative Britain, meaning the continuation of the current dynamics of the UK with their economic, social and cultural prioritisation of a minuscule, increasingly intolerant and anti-social elite, this leaves us with three possible futures.

First, is the future which we could call *progressive Britain*. This is associated with the Labour vision of Britain, but not completely exclusively. If it is to have continued traction and appeal north of the border, its advocates have to tell the rest of us how this is feasibly going to be achieved considering the realities of modern Britain? Labour has much to be proud of in its past at a Scottish and British level (and much not to be), but from a purely factual point since 1945 there has been at a UK level four distinct periods of Labour government covering 30 years. With the exception of the 1945 Attlee administration, not one of the remaining governments has significantly challenged the institutions of 'conservative Britain' or reduced poverty and inequality. If this is the historic evidence, supporters of a progressive Britain have to address why this was the case and why if it all it could be different in the future.

Second, there is what can be described as *continuity, conservative Scotland*. This was once the position of Scottish Labour, but seems to have become the vision of the SNP leadership. It suggests that independence is the best guarantee of continuing the existing order of Scottish society. This approach is about minimalising risk and uncertainty in independence, but begs the question, why would people embrace the degree of upheaval if there were to be little prospect of change?

Third, is the prospect of *the third Scotland*. This I have previously described, emerged particularly through the independence debate, in a host of energetic, dynamic, mostly self-organised initiatives such as National Collective, Jimmy Reid Foundation and the Radical Independence Campaign. This puts social change at the vanguard of constitutional change. A major challenge is that it has to answer how, given its weak institutional voice, it can overcome the entrenched interests of conservative Scotland and adherents to the above two propositions.

Assessing the merits of the above three, the idea of a progressive Britain looks less and less plausible in the foreseeable future. The second, continuity Scotland, looks like the position of 'middle Scotland', and of the old establishment (who combined it within the framework of progressive Britain) and new establishment. Therefore, irrespective of whether Scotland is independent or not this is the mindset of steady as she goes, safety first Scotland which is uninterested in shifting power and facing up to some of our long-term challenges. The 'third Scotland' is nearly entirely but not exclusively pro-independence, but it poses that social change is more important than the formalities of constitutional change, and is made up of a rich array of radical voices, not all of whom can be labelled 'nationalist'. Its challenge is how it translates the energies and creativities into some kind of coherent set of ideas for a future Scotland that can compete with the other scenarios.

If we examine this terrain in relation to possible futures, with the viability of a progressive Britain off the agenda for many years, the realm of debate is between continuity, conservative Scotland and 'the third Scotland'. The former has shaped the parameters of much of mainstream politics, the SNP and previously, Labour in Scotland. The latter is weak institutionally and while it has numerous initiatives, it is going to struggle in the short to medium term to challenge the former. Yet, it has to be said it is in 'the third Scotland' that something interesting is happening about Scottish politics, culture and beyond. This represents both a shift in generational and institutional power, and taps into the prevalent desire for a different Scotland. That manifest feeling has to be addressed and nurtured.

Drawing on ideas in previous chapters – imagination, humour and playfulness are means by which the mantras of institutional and conservative Scotland, including of a left and nationalist kind, can be undermined. For example, are such perspectives really proposing, in the words

'We Love Real Life Scotland' *by Ross Sinclair.*

of cultural activist and artist Ross Sinclair, that 'we love real life Scotland'
(2012) – with all that entails? At least posing the question begins a more
interesting debate.

## Scotland International: The Four Dimensions Geopolitically

Scotland's debate on self-government is not about being 'separatist', 'little
Scotlanders' or 'narrow nationalists'. It is about our country collectively
deciding what it wants to do and aspire to as a society, and then addressing what is the best way of achieving this. Related to this endeavour is the
task of Scotland rethinking and repositioning itself internationally.

This is something numerous other countries have done at crucial
points in their history. Take two examples. Finland (after being in a union
with Sweden), in the 20th century shifted from being part of imperial Russia
to, in the immediate post-war era, operating with cognisance to Soviet
sensibilities before post-Soviet collapse and then shifted to where it currently
resides as Nordic, and European. Turkey was previously the heart of the
Ottoman Empire and the dominant Muslim and Middle East power,
along with being powerful in the Mediterranean. Post-Ottoman it aspired
to become a modern European nation, and in recent times has oscillated
between seeing itself as European and a Middle East regional power.

What these two cases show is that nations more often than not do not
arrive at final destinations which become fixed and immovable: an argument which can be underwritten by the UK's semi-detached, sceptical relationship of 40 years plus with the European Union, currently heading to
some kind of climax in a future referendum.

Scotland geopolitically has at least four critical influences in this
respect. First, there is the British dimension. This is predominantly but not
exclusively about England and what is called in some quarters 'the English
question'. This phrase attempts to describe the English condition as constitutional change happens all round it in the UK leaving England this unreformed, undemocratic entity run by direct rule from Westminster. So far
the English people have shown no inclination to want to change or challenge this state of affairs, but that may not always be the case.

One of the other interpretations of 'the English question' is that it
signals the search for an English identity post-Empire which the English
political classes have clearly painfully struggled with since decolonisation.
Perhaps the evolution of Scottish self-government could, if it led to formal
independence, galvinise England into having these long overdue discussions.

Then there is the UK beyond England. Plaid Cymru former MP Adam Price recently commented that pro-union opinion north of the border talking of Scottish independence along the lines of 'divorce' and 'separation' was not a very helpful way of thinking about matters. Instead, in terms of the UK union, there were Price argued, 'four people in the marriage', by which he meant the Scots, English, Welsh and Northern Irish (*The Guardian*, 23 October 2013). This raises the possibility of a new, more democratic set of arrangements between the four nations of the UK, and irrespective of whether Scotland is formally independent, of a very different kind of union.

This would entail the Westminster classes' unitary state mentality (which is one of the major problems in the current UK), giving way to a more fluid, messy, multi-speed union, made of self-governing nations in a union of states. Linda Colley in her new collection on the crises of the union of the UK notes that 'many of the old sustaining stories and shibboleths… are played out' (2014: 154); and then proposes a complete overhaul of the entire British system: an English Parliament somewhere other than London, a federal settlement and a written constitution, but does not say how this can happen. Change is happening and going to continue, but it is unlikely to follow Colley's neat and ordered prescription.

Second, there is the European dimension. Does Scotland remain part of the UK's rather painful, unsatisfactory, carping from the sidelines relationship with the European Union? Or does it aspire to be part of the core European project with all that entails in terms of political integration? On the one hand, Scotland aspires to be a modern, progressive, European nation, and yet the possibilities of this happening have occurred at a time of multiple crises of the European project: of the euro, of elite Europe, of a seismic democratic deficit in its institutions and decisions, and in the Franco-German alliance.

Arguably there is no feasible future in the short to medium term where the UK political elites suddenly realise that the UK should be a thoroughly European country. The realisation that the UK is slowly detaching itself from the EU is now prevalent with quite a bit of sadness and regret in European political elites, including once traditional allies of the UK. The UK is heading on a major geopolitical journey in relation to the EU. And all of this has huge consequences for Scotland.

Third, there is the American-Atlanticist dimension which can be seen in the defence and security implications around Trident and the NATO military industrial complex situated in Scotland. Then there is the intertwining of UK and US security and intelligence interests and how bodies like MI5 and MI6 share information with the CIA and NSA and co-exist in a mutually reinforcing database state, which Edward Snowden's revelations in *The Guardian* showed to be engaging in mass surveillance on an unprecedented scale.

Then there are the foreign policy dimensions of this debate which stretch beyond the recent controversies of Blair, Afghanistan and Iraq, to how the UK has uncritically positioned itself in the world as an advocate of US strategic interests (the inter-related security and intelligence work of Britain's GCHQ with the US NSA being but one example).

Related to this is how successive British governments have seen it as their role to act as cheerleaders for an Anglo-American capitalism and market fundamentalism, which is predominantly and at times exclusively focused on the interests of the super-rich, finance capital, deregulation and outsourcing or privatising what were once public services. UK Governments, including the Blair-Brown New Labour era, even take pride in evangelicising for this global class ideology across the world; for example, Claire Short as International Development Minister led a huge programme advocating water privatisation across Africa (House of Commons, 19 June 2002). This worldview has completely disfigured British politics and driven it markedly rightwards in the last 30 years.

The Scottish self-government debate is influenced by a revulsion at this trajectory and its consequences, but countering it involves addressing Scotland's position in the NATO military industrial complex, and that Scottish businesses and finances have played a leading role in creating the ethos and inequities of Anglo-American capitalism.

Fourth, there is the northern European and Nordic dimension. This is focused upon the connection between Scotland and the Nordic nations, and the potential of Scotland to advance and institutionalise more social democratic values in its politics and public policy choices. This has been until recently the weakest of the four strands, but in the last few years has become one more Scots have shown an interest in developing.

Acknowledging Scotland's potential as a northern nation and becoming more Nordic addresses the desire to reject the Anglo-American model of capitalism, and to find a more progressive, egalitarian and sustainable future path. It also touches on a desire for an international Scotland to find new alliances and ways of expressing itself, along with a geopolitical interest in the politics and ecology of what is called 'the new north', which stretches far beyond the Nordics to all the lands sharing a similar longitude.

The above four strands cross-sect and influence each other, and whichever way Scotland's debate develops in the future, all four will have a bearing on how it sees itself, acts in the world, the alliances and values it collectively chooses, and how it is seen by others. Post-September 2014, there will not be a final denouement of these four, but a continually shifting and dynamic Scotland as it collectively moves geopolitically and becomes, on existing trends, less British but remaining so in many of its character-istics. It will move towards being less shaped by the ethos of contempo-rary Anglo-American interests, but which will still be influential, and more by European, northern and Nordic norms.

In conclusion, I want to return back to the personal and how this influences and informs the wider political and cultural. This is, after all, the way many if not all of us interpret and understand how we have come to see the world. My father, Edwin, had his politics shaped by a certainty and idealism of the culture of the left. This set of beliefs, and even faiths, ran on a spectrum from believing in the Soviet Union for some, to the idea that Britain could become a socialist country, to an anchoring in working-class identity and organisation, and sense that a more economically and social just future was being created by the actions of the labour movement and progressives of many different types and hues.

All of that now seems a foreign country compared to where we stand in Scotland, the UK and internationally. My father's views represent an elegy for a lost Scotland which could still be seen in the public responses to the Grangemouth oil refinery crisis and the Govan BAE shipyard job losses. The world may have changed: employment, work, trade union attitudes and membership, the shape of society, gender and how men and women act and interact, and so much more in just over a generation. Yet, at the same time, the collective memories of the power of working-class self-organisation and the value of solidarity and inter-connectedness have not been wholly lost. People know hyper-individualism – reducing human beings to mere commodities and brands – is not enough or in any way attractive, and is in fact close often to a grotesque dystopia.

The world then has changed but in other ways it has not. Part of this answer within at least my personal story lies in the politics my mother, Jean, represented. They were more community based, about doing, supporting and aiding others, were activist based without ever using that word, and rooted in an idealism about people that was practical. Somehow I think the authenticity of that approach with its focus on nurturing alliances and groups, and gently creating change without lecturing or hectoring people offers more insights than the route of always being sure of your ground and your correctness.

Our quest for a different Scotland is a historic one. It is beyond the claims and traditions of any one part of our country. We should let no one perspective or viewpoint claim ownership of this cause. Underneath all of these debates we need confidence in an idealism relevant for these times which rises above dogma and inflexibility, but the perils of cynicism and fatalism too. This has to be combined with an attitude of hope and possibility that says we can collectively shape our future, and with an element of certainty and resolution that we can do this in an age filled with uncertainty and doubt.

This is a time which requires a new kind of idealism: humble, generous, pluralist and outward looking. If that sounds a tall order we should also remember that it adds strength for this idealism to be profoundly human and know when it fails or falls short, as it inevitably will. This will not matter if we learn from these, grow and adapt and develop a culture and ecology of self-government and self-determination.

What will the Scotland many of us aspire to live in look like? Can it genuinely be a society and nation which faces up to these challenges? For all the questioning and challenging in the proceeding pages, I believe we are already on this journey. The Scotland of the future, the place that faces up to hard choices, that calls power to account, but at the same time dares to dream and believe in a different Scotland, is already being created by the sum total of thousands upon thousands of Scots up and down this land.

The Scotland of the future is being collectively brought into the here and now by the efforts of countless Scots. The words of the ancient Chinese philosopher Lao Tzu offer a glimpse of the kind of change we need to have the will and desire to make happen:

> As for the best leaders, the people do not notice their existence. The next best, the people honour and praise; the next the people fear; and the next the people hate. But when the best leaders' work is done, the people say 'we did it ourselves'. (quoted in Benn, 1970: front cover)

# Afterword: How to Make a New Democracy

THE UK IS NOT and never has been a fully-fledged political democracy. In numerous elite conversations this fact is implicitly recognised. The UK is described accurately as a constitutional monarchy or as a parliamentary democracy. The reality is that the UK is increasingly influenced by the repackaging and representing of its past by its elites, and the appropriation of the voices of past generations like some once splendid country house fallen on hard times and telling tales of yesteryear.

Scotland, on the other hand, likes to imagine and see itself differently – as democratic, disputatious, argumentative, less hierarchical and deferential. Yet, Scotland now is not and never has been a democracy. For most of its history it has been shaped by powerful institutions, its own establishment and elite opinion.

In both cases – Scotland and the UK – we are only talking about the narrow confines of political democracy, not economic and social concerns. These latter issues which have existed in previous political ages could not currently be more removed from the mainstream of British and Scottish considerations, but they cannot forever be omitted and kept to the margins.

Scottish society professes to be democratic and where political authority is meant to have its source in the popular will, but this is within a constricted, tightly defined and regulated public space. This is then further restricted by the limited nature of what passes for British democracy historically, and which is growing ever weaker due to increased centralisation and the rise of the mass surveillance database state. It is not an accident that *The Economist*'s 'Democracy Index' has seen the UK decline in its ratings for each of the first five years of the index (Economist Intelligence Unit, 2013).

Scotland is not that different from this at the moment. Our democratic areas of consent and legitimacy are small indeed – centring on the Scottish Parliament and the election of Scottish MPs to the House of Commons – leaving aside whether the weathered institutions of local government are in any way worthy of that name given the constraints on them.

It has been the argument of this book that for all this a sizeable, powerful section of Scottish society aspires to live in a democracy – one that is a fully functioning political democracy. One which even begins to explore issues of economic and social democratisation as well. It could of course be argued that such sentiment – particularly the first feeling – could be identified all over the UK – and find voice in England in some future form in relation to two unions: the post-devolution UK and Europe. But for the moment there is little sign of this, whereas in Scotland there is the potential of change now and in the foreseeable future.

To begin to explore and offer some tangible policy recommendations in line with the arguments contained in the book, I offer a programme for the making of a more democratic Scotland below. This may be in places imperfect and not the final word, but it is a realistic, idealistic and deliverable set of policies which would, if implemented, change Scotland in a fundamental manner, and begin to oversee a dramatic shift in power and voice.

In planning this menu of policies I elicited comments and suggestions from 60 people across Scottish society. These came from all walks of life – from academics and journalists, to business people, trade unionists, think tanks, NGOs, campaigners and activists. The sample, while in no way representative of the wider nation, was drawn up with sensitivities on age, class, gender, ethnicity and place, but most of all people had something to say. I restricted each person to two suggestions (all of which are anonymous) on the question of how do we make Scotland a better democracy – a land more egalitarian, inclusive and run by and for the vast majority of the people.

These comments are presented in two ways. First comes a list of 50 which mixes some of the contributors' ideas with some of my own and which are proposed as insights into the way forward for a different Scotland. This is then followed by a further selection of comments that illustrate the wealth and breadth of imagination and engagement proposed by the group of 60 people.

Some observers will note that the definition of a democracy covers the political, economic and social, and also that the list does not take an explicit stance on whether Scotland should or should not be an independent nation. This latter position is a deliberate one. Shifting Scotland to becoming more of a democracy and collectively discussing what kind of society we wish to be should be what leads and informs the independence debate. Discussing and agreeing this first is the best way to make constitutional change alive and relevant to the public, rather than as an arid and specialist subject.

Some may see this as entailing the act of Scotland writing itself a modern constitution, and the processes by which this comes about. Of course it does. However this may make it sound like a legal confinement, not the inspiring aspiration that establishes what constitutions mean. This is both fundamental and far-reaching. We cannot create and then inhabit a constitution without the more important democratic spaces and cultures coming into being at the same time. What we are talking about is voice in its deepest sense: becoming a people and a polity.

This is, to put it simply, an outline for a comprehensive programme for shifting Scotland from a debate and focus on self-government to one based on self-determination. There is a fundamental difference between the two: the first has become focused on institutions, a confined version of politics, and politicians as the main agents of change. The second is about a much more fluid notion of change and wider idea of politics, less focused and owned by institutions. The latter can inform and make more relevant the former so that this is not an either/or.

## A Menu of Fifty Possible Policy Actions

1   Every Scottish citizen should have opportunity to contribute to and help shape a new Scottish constitution. This should not be done by the time-old gathering of the great and the good invoking the people in a Constitutional Convention, but should instead directly involve the people and learn from the new constitutionalism breaking out around the world.

2   Change the Scottish Parliament electoral system from the Additional Member System (AMS) with its closed lists to either the Single Transferable Vote (STV) or open lists.

3   Encourage all political parties to have open primaries for their parliamentary candidates.

4   A right of recall of MSPs/MPs subject to petition signed by ten per cent of the local electorate.

5   Establish a Second Chamber elected by STV open list.

6   Draw up a legal framework protecting local self-government – a constitution of local democracy. This would formally protect not just the autonomy and status of local government – something Westminster has never done – but would provide a commitment to real subsidiarity across a range of political, economic and social areas.

7   Establish structures of substantive local government – with significant powers and autonomy – and a clear, direct link between local taxation and local spending.

8   Increase the number of local councils from the current 32 based on 163,200 people per local council to closer to the European Union average of 5,630 people, depending on demand and interest.

9   Limit the number of terms that local councillors are allowed to serve on local councils to a maximum of two terms.

10  Immediate abolition of council tax freeze.

11  To eliminate land speculation and stabilise land markets, introduce land value taxation as a replacement for council tax, business rates and land and buildings transaction tax.

12  Community ownership of energy development and companies.

13  Secure Scotland's renewable energy dividend with it made a condition of planning consent that a percentage of each project's equity be put aside for local ownership or into a National Renewables Fund for the common good.

14  A network of local tax and welfare advice centres established based in the main local authority buildings.

15  A citizen's income is created which is an unconditional, non-with-drawable income payable to each individual as a right of citizenship.

16  Adopt a policy of reducing the gap between the highest and lowest paid. This should include within it a ratio between the highest and lowest paid as proposed in the recent Swiss referendum.

17  All enterprises whether public, private or voluntary employing more than 100 people should once a year have to publicly report the average rewards including bonuses, stock options and any other related income. This would be cost neutral as those organisations which were more ethical and socially concerned would attract more business and custom.

18  A new honours system aimed at celebrating our highest paid taxpayers. Those who pay the most tax (in percent) in every community would be celebrated in a local new year's honours list. Basic information on the amount of tax that everyone pays would be available as a matter of public record as in Norway.

19  Replace GDP as the major indicator of national progress with a measurement such as Oxfam Scotland's Humankind Index. This will include economic, social, sustainable, equitable and democratic indices.

20  Employers and communities have a statutory right to convert an enterprise into an employee or community owned one whenever there is a takeover bid or proposed closure. A limited version of this has existed in Italy since 1985 called the Marcora law.

21  Change the UK Treasury rule that forbids Danish style employee pensions which are run with very low fees and fair pay outs. Currently Scots are shortchanged to the tune of £3 billion per annum in existing employment pensions.

22  Limit the number of boards which directors can sit upon at any one time to two.

23  Term limits for all public appointments to public boards to two successive terms.

24  A central bank under democratic control.

25  A legal right for children (whether minors or adults) to inherit land and property.

26  Accountability of the Crown Estate in Scotland to the Scottish Parliament along with the administration and revenues of the Crown's property rights to Scotland's territorial seabed and adjoining continental shelf area.

27  Introduce an initial gender quota of 30 per cent on all public bodies rising to 50 per cent within ten years.

28  Apply equality laws to religious organisations, including faith schools.

29  Invest in health visitors. Currently the vast majority of health visitors stop visiting babies when they have reached six weeks. Only recently has a second stage been added at 30 months – for a range of tests for all children. In Holland and Germany the number of visits over this 30 month period would be ten. Yet Scotland is cutting rather than increasing the number of health visitors.

30  Prevent GPs working for the NHS as autonomous private businesses which is currently commonplace and detrimental to national health priorities and hugely expensive.

31  Scotland's schools should become learning centres able to encourage talent in any field and facilitate individual learning. They should be able to offer education to anyone irrespective of their age, ability or background.

32  Family studies and healthy relationships should be taught to all children. Future generations of Scotland need to know how to value themselves and others and to have confident life and social skills to aid them in forming and maintaining better relationships.

33  Every child aged from 12 months until they start school is entitled to free, high quality nursery care three days a week. This will assist in child development and allow parents, especially mothers, to work, so contributing to the economy and society.

34  Every child when they start primary school is automatically enrolled in their local library.

35  A Young Scots volunteers (YSV) programme. Every young person between the ages of 17 and 21 years has to compete a placement of at least six months, volunteering at home or preferably abroad. The

scheme would award places competitively, not based on academic achievement, but on a young person's perceived needs and commitment.

36  Abolish illiteracy. Too many Scottish children leave school unable to read which blights their entire lives. This can be done and does not involve huge sums of money or paying teachers large amounts more, and will more than pay for any additional resources from the contribution to society of those who have been aided.

37  Self-directed support for those who need social care is now a right. The principle should be extended to community nursing, employability support services, post-school services, ex-offender services and anywhere else in public life where people can exercise real control over the services they use.

38  Abolish the charitable status of private schools.

39  Establish deliberate democratic processes in every local area alongside official local government structures.

40  A prohibition on government established expert groups filled solely with professionals. All official groups and reviews to have a statutory duty to have direct representation from the groups affected. Government to have a legal duty to reply to any recommendations from such groups within one year of a report publication.

41  All government legislation and policies to have a built-in obsolescence clause. This will state that when the law or policy achieves its result that the relevant professional group(s) to which the legislation pertains is reviewed are not automatically continued and in places abolished. Legislation should recognise that professions have lifespans. There should be time called on the continual cycle of the professional classes.

42  A Scottish Broadcasting Corporation should be set up.

43  A Scottish public sector procurement strategy should be developed given this is big business currently worth £11 billion a year and one which by bundling projects means that few Scottish firms are big enough to apply. A longer-term approach is required with a focus on growing Scots companies, research and development, and employment opportunities.

44  A national 'Get the Vote Out' programme should be rolled out for elections and referenda which is led by a non-politically aligned body. Its aim should be to assist in civic and political citizenship to encourage people to vote and take part in public life. This could draw on examples of political and civic engagement such as the Vincentian Partnership for Social Justice in Ireland which has had marked success in driving up turnout at elections.

45  Priority should be given to improving the take up on the electoral register via a national electoral registration drive. Registration rates have been in long-term decline for four decades, with on some estimates less than 90 per cent of eligible voters on the register, and this is significantly lower among younger and poorer voters.

46  Make the internet a basic utility and universally provided. There should be a universal service obligation on companies to provide a free basic service with people able to upgrade to faster and better speeds if they so wish.

47  A community garden in every primary school. Urban wasteland should be cultivated. Where no land is available, householders could donate their gardens for a reduction in council tax.

48  Allow taxpayers to devote proportions of a set amount between £50–100 per annum to non-profit digitally based news content and research organisations.

49  The national arts and cultural organisation to not see the arts as an extension of economic policy but as a good in themselves. The arts should not be seen as a branch of government policy but should have artists and practitioners at their heart.

50  An Oil Fund for the Mind to be established based on one per cent of the Oil Fund and divided between social justice at home and conflict resolution abroad. This would follow the example of the Norwegian Oil Fund which has earmarked a small percentage for international conflict resolution and played a constructive role in the Tamil Tiger-Sri Lanka civil war.

Finally, and most importantly, Scotland should become a modern country and democracy.

APPENDIX

# Some More Detailed Thoughts and Suggestions

HERE ARE A sample of some of the comments and suggestions made when people were invited to make suggestions on how to make Scotland more democratic:

- Encouraging more community ownership of football clubs sends the right kind of signals about what is possible to the average football fan. Previous experience of local football clubs being in the patronage of businessmen as their playthings have shown the weakness of that way of doing things and often with disastrous results. With community ownership there might also be a recognition of operating with available resources rather than with an impossible dream.

- Public Buildings built by and for the Public: abandon the ideological idiocy of asking/begging/bribing banks and construction conglomerates to borrow money expensively to lead the provision of our schools, hospitals, homes and other essential public buildings for their own benefit: instead empower and equip our local authorities to borrow and invest, putting the interests of people at the hearts of their communities.

- Allowing some people to work less would be more reflective of the dramatic changing patterns of work which are far more precarious than ever before with zero hours contracts being endured by increasing numbers of the population. It would be much easier to administer than requiring people to sign on and sign off every time they get some piecemeal work. I also think it would give people stability in uncertain economic climates which has been shown to have massive impacts on both mental and physical health.

- A New Land Economy: development rights should be devolved from government to local communities, with residents as 'community shareholders'. They would vote on whether or not to lease or sell development rights, with the price determined by the environmental impact of development v. its economic benefits. We would move from an adversarial planning regime to a contractual one, with local people sharing the benefits of development and developers having incentives to enhance rather than degrade the landscape. With such an income stream, communities could pay to attract or keep 'loss making' infrastructure such as local shops, transport links or even pubs.

- Scotland has a fantastic history of engineering talent and innovation, so we should really focus on it. Everyone says that we can become the renewables capital of the world, but we need a Green Industrial Strategy to maximise our opportunities and ensure that all Scots benefit from the renewables revolution. For instance, Clyde shipyards should diversify to build turbine blades and other green infrastructure – just like the high-wage economies of Denmark and Germany already do. Scotland needs once again to be proud of a renewed blue-collar identity.

- Scottish football. Ah, such a history, such a difficult present! One simple prescription: look to Germany. Fan ownership, lower prices, home-grown talent. Return the beautiful game to the people and you can't go wrong.

- Shift tax to immobile things like land and to usage (e.g. road use) – thus making tax progressive in assets and behaviour. You'll barely tax the poor at all but have more efficient collection elsewhere. In the process you scrap council tax, corporation tax and others.

- Childcare allowance for those with joint income of under £25,000 to be allowed to be paid to family members (rather than using child minders) i.e. grandparents etc. Lowest earners spend their money locally so this would help both the extended families of the poorest in society and the local economy.

- The Scottish Parliament should agree a three year moratorium on new bills since the current suite (Children's Services, Public Bodies, Procurement, Empowerment) are all vanity projects designed to achieve resource traction but with no real legislative purpose. MSPs could apply their time to driving reforms of the public sector and public services so that they meet the aspirations of the public and are more sustainable.

- In no area is early years intervention more critical than for children and young people 'in care' where 33 per cent are in care still at home, the majority are over 14 years of age, and the complexities of their needs are the same as young people removed from home. Policy and resource investment needs to shift to ensure provision of effective support to families to build resilience, prevent breakdown and unnecessary use of residential placements, where currently the bulk of funding is directed, and which some refer to as demand failure.

- I think Scotland is dominated by a sincere but complacent social democratic elite, which seeks to delimit the boundaries of acceptable analysis, and in effect controls the media. It excludes the majority of the population from power: a curious situation indeed!

- There is in Scotland a long, deep and justified hatred of feudalism, yet we still have the bizarre situation of our so-called noble families, our nouveaux riches, our private equity funds and our biggest companies owning vast tracts of land and property. I am in favour of a Scottish law to replace private property with community property, not on the basis of expropriation, but on the basis that all resources (land, houses, bonds, equities, trusts and money) are to be held and used in trust for and with the direct involvement of wider communities, with strong rights of intervention when this objective is resisted or evaded.

- Renew local democracy – whatever the problem the solution is always more democracy. Scotland's 32 local authorities are the wrong size – too large to be considered 'local' and too small to deliver the cost efficiencies demanded of the public sector. Proposition: establish 14 'super-sized' local authorities (co-terminous with health boards) to deliver strategic public services and back office functions for a new breed of 'burgh-sized' local councils.

- Orkney, Shetland and the Western Isles to be given special status recognising their unique character which legally protects their fiscal and general autonomy. The last thing islanders or any Scots want is to replace one kind of centralisation and distant rule from London with another from Edinburgh.

- The legal freedom to withdraw labour collectively and without restriction combined with powers for the Scottish Parliament and local authorities to own and run public utilities and productive resources without legal restriction by the European Union or the British Parliament.

- A legal requirement for national referenda on any Scottish-wide changes in public ownership. A pro-active right to call referenda via petition of one per cent of the electorate for extending public ownership or privatisation.

- In education we should be looking North to Finland, not South to England and thus West to Chicago...

- A national strategy for airline routes in and out of Scotland. A tax on the transfer of young footballers to major leagues to encourage a national trust for talent development.

- An expansion of 'hutting'. I am stuck by the fact that in the 1930s one of the responses to economic crisis was unemployed workers from Clydeside building huts and growing their own food in places like Carbeth. I think there needs to be a renewed focus on how we enable people to get back to the land in Scotland as part of a process of restoring a landscape that is often lacking both people and bio-diversity.

- Voting to be compulsory. We need to repair our democracy. Our politics would shift if vested interests didn't hold sway and it wasn't about targeting towards who votes. Parties would need to be more universal in their thinking, more whole population focused, less sanguine about inequalities if every vote counted. And we'd be more committed to and value more democracy at all levels as education would go alongside education. No more missing Scotland!

- Bring in substantial tax breaks for venture capital investment in Scotland to promote business investment and encourage an alternative source of finance to bank lending. We need ISA-type tax sheltered investment for young Scottish business start-up and innovation, not for buying shares in Glaxo, BP and Rio Tinto. And non-Scots should be free to subscribe and apply!

- Create neighbourhoods, not thoroughfares. This means the places where people live should be designed to prioritise their needs – not those of passing motorists. Beyond a few lucky '20s-Plenty' zones, many villages, towns and cities are dominated by fast-moving traffic, which makes moving around local streets on two feet or two wheels an unpleasant and dangerous experience. This is particularly acute in poorer areas, where car ownership is lowest yet child pedestrian casualty rates are highest. Mandatory 20mph speed limits within all residential areas – including tenemented streets currently defined as 'main roads' – and designing streets to prioritise the needs of pedestrians and cyclists rather than motorists, would make everyone's life quieter, happier and safer.

- Denmark has folk schools which allow adults to undergo ongoing, subsidised, cultural education. I propose that Scotland should offer free folk holidays to all families allowing them to experience life in different area of Scotland from the one in which they live for one or two weeks a year. Whilst on holiday a curriculum of cooking, music, outdoor activities and craftwork would be available to widen horizons and fire the imagination.

- No businesses are welcome in Scotland unless they contribute to the common good, robustly, not just superficially. So beyond Amazon jobs to true quality work in sustainable industries that pro-actively support local communities. And all state support contingent on delivery of the common good.

- That a modern and dynamic future Scotland will ensure that its teacher workforce matches as far as possible the diversity of its pupil population, to take into account characteristics such as ethnicity, colour, language, faith and belief, disability, sexual orientation and social class.

- The record of the BBC in Scotland, particularly in current affairs and drama, is a national disgrace. With or without independence, Scotland needs a national broadcasting corporation committed to high-quality output on both television and radio.

- One of the fundamental challenges we experience in Scotland is how to transform cultures of fear (or mistrust, disempowerment, blame etc.) into cultures of trust (or collaboration, empowerment and nonviolence). The transition from one to the other relies on creating conditions (or environments) that nurture trust at all levels of society (families, schools, organisations of all kinds). My policy recommendation would be to create a Scotland-wide network of practitioners in the art and craft of collaborative leadership with the aim of embedding collaboration at all these levels of society. Skills and practices they would spread include how to speak truth with care, facilitate empathic dialogue, give and receive feedback without criticism, make decisions collaboratively, transform conflict etc.

- If we want to regenerate Scottish business why not enshrine at the heart of planning support for Scottish business? If a supermarket, if a multinational wishes to move or expand in Scotland then surely they should be asked what they are doing for the businesses of that country? And if they will not sign up to a sustainable code of conduct and practice, do we really want them here?

# Bibliography

Aitken, Keith, *The Bairns O'Adam: The Story of the* STUC, Polygon, 1997

Alexander, Douglas, 'With a year to go, it's time to go deeper...', speech at Wynd Centre, Paisley, 20 September 2013, on Labour Hame, http://www.labourhame.com/archives/3925

Anderson, Benedict, *Imagined Communities: Reflections of the Origins and Spread of Nationalism*, Verso, 1983

Ascherson, Neal, *Stone Voices: The Search for Scotland*, Granta Books, 2002

Bauman, Zygmunt, *Liquid Modernity*, Polity Press, 2000

Benn, Tony, *The New Politics: A Socialist Renaissance*, Fabian Society, 1970

Benn, Tony, *Arguments for Socialism*, Jonathan Cape, 1979

Berlin, Isaiah, Against the Comment: Essays in the History of Ideas, Oxford University Press, 1981

Beveridge, Crawford, Neil McIntosh and Robert Wilson, *Independent Budget Review: The Report of Scotland's Independent Budget Review Panel*, Scottish Government, 2010

Bloch, Ernest *The Principle of Hope* (three volumes), MIT Press, 1986

Bogdanor, Vernon (ed.), *The British Constitution in the Twentieth Century*, Oxford University Press/The British Academy, 2003

Bonnett, Alastair, *Left in the Past: Radicalism and the Politics of Nostalgia*, Continuum, 2010

Bort, Eberhard, McAlpine, Robin and Morgan, Gordon, *The Silent Crisis: Failure and Revival in Local Democracy in Scotland*, Jimmy Reid Foundation, 2012

Bowie, James A., *The Future of Scotland: A Survey of the Present Position with Some Proposals for Future Policy*, W. & R. Chambers, 1939

Brivati, Brian, *The End of Decline: Blair and Brown in Power*, Politico's Publishing, 2007

Brocklehurst, Alex, *Peerages Created 1958–2008*, House of Lords Library, 2008

Brown, Alice, 'The changing shape of Scottish politics and identities', *Renewal*, 1998, Vol. 6, No. 4, 14–22

Brown, Gordon (ed.), *The Red Paper on Scotland*, Edinburgh University Student Publication Board, 1975

Brown, Roger and Kulik, James, 'Flashbulb Memories', 1977, 5 (1), *Cognition*, 73–99

Bryan, Pauline and Kane, Tommy (eds), *Class, Nation and Socialism: The Red Paper on Scotland 2014*, Glasgow Caledonian University Archive, 2013

Bunt, Laura, Harris, Michael and Patrick, Ruth, *Radical Scotland: Confronting the Challenges facing Scotland's Public Services*, NESTA, 2010

Cable, Vince, *Free Radical*, Atlantic Books, 2009

Caryl, Christian, *Strange Rebels: 1979 and the Birth of the Twentieth Century*, Basic Books, 2013

Castells, Manuel, *The Rise of the Network Society* (three volumes), Polity Press, 2000–2004

Christie, Campbell (chair), *Commission on the Future Delivery of Public Services*, Scottish Government, 2011

Colley, Linda, *Acts of Union and Disunion: What has held the* UK *together – and what is dividing it?*, Profile Books, 2014

Craig, Carol, *The Scots' Crisis of Confidence*, Big Thinking, 2003

Crick, Bernard, *Socialist Values and Time*, Fabian Society, 1984

Crompton, Tom, *Common Cause: The Case for Working with Our Cultural Values*, Oxfam UK, 2010

Crouch, Colin, *Post-Democracy*, Polity Press, 2004

Curtice, John and Ormston, Rachel, 'Is Scotland more left-wing than England?', *British Social Attitudes 28 Special Edition*, December 2011

Deci, Edward L. and Ryan, Richard M., (eds), *Handbook of Self-Determination Research*, University of Rochester Press, 2002

Devine, Tom, *The Scottish Nation 1700–2000*, Allen Lane, 1999

Deutsch, Karl, *Nationalism and Social Communication: An Inquiry into the Foundations of Nationality*, MIT Press, 2nd edn. 1966

Dickson, Tony, 'Scotland is Different, OK?', in David McCrone, Stephen Kendrick and Pat Straw (eds), *The Making of Scotland: Nation, Culture and Social Change*, Edinburgh University Press in conjunction with the British Sociological Association 1989, 53–70

Diffley, Mark, 'Public services reform and public opinion', in Ipsos MORI Scotland, *Spotlight on Scotland*, 2013

Dorling, Danny, *Fair Play: A Danny Dorling Reader on Social Justice*, Policy Press, 2012

Duncan, Bill, *The Wee Book of Calvin*, Penguin, 2004

Duncombe, Stephen, *Dream: Re-imagining Progressive Politics in an Age of Fantasy*, New Press, 2007

Economist Intelligence Unit, *Democracy Index 2012: Democracy at a Standstill*, Economist Intelligence Unit, 2013

Edwards, Owen Dudley, (ed.), *A Claim of Right for Scotland*, Polygon, 1989

Ehrenreich, Barbara, *Dancing in the Streets: A History of Collective Joy*, Granta Books, 2007

Ehrenreich, Barbara *Bright-Sided: How the Relentless Promotion of Positive Thinking has Undermined America*, Metropolitan Books, 2009

Electoral Commission, *The Completeness and Accuracy of Electoral Registers in Great Britain*, Electoral Commission, 2010

Elliott, Larry and Atkinson, Dan, *Fantasyland: Waking Up to the Economic, Political and Social Illusions of the Blair Legacy*, Constable, 2007

European Trade Union Institute, *European Participation Index*, European Trade Union Institute, 2010, http://www.worker-participation.eu/About-WP/European-Partici-pation-Index-EPI

Finlayson, Alan, 'Making Labour Safe: Globalisation and the Aftermath of the Social Democratic Retreat', in Gerry Hassan (ed.), *After Blair: Politics after the New Labour Decade*, Lawrence and Wishart, 2007, 37–46

Florida, Richard, *The Rise of the Creative Class: And How It Is Transforming Work, Leisure, Community and Everyday Life*, Basic Books, 2003

Flynn, Laurie (ed.), *We Shall Be All: Recent Chapters in the History of Working Class Struggle n Scotland*, Bookmarks, 1978

Foley, James and Ramand, Pete, *Yes: The Radical Case for Scottish Independence*, Pluto Press, 2014

Fraser, Ian, *Shredded: The Rise and Fall of the Royal Bank of Scotland*, Birlinn, 2014

Freedman, Lawrence, *Strategy: A History*, Oxford University Press, 2013

Friedli, Lynne, ''What we've tried, hasn't worked': the politics of asset based public health', *Critical Public Health*, 2012, http://www.centreforwelfarereform.org/uploads/attachment/353/the-politics-of-assets-based-public-health.pdf

Fry, Michael, *Patronage and Principle: A Political History of Scotland*, Aberdeen University Press, 1987

Gall, Gregor (ed.), *Is There a Scottish Road to Socialism?*, Scottish Left Review Press, 2007

Gall, Gregor (ed.), *Scotland's Road to Socialism: Time to Choose*, Scottish Left Review Press, 2013

Gallagher, Tom, *The Illusion of Freedom: Scotland under Nationalism*, Hurst and Company, 2009

Gamble, Andrew, *The Conservative Nation*, Routledge and Kegan Paul, 1974

Gamble, Andrew, *Between Europe and America: The Future of British Politics*, Palgrave Macmillan, 2003

Gay, Doug, *Honey from the Lion: Christianity and the Ethics of Nationalism*, SCM Press, 2013

Goldblatt, David, *The Ball is Round: A Global History of Football*, Penguin, 2007

Hannan, Daniel, *How We Invented Freedom and Why It Matters*, Head of Zeus, 2013

Harvie, Christopher, *Scotland and Nationalism: Scottish Society and Politics, 1707–1977*, George Allen and Unwin, 1977

Hassan, Gerry, *Independence of the Mind: Elite Narratives, Public Spaces and the Making of Modern Scotland*, Palgrave Macmillan, forthcoming 2014

Hassan, Gerry and Barnett, Anthony, *Breaking Out of Britain's Neo-Liberal State*, Compass, 2009

Hassan, Gerry, Mean, Melissa and Tims, Charlie, *The Dreaming City: Glasgow 2020 and the Power of Mass Imagination*, Demos, 2007

Hassan, Gerry and Shaw, Eric, *The Strange Death of Labour Scotland*, Edinburgh University Press, 2012

Heath, Anthony, Savage, Mike and Senior, Nicki, 'Social Class: The Role of Class in Shaping Social Attitudes', in Alison Park, Caroline Bryson, Elizabeth Clery, John Curtice and Miranda Phillips (eds), *British Social Attitudes 30*, NatCen Social Research, 2013, 173–99

Herman, Arthur, *The Scottish Enlightenment: The Scots' Invention of the Modern World*, Fourth Estate, 2002

Hicks, Joe and Allen, Grahame, *A Century of Change: Trends in UK Statistics since 1900*, House of Commons Library, 1999

Hirschman, Albert O., *Exit, Voice and Loyalty: Responses to Decline in Firms, Organisations and States*, Harvard University Press, 1970

Hitchens, Christopher, *The Monarchy: A Critique of Britain's Favourite Fetish*, Chatto and Windus, 1990

Hitchens, Christopher, *Orwell's Victory*, Allen Lane, 2002

Hyman, Peter, *1 Out of Ten: From Downing Street Vision to Classroom Reality*, Vintage, 2005

Ipsos MORI, 'How Britain Voted in 2010', *Ipsos MORI, 2010*, http://www.ipsos-mori. com/researchpublications/researcharchive/poll.aspx?oItemId=2613

Jacoby, Russell, *The End of Utopia: Politics and Culture in an Age of Apathy*, Basic Books, 2000

James, Oliver, *Affluenza*, Vermillion, 2007

Johnston, Thomas, *Our Scots Noble Families*, Forward Publications, 1909

Johnston, Thomas, *The History of the Working Classes in Scotland*, Forward Publications, 1923

Johnston, Thomas, *Memories*, Collins, 1952.

Keating, Michael and Bleiman, David, *Labour and Scottish Nationalism*, Macmillan, 1979

Kuper, Simon and Szymanski, Stefan, *Why England Lose: And Other Curious Phenomena Explained*, Harper Collins, 2009

Levitt, Ian, 'Poverty in Scotland', in Gordon Brown (ed.), *The Red Paper on Scotland*, Edinburgh University Student Publication Board, 1975, 317–333

MacKenzie, W.J.M., *Political Identity*, Penguin, 1978

MacLeod, Dennis and Russell, Mike, *Grasping the Thistle*, Argyll, 2006

Macleod, Donald, 'Scottish Calvinism: A Dark Repressive Force?', originally published in the *Scottish Bulletin of Evangelical Theology*, 2001, 19 (2), http://www.freescot-coll.ac.uk/files/Articles/Scottish-Calvinism.pdf

Macwhirter, Iain, *Road to Referendum*, Cargo Publishing, 2013

Mair, Peter, *Ruling the Void: The Hollowing of Western Democracy*, Verso, 2013

Marr, Andrew, *A History of Modern Britain*, Macmillan, 2007

Martin, Iain, *Making It Happen: Fred Goodwin, RBS and the Men Who Blew Up the British Economy*, Simon and Schuster, 2013

Marquand, David, *Britain since 1918: The Strange Career of British Democracy*, Weidenfeld and Nicolson, 2008

Mathiesen, Thomas, *Silently Silenced: Essays on the Creation of Acquiescence in Modern Society*, Waterview Press, 2004

Maxwell, Stephen, *Arguing for Independence: Evidence, Risk and the Wicked Issues*, Luath Press, 2012

McAlpine, Robin, 'We have to stop complaining and raise our game', in Gregor Gall (ed.), *Scotland's Road to Socialism: Time to Choose*, Scottish Left Review Press, 2013, 126–35

McCabe, Mike, '"On Jordan's Stormy Banks": Evangelicalism and the Socialist Revival in Scotland, *c.*1890–1914', in Andrew R. Morton (ed.), *After Socialism? The Future of Radical Christianity*, Centre for Theology and Public Issues, 1994, 23–37

McConnell, Allan, *Scottish Local Government*, Edinburgh University Press, 2004

McCrone, David, *Understanding Scotland: The Sociology of a Nation*, Routledge, 2nd edn., 2001

McIlvanney, William, *Surviving the Shipwreck*, Mainstream, 1992

McKnight, David, *Murdoch's Politics: How One Man's Thirst for Wealth and Power Shapes Our World*, Pluto Press, 2013

McLean, Iain, 'Scottish Labour and British Politics', in Gerry Hassan (ed.), *The Scottish Labour Party: History, Institutions and Ideas*, Edinburgh University Press, 2004, 46–59

Miller, Jim, *The Dam Builders: Power from the Glens*, Birlinn, 2003

Mitchell, James, *Strategies for Self-Government: The Campaigns for a Scottish Parlia-ment*, Polygon, 1996

Mitchell, James, *The Scottish Question*, Oxford University Press, 2014

Momus, *Solution 11–167: The Book of Scotlands*, Sternberg Press, 2009

Momus, *Solution 214–238: The Book of Japans*, Sternberg Press, 2011

Mouffe, Chantal, *On the Political*, Verso, 2005

Muir, Edwin, *John Knox: Portrait of a Calvinist*, Jonathan Cape, 1929

Nairn, Tom, *The Enchanted Glass: Britain and its Monarchy*, Radius, 1988

Neil, Andrew, *Full Disclosure*, Macmillan, 1996

Obama, Barack, *Dreams from my Father: A Story of Race and Inheritance*, Canongate, 2008

Oborne, Peter, *The Triumph of the Political Classes*, Simon and Schuster, 2007

Oliver, Neil, *A History of Scotland*, Weidenfeld and Nicolson, 2009

Orwell, George, 'Inside the Whale', originally published in 1940, reprinted in *Inside the Whale and Other Essays*, Penguin, 1957

O'Toole, Fintan, *Ship of Fools: How Stupidity and Corruption Sank the Celtic Tiger*, Faber and Faber, 2009

O'Toole, Fintan, *Enough is Enough: How to Build a New Republic*, Faber and Faber, 2010

Oxfam Scotland, *Our Economy: Towards a New Prosperity*, Oxfam Scotland, 2013

Paterson, Lindsay, *The Autonomy of Modern Scotland*, Edinburgh University Press, 1994

Paterson, Lindsay, Bechhofer, Frank and McCrone, David, *Living in Scotland: Economic and Social Change since 1980*, Edinburgh University Press, 2004

Peterson, Christopher, Maier, Stephen F. and Seligman, Martin E.P., *Learned Helpless-ness: A Theory for the Age of Personal Control*, Oxford University Press, 1995

Rafeek, Neil C., *Communist Women in Scotland: Red Clydeside from the Russian Revolution to the end of the Soviet Union*, Tauris, 2008

Rawnsley, Andrew, *The End of the Party: The Rise and Fall of New Labour*, Penguin Viking, 2010

Reid, Harry, *Reformation: The Dangerous Birth of the Modern World*, Saint Andrew Press, 2010

Renan, Ernest, 'What is a Nation?', originally published in 1882, reprinted in Homi K. Bhabha (ed.), *Nations and Narration*, Routledge 1990, 8–22

Riddoch, Lesley, *Blossom: What Scotland Needs to Flourish*, Luath Press, 2013

Roberts, Alasdair, 'The Independent Sector', in Byrce, T.G.K., Humes, W.H., Gillies, D. and Kennedy, A. (eds), *Scottish Education: Fourth Edition: Referendum*, Edinburgh University Press 2013, 120–28

Roy, Kenneth, *The Invisible Spirit: A life of post-war Scotland 1945–75*, ICS Books, 2013

Sampson, Anthony, *Anatomy of Britain*, London: Hodder and Stoughton, 1962

Sampson, Anthony, *Anatomy of Britain Today*, Hodder and Stoughton, 1965

Sampson, Anthony, *Who Runs This Place? The Anatomy of Britain in the 21st Century*, John Murray, 2004

Samuel, Raphael, *The Lost World of British Communism*, Verso, 2006

Sandbrook, Dominic, *Seasons in the Sun: The Battle for Britain, 1974–1979*, Allen Lane, 2012

Save the Children Scotland, *Child Poverty in Scotland: The Facts*, Save the Children
    Scotland, March 2013, http://www.savethechildren.org.uk/sites/default/files/images/
    child_poverty_facts_2013.pdf

Schlesinger, Philip, 'Cultural Policy and the Constitutional Question', in Gerry Hassan
    and James Mitchell (eds), *After Independence*, Luath Press, 2013, 272–82

Scottish Government, *Scotland's People Annual Report: Results from the 2011 Scottish
    Household Survey*, Scottish Government, 2012

Scottish Government, *Scotland's Future: Your Guide to an Independent Scotland*,
    Scottish Government, 2013

Shaxson, Nicholas, *Treasure Islands: Tax Havens and The Men Who Stole the World*,
    Bodley Head, 2011

Sillars, Jim, *In Place of Fear II: A Socialist Programme for an Independent Scotland*,
    Vagabond Voices, 2014

Sinclair, Ross, *We Love Real Life Scotland: Art, History and Place: A Reader exploring
    the heritage of Huntly's Gordons and other Scottish Incidences*, Deveron Arts,
    2012

Smout, T.C., *A Century of the Scottish People 1830–1950*, Collins, 1986

Thompson, E.P., 'Outside the Whale', in E.P. Thompson (ed.), *Out of Apathy*, Stevens
    and Sons, 1960, 141–94

Thomson, Ben, Mawdsley, Geoff and Payne, Alison, *Renewing Local Government*,
    Reform Scotland, 2012

Torrance, David, *'We in Scotland': Thatcherism in a Cold Climate*, Birlinn, 2009

Tourish, Dennis, *The Dark Side of Transformational Leadership: A Critical Perspective*,
    Routledge, 2013

Toynbee, Polly and Walker, David, *The Verdict: Did Labour Change Britain?*, Granta,
    2010

The Vicentian Partnership for Social Justice, presentation at the National Conference
    for the Community and Charity Sector, Dublin, 31 May 2012, http://www.
    slideshare.net/THEWHEEL12/slides-at-national-conference-for-the-communi-
    ty-and-charity-sector-2012

Wightman, Andy, *The Poor Had No Lawyers: Who Owns Scotland (and How They
    Got It)*, Birlinn, 2010

Wilkinson, Richard and Pickett, Kate, *The Spirit Level: Why More Equal Societies
    Almost Always Do Better*, Allen Lane, 2009

Williams, Raymond, *Orwell*, Fontana, 1971

Wright, Kenyon, *The People Say Yes: The Making of Scotland's Parliament*, Argyll, 1997

Wright, Patrick, *On Living in an Old Country: The National Past in Contemporary
    Britain*, Verso, 1985

Zerubaval, Eviatar, 'Social Memories: Steps in a Sociology of the Past', *Qualitative
    Sociology*, 1996, 19 (3), 283–99

# Index

### After Independence: The State of the Scottish Nation Debate

Edited by Gerry Hassan and James Mitchell
ISBN: 978-1-908373-95-3 PBK £12.99

At the height of the Scottish Independence debate, *After Independence* offers an in-depth and varied exploration of the possibilities for Scotland from both pro- and anti-independence standpoints.

Drawing together over two dozen leading minds on the subject, *After Independence* offers a comprehensive and balanced analysis of Scotland's current and prospective political, economic, social and cultural situation.

Brought together in an inclusive, accessible and informative way, *After Independence* asks and answers a range of questions crucial to the Independence debate and invites its readers to become involved at this crucial moment of Scottish history in the making.

# Radical Scotland: Arguments for Self-Determination

Gerry Hassan and Rosie Illet
ISBN: 978-1-906817-94-7 PBK £12.99

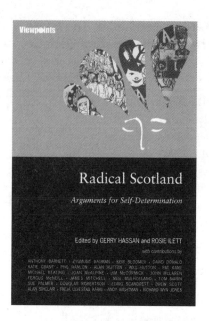

*The era of devolution as we have known it is over.* Radical Scotland *challenges conventional wisdoms, and poses solutions which encourage us to become more active agents of our own destiny.*

Scotland believes it is a radical, egalitarian, inclusive nation. It was hoped that the establishment of the Scottish Parliament was going to give expression to this. Instead, we have witnessed a minimal, unattractive politics with little to choose between the main parties. This might be adequate in the good times, but no more.

*Radical Scotland: Arguments for Self-Determination* explores how we can go beyond the limited politics we have experienced and makes the case for shifting from self-government politically to self-determination as a society and a nation. It asks how do we shake up institutional Scotland? How do we shift power and give people voice?

The editors Gerry Hassan and Rosie Ilett have brought together in one volume some of the most original thinkers in our nation making the case for a very different politics and society. It includes conversations with leading global figures on some of the key issues facing the world which impact on Scotland. This book is a must read for all those interested in Scotland at a crucial time, for its future, for the Parliament, and for those who want our politics and public policy to be more effective, imaginative and bold.

## Blossom: What Scotland Needs to Flourish

Lesley Riddoch
ISBN: 978-1-908373-69-4 PBK £11.99

 Weeding out vital components of Scottish identity from decades of political and social tangle is no mean task, but it's one journalist Lesley Riddoch has undertaken.

Dispensing with the tired, yo-yoing jousts over fiscal commissions, devo something-or-other and EU in-or-out, *Blossom* pinpoints both the buds of growth and the blight that's holding Scotland back. Drawing from its people and history, as well as the experience of the Nordic countries and the author's own passionate and outspoken perspective, this is a plain-speaking but incisive call to restore equality and control to local communities and let Scotland flourish.

*Not so much an intervention in the independence debate as a heartfelt manifesto for a better democracy.*
THE SCOTSMAN

## The Case for Left Wing Nationalism

Stephen Maxwell
ISBN: 978-1-908373-87-8 PBK £9.99

 Spanning four politically and socially tumultuous decades, Stephen Maxwell's essays explore the origins and development of the Scottish Nationalist movement. As an instrumental member of the SNP, life-long activist and intellectual, Maxwell provides a unique insight into the debate over Scottish independence.

*The Case for Left Wing Nationalism* considers the class dynamics of the constitutional debate, deconstructs the myths that underpin Scottish political culture and exposes the role Scottish institutions have played and continue to play in restricting Scotland's progress.

In this wide-ranging analysis, Maxwell draws on a wealth of cultural, economic and historical sources. From debating the very nature of nationalism itself, to tackling the immediate social issues that Scotland faces, Maxwell establishes a very real picture of contemporary Scotland and its future.

*It stands as a fine contribution by a fine man.*
ALEX SALMOND

Details of these and other books published by Luath Press can be found at:
**www.luath.co.uk**

## **Luath** Press Limited
*committed to publishing well written books worth reading*

LUATH PRESS takes its name from Robert Burns, whose little collie Luath (*Gael.,* swift or nimble) tripped up Jean Armour at a wedding and gave him the chance to speak to the woman who was to be his wife and the abiding love of his life. Burns called one of 'The Twa Dogs' Luath after Cuchullin's hunting dog in Ossian's *Fingal*. Luath Press was established in 1981 in the heart of Burns country, and now resides a few steps up the road from Burns' first lodgings on Edinburgh's Royal Mile.

Luath offers you distinctive writing with a hint of unexpected pleasures.

Most bookshops in the UK, the US, Canada, Australia, New Zealand and parts of Europe either carry our books in stock or can order them for you. To order direct from us, please send a £sterling cheque, postal order, international money order or your credit card details (number, address of cardholder and expiry date) to us at the address below. Please add post and packing as follows: UK – £1.00 per delivery address; overseas surface mail – £2.50 per delivery address; overseas airmail – £3.50 for the first book to each delivery address, plus £1.00 for each additional book by airmail to the same address. If your order is a gift, we will happily enclose your card or message at no extra charge.

**Luath** Press Limited
543/2 Castlehill
The Royal Mile
Edinburgh EH1 2ND
Scotland
Telephone: 0131 225 4326 (24 hours)
Fax: 0131 225 4324
email: sales@luath.co.uk
Website: www.luath.co.uk